THE GREATEST RANGER EVER?

THE GREATEST RANGER EVER?

DAVIE MEIKLEJOHN
THE CASE FOR THE ORIGINAL IBROX LEGEND

JEFF HOLMES

First published by Pitch Publishing, 2014

Pitch Publishing
A2 Yeoman Gate
Yeoman Way
Durrington
BN13 3QZ
www.pitchpublishing.co.uk

A CIP catalogue record is available for this book from the
British Library.

ISBN 978-1-90962-649-2

Typesetting and origination by Pitch Publishing

Printed in Great Britain

Contents

For my brother-in-law John Taylor

(formerly Allanach) 1967–1979

Acknowledgements

THANKS are due to Kenny McDonald for proofing and much more; to Richard McBrearty and David Miller of the Scottish Football Museum, and my father-in-law Jim Gahagan, for the use of photographs. To Brian Reilly and Freddie Duda Jnr of Maryhill Football Club for assistance. To my wife Elaine, children Derek and Carey, daughter-in-law Jayne and grandson Josh, and friends Willie Brown and Jamie McGregor – thank you for the constant encouragement.

To Paul and Jane, and all at Pitch Publishing, for their continued faith, and to Duncan Olner for another wonderfully eye-catching cover.

And last, but by no means least, to lifelong Rangers fan – and my stepbrother – Andy Madden, gone, but certainly not forgotten.

Introduction

JOHN GREIG was voted the Greatest Ever Ranger in a poll of supporters in 1999. It was a tough call given the number of exceptional players who have flourished in light blue during the last five or six decades. I voted for Greig; it was hard not to. The status he enjoys on the south side of Glasgow since making his debut for Rangers in 1961 is unrivalled, but was the vote a fair reflection on those who have played for one of the most famous clubs in the world or should it have been called 'The Greatest Ranger in Living Memory?'

Naturally, Greig was a popular winner: A legendary, wholehearted one-club man who served Rangers with great distinction, and in every capacity going. Greig ticks all the boxes. He won three trebles and captained Rangers to European Cup Winners' Cup glory in 1972. He is a genuine contender, as are countless others, but in my mind it's nigh-on impossible to pin such a weighty accolade on any individual, especially as Rangers Football Club has been in existence for over 140 years – but we can certainly have a stab at it.

Davie Meiklejohn and John Greig played in totally contrasting eras but share many a similarity which, I believe, allows the inevitable comparison. The tale of the tape, as it were. Both were born leaders and played at right-half for a significant part of their careers. Greig also played at inside-right and latterly at left-back. After starting out as a right-back in youth football, Meik blossomed into a right-half of genuine quality before eventually playing some of his finest games at centre-half. Like all good players he was versatile and filled many other positions in times of need.

Both Meik and Greig proudly represented Scotland on a number of occasions. Greig amassed 44 caps while Meiklejohn played for his country 15 times, although his opportunities were restricted given Scotland played far less games during his era; just the Home International series and the odd challenge match against foreign opposition for the stars of yesteryear.

Meiklejohn's rise to prominence on Edmiston Drive was frighteningly quick. He started off the 1919/20 season with Maryhill Juniors and ended it with Rangers, and a Scottish League First Division winners' medal. The buffer was a handful of games for the Gers' second string. Perhaps manager William Wilton's preferred maxim was, 'If you're good enough, you're old enough.'

I started watching Rangers in the early 1970s and was a massive Greig fan. That adulation continued until he hung up the boots in 1978. I have watched just a short film of Meiklejohn in action, which hardly supplied the ammunition required to make a valid case for the Govan man over Greig, but having researched this book for around two years I've read enough comment and match reports to know that Meiklejohn was a colossus: a giant among men.

Contemporary players, managers and reporters sang his praises with alarming regularity; they spoke of his indomitable spirit, determination and undying love for his team but, more importantly, they spoke of his talent, his tactical nous and his composure on the ball when collective backs were against the wall: someone who could put his foot on the ball and make a pass, which reminded me of the late Jim Baxter (another contender?).

Whenever Rangers or Scotland travelled abroad, everyone wanted to speak to Meiklejohn. It didn't matter a jot that he was in Berlin or Vienna, New York or New England, everyone knew Davie Meiklejohn. No worldwide web in those days, but he still managed to become a global name long before the days of David Beckham!

When there was talk of him retiring from the international scene, one reporter commented, 'I've heard it rumoured that Meik is finished with representative football. If I were a selector I'd place a pistol at the back of his neck and drive him to Hampden!' On another occasion, just after a starring role for the Scottish League against the English, *Daily Record* reporter Waverley said, 'It isn't too much to say that we won because we had a Meiklejohn, and England lost because they didn't!'

We could chat all day, but let's allow the following chapters to do the talking on behalf of the man I believe to be the Greatest Ever Ranger. Ladies and gentlemen, I give you 'The Case for Davie Meiklejohn'.

Jeff Holmes, October 2014

Prologue

HE WAS once labelled the greatest ever Ranger by Ibrox legend Willie Thornton. It was quite a compliment from a man who knew the game inside out. But David Ditchburn Meiklejohn stood out from the rest – as a great motivator, incredibly versatile and, more than anything, a tactical genius.

Born a stone's throw from Ibrox, in nearby Govan, Meik chose football over the shipyards, a decision which didn't sit too well with his parents but one legions of Rangers fans would become thankful for in many 'hours of need' over almost two decades.

Despite being known as the 'thinking man's player' he was never shy at putting his head in where it hurt, and was injured on numerous occasions as a result.

But if ever there was a moment which defined Meik as a true leader, it arrived on Saturday 14 April 1928. Winning the title hadn't presented the talented half-back with too many problems, as borne out by 13 championships in his 17 seasons with Rangers, a phenomenal record, but quite clearly annexing the Scottish Cup had become a thorny issue for both player and club with some even suggesting that a Scottish Cup hoodoo – or curse by a disgruntled traveller – hovered over Ibrox.

Rangers hadn't won the cup for 25 years, since 1903 to be precise, and on that occasion it had taken three matches – two of them at Celtic Park – to dispose of Hearts. That was the fourth time the club had won the cup since the inaugural final of 1874, but given their almost total domination of the league it was a mystery as to why they hadn't accumulated many more national trophies.

Old foes Celtic were their opponents in 1928, in a match played at Hampden Park in front of 120,000 fervent supporters. During those 25 barren cup years, Rangers had lost five finals, twice to Celtic, but still Meiklejohn was convinced this could be their year.

And how many players, with such an incredible career behind them, would be capable of looking back years later and focusing on one particular moment from a lifetime of great memories? Not too many, I would imagine, but that's exactly what Meiklejohn did. Perhaps the 1928 Scottish Cup Final had become indelibly etched in his psyche.

With 11 minutes of the second half gone – and the game still goalless – Rangers were awarded a penalty. The majority of Gers players turned their back, refusing to even contemplate stepping forward.

As skipper of the team, Meik insisted that responsibility should rest with him and placed the ball carefully on the spot. He paused for a few seconds before taking no more than a couple of steps back, and with that he rushed forward and thumped the leather past a despairing John Thomson and into the net – the cue for half of the stadium to erupt in unbridled joy.

Later, he would say, 'I never felt so scared in all my life, for I realised that failure on my part might lead to yet another cup final defeat.

'For ten minutes afterwards I was in a trance. I have only a hazy recollection of that period, and now feel that if Celtic had realised my condition, and played on it, I would have been clay in their hands.'

Rangers dominated the remainder of the match and triumphed 4-0 with Sandy Archibald scoring twice and Bob McPhail, the regular penalty taker, registering the other.

It wouldn't be the only time in his long and illustrious career that Meiklejohn would lead from the front; while off the park, he upheld the traditional values of Rangers Football Club at all times and proved the perfect ambassador for the Light Blues.

Whenever the club ventured to foreign lands, Meik was the centre of attention. His unblemished reputation preceded him. Perhaps a mark of his popularity was summed up perfectly when a touring Austrian side arrived in Glasgow for a friendly match. Meik was a major doubt due to injury, a fact that disappointed the Austrian players and coaches in equal measures. At that time, the Nazi war machine was on the move in Europe, and everyone was wary of Hitler's intentions, which led one reporter to say, 'Meiklejohn is as popular in Austria as Herr Hitler would like to be!'

Says it all, really.

1

Decision day for young Meik

ONE can only imagine the concern felt by Alexander and Agnes Meiklejohn when the latter announced that she was having the couple's second child. It was May of 1900 and traces of the Bubonic Plague had just been discovered in Govan, centuries after the disease had killed upwards of 100,000 people in London alone. More than 100 cases were reported locally, which prompted the health and sanitation authorities to move quickly and open a 'quarantine house', where all new cases could be taken. It was believed that the disease had originated in Africa or Asia and reached Govan via one of the many ships that docked in the area. It was certainly a worrying time for the residents of Govan, as well as the wider population.

Thankfully the disease had kept its distance from the Meiklejohn household, which was situated in Sharp Street, a mere free kick from Govan Wharf and the Govan Landing Stage, and on the morning of Wednesday 12 December, close number seven played host to a birth that raised eyebrows only due to the unusual nature of the child's middle name, Ditchburn.

Otherwise, David Meiklejohn was a regular, healthy baby boy, and the family toasted his arrival with a dram of Scotland's favourite tipple. David had an elder brother, Adam, five years his senior, while

Jean, a young sister, would come along ten years later. Ditchburn, a name originating in Northumberland, had been in the family for several generations.

From the family's tenement windows to the front of their two-room flat they had views across the River Clyde to Meadowside, where the world-famous granary works were just a few years off. However, to the rear of the Meiklejohns' close was St Constantine's Church – and its adjacent burial ground. No doubt the youngsters of the area enjoyed playing hide and seek in the graveyard and the myriad surrounding buildings.

And were Sharp Street still there today, peering from the side window would have given tenants a view of the new Glasgow; of the Tall Ship, the Riverside Museum and the newly-built Hydro concert venue.

In 1900, though, Govan – the fifth largest burgh in Scotland – was awash with shipyards, and the likes of Fairfield, Middleton and Govan shipbuilding yards were all within a couple of hundred yards of the Meiklejohn household. In the early 20th century Govan was a bustling and vibrant community, with jobs aplenty, and an all-pervading sense of community spirit that was second to none. Indeed, it was a far cry from the present day where unemployment is rife and the chance of securing a job on leaving school is minimal. Life expectancy is sadly among the lowest in the city.

But despite eventually travelling the world playing for Rangers and Scotland, Meiklejohn never strayed too far from home and would live his entire life within a ten-mile radius of Ibrox Stadium. The same could hardly be said of his father, though. Born and raised in the small Fife village of Carnock, Alexander was forced to move around in search of employment. Coming from a long line of iron ore miners, he moved the 20 or so miles to East Wemyss to take up a position in a pit, before moving again to Dunfermline. He was then offered a job in Govan, as a marine engineer fitter, and took on the tenement flat at 7 Sharp Street.

At the age of 15, David's older brother Adam secured a job as a clerk in a city centre chartered accountant's office and was able to contribute to the weekly bills. By that time, the family had moved the short distance to Church Street.

David attended Bellahouston Academy and was a member of the Boys' Brigade, the 103rd company, which was based at Bellahouston Parish Church. It was one of the oldest companies in the city and every Friday night he would walk from his Church Street home to Clifford Street, a trek of no more than five minutes. The church would eventually join forces with neighbouring Steven Memorial Church to form what is known today as Ibrox Parish Church.

The Boys' Brigade, a Christian organisation, offered young males an opportunity to take part in team sports at weekends, a regular weekly club night and Bible classes at Sunday School. It is still as popular an organisation in the Glasgow area today as it was back then, with thousands of young members and hundreds of volunteer leaders still actively involved.

A young Meik played at right-back for the Boys' Brigade football team, of which future Queen's Park centre-forward J.B. McAlpine was a team-mate. McAlpine would go on to score a hat-trick against Celtic in a 1923 Glasgow Cup match that the Spiders won 4-3, as well as becoming Queen's Park's all-time record goalscorer.

But when David left school he hadn't the slightest notion of becoming a professional footballer. Like many other youngsters he had enjoyed playing football for his school team, but that was where it ended. He had set his heart on following in the footsteps of his father and securing a job with a Govan engineering firm, and was made well aware of the value of an apprenticeship, and the need to study.

So after enjoying Boys' Brigade and schools football, the old leather boots were tossed to the back of a cupboard and the steely determination he would go on to show in his future career was firmly fixed on an apprenticeship in the nearby yards. He was ideally placed, geographically, as his Govan home was just a short walk from the centre of the shipbuilding universe, and opportunities often knocked for the brightest and most ambitious kids in the neighbourhood. Whether or not they were grasped with both hands was another story.

But just as the youngster was knuckling down in his chosen profession, a knock on his front door would unwittingly change the course of young Meiklejohn's life forever. He was just 18 months into his apprenticeship when, in April of 1919, the manager of a crack local juvenile team, Greenfield United, tracked down David to Church

Street. He begged the young engineer to answer a personal SOS – Save Our Season!

Greenfield were arguably one of the top juvenile teams in the country at that time, and had made it to the final of four competitions. They were also in the running for the league championship but their regular right-back had suffered a nasty injury and the manager was on the lookout for a replacement defender of equal quality. It was well known throughout Govan that the teenage Meik was a talented footballer and, faced with all these crucial matches within just 21 days, they knew exactly who they wanted to fill the void.

It was a difficult decision. Meik was well aware that five matches – and all significantly important – within such a short space of time would impact on his studies, but nevertheless took the decision to help out the local combine. It would be a decision which would kick-start the most incredible seven-month period, and one which would necessitate the purchase of a display cabinet fit to hold a rapidly growing medal collection.

Within that short three-week period, David helped Greenfield win the Southside Cup, Govan Juvenile Cup and Glasgow Cup. The team lost the final of the Scottish Cup but, as a 'consolation', won the league title. Five medals – four of them coloured gold – would form the nucleus of the Meiklejohn medal collection for years to come.

But there was more. A scout from Maryhill Juniors had watched him play a starring role for Greenfield and invited him up to Lochburn Park, where he would play right-back for the remainder of the season. Medal number six was just a matter of weeks away as Hill won the Maryhill Charity Cup, which in those days was viewed as a prestigious competition.

In the final, Maryhill faced local foes Ashfield, and the 18-year-old rookie defender played well in a 0-0 draw at Lochburn. In the replay, Hill thrashed Ashfield 5-0 and Meik hopped on a bus home with another medal in his pocket.

He was a wanted man. The jungle drums were beating and his incredible achievements had alerted those on the lookout for a young right-back with great potential. A few more managers made their way to his Church Street home, with registration forms requiring just a signature, but the player showed loyalty to Maryhill and duly signed on for the new season.

Loyalty would become a byword for Meiklejohn throughout his life. He played a handful of games for Hill but the most significant was back in his native Govan. Maryhill were paired with St Paul's United in a North Eastern Cup tie at the beginning of September and the match was played at Moore Park, just a couple of hundred yards from the Meiklejohn household.

It was a pulsating tie and the Govan youngster, who was by this time playing at half-back, was thrilled when Maryhill were awarded a late penalty and he was asked to take on the responsibility of firing his side into the next round. That he did, but the tie was abandoned with just a few minutes to go due to fading light and the result was declared null and void. The teams would have to do it all again, although David wouldn't be around when the tie was replayed some three months later.

In the crowd at Moore Park that night was a Rangers scout who immediately reported back to manager William Wilton about this talented young player. Wilton wasted no time at all in attempting to recruit the youngster. It was decision time. Engineering or football? Thankfully for Rangers fans, he chose the latter. The transfer 'fee' paid to Maryhill was an interesting one – £10 and a new corrugated iron fence for Maryhill's Lochburn Park. The perfect legacy!

It was a meteoric rise from juvenile football to the cream of the Scottish senior game, with a brief stop-off at the juniors. The streets of Govan would prove an ideal breeding ground for many a youngster with high hopes and aspirations of a grand future and young Meik was about to make the breakthrough. With boots slung over his shoulder, he would walk the Golden Mile to the front door at Ibrox Park every day for training and home games – no luxury coach travel for the man who would become king.

Mind you, things could have been very different had another admirer acted with a little more haste. Everton also watched the youngster at Moore Park that night, and had been impressed by his performance. The Merseyside club had been keeping tabs on the young half-back and had watched him play several times but dragged their heels when it came to the crunch. They wanted him but a decent offer was made days after Rangers had made their move and, from the moment he had set foot inside Ibrox for the first time, Meiklejohn's mind was made up. It was Rangers or bust – and his timing was impeccable.

He made the step up at exactly the right time. Up until the 1919/20 season, there hadn't been a great deal of opportunities for young Scottish players, save for going straight into the first team, or sitting clicking their frustrated heels in the stand on a Saturday afternoon. It was the top team or nothing until the advent of a new competition – the Scottish Alliance League, specifically designed for up-and-coming players and senior players on the fringes of the main team.

It was an ideal learning ground for Meik. So he signed off from his short, but enjoyable, time at Maryhill by scoring in a 6-1 Scottish Cup win over Rutherglen Comrades, a first-year junior combine. It was goodbye Lochburn, and hello Ibrox. A measure of Meik's importance to Maryhill was shown when the Lochburn Park side lost five matches in a row immediately after his departure.

But he was a Rangers player now and along with the Light Blues, others to throw their hat into the 'A' League ring were Celtic, Clyde, Ayr United, Motherwell, Kilmarnock, St Mirren, Clydebank and Partick Thistle. David made his debut for Rangers Football Club on Saturday 11 October 1919, in a Scottish Second XI Cup tie at Ibrox against Clyde. The match finished 1-1 and by all accounts, the youngster acquitted himself very well.

It had been quite a year, but that second XI game against Clyde heralded the start of a love affair with his one and only senior club that would last 18 happy years. This was one Govan lad who was destined to play his way to the top.

2

Tragic end to a glorious season

MEIKLEJOHN had far more than a trip to the beach on his mind when the Rangers second team motored down the coast to Somerset Park, Ayr, at the start of November, 1919. With the traditionally busy festive period looming, Wilton had chosen to join the party over the stay-at-home option of watching the first team in action at Ibrox. The Colts beat Ayr United 2-0 and the Light Blues' first manager no doubt made some important notes on the younger players he believed he could call upon in the event of a first-team emergency.

Meiklejohn was happy to carry on his soccer apprenticeship in the Alliance League, where he showed his versatility by turning out at right-half and centre-half. Meik was a standout in a Second XI Cup tie against Third Lanark, which was watched by more than 10,000 spectators, with adults paying 8d (4p) and 'boys' just 4d. Rangers thumped the Cathkin side 6-1.

As the first snowfalls of Christmas appeared, the Rangers first team sat proudly at the top of the Scottish League and with the Gers boasting the meanest defence in the country, the prospect of Meiklejohn and other youngsters 'getting a game' looked slim. In 18 matches they had shipped just nine goals. But playing for Rangers' reserves certainly had its moments as more than 20,000 fans turned out at Parkhead in the middle of January 1920 to witness the first Old Firm Alliance match. It was a tough afternoon for the young Rangers defence as Celtic, with five first-team regulars on parade, remained in the ascendancy for the bulk of the match, with the Light Blues eventually doing well to lose by just a single goal.

The club's Alliance League results were a bit up and down but Wilton was more concerned with bringing on youngsters than winning titles, and on Saturday 20 March, when the Colts lined up against Kilmarnock at Ibrox for a league match, 19-year-old Meiklejohn was nowhere to be seen.

A Scotland v England League international at Hampden Park had robbed Rangers of first-team stars Jimmy Gordon, Andy Cunningham and Jimmy Bowie and that opened the top-team door for several youngsters, Meiklejohn included. Scotland were on the receiving end of a 4-0 hammering but life couldn't have been any sweeter for the young boy from Govan. He played a starring role as Rangers extended their lead at the top of the league by beating Aberdeen at Pittodrie.

It was a nerve-shredding day for the teenager as the manager waited until the final moments before naming his starting 11. It was normal practice for team selections to be printed in the national press days before a game but, on rare occasions, final decisions would be delayed. On this occasion, Wilton waited until the train arrived in Aberdeen before revealing his selection. One can only imagine the tension and excitement felt by Meiklejohn as the train trudged through town after town on the four-hour plus journey north.

On the morning of the match, a newspaper correspondent pointed out that Celtic, with five players in the national team, had asked for a cancellation of their league match with Falkirk. Rangers, with three, had opted to play for points at Pittodrie. The reporter added, 'I can't see Rangers leaving a point in Aberdeen, because they have first-class reserves. In fact, I hear that young Meiklejohn, once of the Maryhill, will appear at half back.' And start, and finish, he did.

Goals by Dr James Paterson and James 'Fister' Walls, allied to an exemplary performance by Meik, helped ease Rangers nine points ahead of rivals Celtic in the race for the title, although the Parkhead club had two games in hand. With just two points for a win back then, though, realistically the title was Rangers' to throw away. There were ten games left to play and the Light Blues also had a far superior goal difference. In Meik, Rangers had unearthed a young lad who was on his way, if not to fortune, then certainly to fame.

The following week, though, Meiklejohn was back in the Rangers Colts team that tackled Partick Thistle in the first of their home and away Glasgow Reserve Cup ties, while the first team made the short journey to Celtic Park for a Scottish Cup semi-final tie against an Albion Rovers side who would end the campaign bottom of the table and a massive 43 points behind the champions.

Surprisingly, the Scottish tie ended 1-1 and the teams met at Celtic Park four days later in a replay. They could not be separated, though, and 90 goalless minutes ensued. Meik was brought back the following Saturday for a league match against Airdrie at Ibrox, in place of the injured Jimmy Gordon. A nervy 3-2 win – and a competent individual performance described by the media as 'quietly effective' – saw Meik retain his place for the match against Clydebank just 48 hours later – the second game of ten that Rangers would play during April.

A 2-1 loss to the Bankies, who would eventually finish fifth in the 22-team league table, put a dent in Gers' title hopes, but they were given an opportunity to make amends at Celtic Park in the Scottish Cup semi-final second replay 48 hours later. Rangers welcomed back Gordon from injury but there was good news for Meik as he kept his place in the team and lined up at centre-half.

Sadly that's where his good fortune ended as the Cliftonhill minnows sprang the biggest shock of the season by edging a tight contest 2-0 at the home of Rangers' greatest rivals. Ten days later, 95,000 spectators turned up at Hampden for the Scottish Cup Final between Kilmarnock and Albion Rovers and despite losing 3-2 to mid-table Killie, the Rovers were not disgraced, even though contemporary match reports described their brand of football as 'kick and run'.

But Meiklejohn and Rangers had bigger fish to fry and set their sights on wrestling back the title won by Celtic the previous season. Gordon was again on international duty (a 5-4 loss against England at Sheffield) when Rangers travelled through to Tynecastle to face Hearts, and Meik played his part in 'shutting up shop' in a 0-0 draw.

Afterwards, though, it was back to the reserves as Rangers beat Queen's Park 3-1, but following that game, he played for the first team in their remaining five games, starting with the trip to Easter Road, where he scored his first senior-team goal which earned the Light Blues a crucial point in a 1-1 draw.

He scored again six days later in the win over Third Lanark and, sandwiched in between, was commended for putting the shackles on Dundee dangerman Alexander Troup in a 6-1 rout at Ibrox.

And the youngster was a starter as a 0-0 draw at Dumbarton clinched the league title for the Gers, although the real celebrations started on Saturday 1 May when a double by Sandy Archibald and a Doc Paterson goal in a 3-1 win over Morton, saw the championship rubber-stamped in front of just 30,000 at Ibrox.

A major factor in Rangers clinching the league title had been their ability to regularly find the net. An astonishing 106 goals in 42 league games told its own story, with Celtic next highest scorers on 89. The Light Blues also had the meanest defence in the country, losing just 25 goals over the course of the season.

Meik's incredible habit of accumulating silverware had continued, and a league winners' badge joined six others, all won in a remarkable 12-month period. But the cheers soon turned to tears as a freak overnight accident led to the tragic death of manager William Wilton. It was a catastrophe the club would struggle to come to terms with. Within just eight months of joining Rangers, Meiklejohn had lost his guiding light – the man who had made him a Ranger.

As fans streamed out of Ibrox Stadium and made their way down Copland Road, still high on a three-point championship win over Celtic, little did they know that one of the most tragic events in the club's 48-year history was about to unfold.

In the famous Blue Room, Wilton toasted title success in the company of Sir John Ure Primrose, the Rangers president, and others. He then made his way from the stadium to a waiting car where he was bound for the Inverclyde port of Gourock to spend the night on board a friend's yacht.

Prior to leaving, he had confessed to Sir John that he had been feeling fatigued with the season's heavy workload, and welcomed the prospect of inhaling the sea air in the smog-free Firth of Clyde.

Wilton was with Joseph Buchanan, a Rangers director and native of Govan, and James Marr, a chartered accountant from Bellahouston. It was the latter who owned the 19-tonne auxiliary yawl (a two-masted sailing craft) named *Caltha*. Also on board was a skipper and a mate, making a party of five.

The yawl was moored to a buoy in Cardwell Bay but shortly before midnight an easterly gale started to blow, which slowly increased in ferocity, and between two and three o'clock in the morning the yawl broke free from her moorings and was driven hard against the wall of the Caledonian Railway Pier.

The five were in their bunks at the time and the first they knew of their perilous position was when the yawl slammed against the pier. They had no means of communicating with other vessels and, on rushing up to the deck, found themselves in the midst of an incredibly alarming storm with the yawl in real danger of breaking up as a result of the heavy seas battering her against the harbour wall.

They made the decision to try and get ashore by climbing the mast and leaping on to the pier, when the sea swung the mast inwards. This was successfully accomplished by all except Wilton. When his turn came to make the leap, a rope was thrown for him by those who had made it to safety. Holding the rope with one hand, and retaining his grip on the mast, he managed to get his knee on to the pier when the yawl swung outwards. But no sooner had he managed that than he was beaten back by the fierce gale.

Again he tried and succeeded once more in getting his knee on to the pier wall. His friends were trying to grab him by the arm when he suddenly lost his hold on the mast and rope and fell into the sea. He was heard crying out for help, and Marr immediately jumped into the water in a brave bid to rescue him. He was able to get hold of Wilton's arm but unfortunately owing to the heavy sea current, was unable to retain his grip. Wilton disappeared and was not seen or heard again.

Later in the morning the yawl, which had been left badly damaged but was still afloat, was secured by the employees of yacht builder Provost Adam and again moored in Cardwell Bay, where it was the subject of much interest throughout the day.

Dredging operations were carried out under the supervision of William Adam, brother of Provost Adam, but no trace of Wilton's body was found. It would, in fact, be a further 53 days until it was located. It was the most tragic of incidents.

William Wilton had been as honest and reliable as the day was long and the perfect ambassador for Rangers Football Club. He had been associated with the club for many years, and a prime mover in the relocation from their former Kinning Park base to the first Ibrox.

His own playing career had been unspectacular. He had started out with the Rangers Swifts, the second team of the club, and acted as secretary of that 11 when James Gossland, a former international player, took over the same job with the Ibrox first team.

At the end of his playing days Wilton joined the committee at Ibrox and became Rangers' voice at the Scottish League. He was one of the principal founders of the league and his services to that body were long and appreciated. He was also attached to the Scottish Football Association but severed his connections when Rangers FC became a limited company. He also stood down from his duties with the firm of Messrs Mirelees, Watson, Yaryan and Co in order to devote all his time and energy to his beloved Rangers.

As for his duties as manager, Wilton, who led Rangers for 21 years, brought the qualities that were required to maintain the high standing of the club, and its very success was a tribute to the manner in which he guided its affairs.

Sir John Ure Primrose was said to be distraught on learning of his manager's tragic death. He regarded Wilton as a 'prince among football managers', and a man who strove at all times to keep the game of football free from all blemish. Wilton's record as manager had been second to none.

During the First World War the popular man had devoted himself to making life more pleasant for returning wounded soldiers resident at Bellahouston Red Cross Hospital. His endeavour in organising concerts and entertainments was greatly appreciated by soldiers and staff and he went about his business with a quiet enthusiasm that was highly valued by those in authority. Had he so wished, he could have secured a permanent and lucrative post with the Red Cross Society but once the need of his services at Bellahouston Hospital were over, he preferred to return to the Rangers.

Away from football, the social and artistic side of his character found expression in his love of music. He was an accomplished tenor singer, and a member of the Glasgow Select Choir, as well as the Choral Union. He enjoyed other sports such as bowling and golf.

Wilton was 54 when he died and lived in Kilburn Avenue, Dumbreck, on the south side of Glasgow. He was married and was a father to three daughters.

Daily Record reporter 'Brigadier' said, 'By the tragic death of Mr William Wilton, football has lost one of its best-known personalities. Of a reserved nature, he had a firmness of character that made itself apparent only when the situation demanded.

'He was associated with the Rangers club practically since its beginning and, though I cannot go back so far, he has often related to me the story of the struggles of the team in those far off days. He knew what defeat was, and when more successful times came, and the Rangers team was sweeping the boards, he was just as modest – although quietly proud – as he was in the midst of reverses.

'With players and officials in all circles, he was held in the highest esteem and I know of no football official more worthy of his popularity. Courtesy to reporters was one of his unfailing virtues. If he could not divulge his club's private affairs, he was never abrupt with those who might venture beyond the line of reasonableness in their search for information.

'At Ibrox his death will be regretted by everyone as a personal loss. He was loved by his "boys", by trainer, groundsmen and directors, and his place will be difficult to fill.'

With Wilton still missing, and naturally presumed dead, a testimonial match for club stalwart Jimmy Gordon went ahead as scheduled just two days after the final league game of the season. Rangers beat a select side 1-0 in a match played with the format of 35 minutes each way. To keep the 16,000 crowd entertained, there was an exhibition of boxing and a sprint competition. Meiklejohn played in the match which added £710 to Gordon's fund.

On Saturday 15 May the last Rangers fixture of a long and weary campaign took place on the beautiful island of Arran. The match, at Lamlash, raised £25 for the Arran Memorial Hospital – and Meiklejohn had firmly established himself as a first-team regular. It was a season which had brought an impressive haul of seven medals, but also tragedy on an unimaginable scale.

3

The honeymoon
is over

AS SHORT as it was, Meik had served his football apprenticeship and, despite being still just 19 years old, he was an integral part of the first-team set-up at Ibrox. But the first business of the new season didn't directly involve the playing staff. The club's Annual General Meeting was held at the Trade's Hall, in Glassford Street, Glasgow, where the financial position at Ibrox was described as healthy.

The club had a balance, after the deduction of operating costs, of £8,412 2s 6d. Just over £40,000 had been taken through the gate, and a total of £12,172 shelled out on players' wages, expenses and transfers. One can only wonder how much of that found its way into the pocket of big Davie.

In the middle of June, Bill Struth was promoted from trainer to manager. The chairman, Sir John Ure Primrose, had watched the players blossom under Struth's tutelage over the past six years and felt the time was right to allow the former Clyde trainer a free rein on team matters. Struth was well thought of in the football world, having taken Clyde to a Scottish Cup Final.

And one of the first decisions the new manager made was a splendid one. He signed Alan Morton, the 'Wee Blue Devil', from the amateurs of Queen's Park. He was 'acquired' to replace the flying doctor, James

Paterson, who was on the verge of accepting a clinical post in London and signing for Arsenal. Morton cost Rangers £3,000 and would go on to become one of the best buys, pound-for-pound, made by the club.

But while Morton was a fully-fledged Ranger, the business of bringing five-a-side glory to the club passed him by. During the 1900s, club sports days were the staple of the close-season and the Rangers offering was among the best run and attended in the country.

As a former athlete, the sports day was the domain of Struth, and while many folk turned up to see the big-name runners, a large chunk of the afternoon was held over for the five-a-side tournament contested by first-team players from leading Scottish League clubs. Much kudos was attached to the outcome with attractive prizes up for grabs.

First on the calendar was the Ibrox Sports Day (which differed from the Rangers Sports Day), and the stands were packed as Rangers – represented by Harold McKenna, Arthur Dixon, Meiklejohn, Andy Cunningham and Archibald – grabbed the honours, seeing off Clyde and Third Lanark before disposing of Clydebank in the final.

Just days after the tournament, though, divers recovered the body of William Wilton from the River Clyde. His funeral, at Cathcart Cemetery, took place on Tuesday 29 June 1920 and was attended by a large number of family, friends and Rangers supporters. The players walked behind the cortege as it made its way into the cemetery.

The following weekend Rangers won the fives at the Glasgow Police Sports event, which was held at Ibrox. Archibald and Dixon were replaced by Walls and Tommy Cairns and after seeing off Clyde, in which Meiklejohn scored, Rangers thumped Celtic 5-0 in the final with Meik scoring twice.

The Gers then won the Harland and Wolff Sports Day Fives to become the kings of small-sided soccer before adding the Firhill Sports Day competition, courtesy of a Meiklejohn counter in the final. Success followed at the Clyde Sports Day at Shawfield.

Off the park things were moving along nicely and a new club secretary had been appointed. Mr W. Rogers Simpson's first duty was to organise the sale of season tickets, which sold out within a couple of hours at the Ibrox ticket office. Mr Rogers Simpson was a chartered accountant based at St Vincent Street, in Glasgow city centre.

Back to the fives and Rangers continued to dominate by winning their own competition. Rangers Sports took place just ten days before the new season and 700 entrants in track and field assured some great entertainment for spectators.

In the football, Clydebank were brushed aside in the quarter-finals, with Meiklejohn scoring twice in a 3-0 win. A narrow defeat of Clyde followed and in the final, against Partick Thistle, Meik scored once again in a 4-0 win. Cunningham bagged a hat-trick.

More than £1,000 was taken at the gate, as well as a 'pot of money' from the stand, but one season ticket holder complained that his brief hadn't allowed him access to the seated area as it had done for years. He was forced to hand over an extra shilling to gain admittance to the stand.

Rangers moved on to the final sports day of the pre-season hosted by arch-rivals Celtic. Meiklejohn was joined by Walls, Cunningham, Tommy Muirhead and McKenna, and they were red-hot favourites to continue their winning streak, but the best-laid plans...

In the semi-finals, against Celtic's 'B' team, an 'awful collision' between Meiklejohn and Tommy McInally looked likely to put both players in hospital, although thankfully, despite being badly shaken, both were able to carry on after lengthy treatment. Celtic won 3-0 but Meik's injury wouldn't be the last suffered by this wholehearted Ranger.

It was a disappointing manner by which to end the five-a-side 'season' although I'm sure a fantastic start to the new league campaign, with Rangers defending the title, would help the Light Blues overcome the disappointment.

Prices for the new season had been set at 1s (5p) for adults (which included the dreaded Entertainment Tax), 6d for soldiers, sailors and boys, 1s for admittance to the grandstand, and 7d for the North Stand.

But the first match, against Airdrie at Ibrox, drew just 12,000 supporters due in part to the awful weather. The game was played on a Tuesday night with a 7pm kick-off and Rangers lined up thus: Robb, Manderson, Smith, Muirhead, Dixon, Walls, Archibald, Bowie, Cunningham, Cairns (who had missed out on the Celtic fives due to injury), and Morton.

Meiklejohn had picked up an injury in training and was replaced by Muirhead while Morton, making his Rangers debut, was forced off after being injured in a tackle with Airdrie's Dick. But Rangers were still strong enough to win 4-1.

Meik was back for the next game, against Aberdeen, but was one of six players injured in a fierce contest. The day after the match, Jimmy Gordon, 13 years a Ranger, left Ibrox to sign for Dunfermline Athletic in the second-tier Central League.

In the 1920s, players were rewarded with a benefit match for five years' service, unlike today's testimonial criteria of ten years. Meik's team-mate Bert Manderson, the Northern Irishman, was one such player granted a benefit game. Celtic were the visitors and 10,000 turned up, producing gate receipts of £500.

During the game, which Rangers won 2-1, the Celtic keeper Charley Shaw suffered a hand injury and was forced to leave the field. With no substitutes allowed in those days, Celtic called on the services of Rangers centre-back Arthur Dixon, who was running the line. A quick change of attire saw him take over between the sticks and he was credited with making some fine saves. Manderson, nicknamed 'McHinnery' by Gordon, had been signed from Belfast Celtic and converted by the Light Blues from a centre-forward to a full-back of some note.

The Light Blues maintained their fantastic 100 per cent league record with a 2-0 win over Morton in front of 41,000. Their seventh successive win saw them move three points clear of Airdrie at the top of the league.

Another difference between football in Meiklejohn's day and modern times was the importance placed on the Glasgow Cup. Nowadays the competition is contested between Glasgow's youth sides. Not in the 1920s. It was a must-win competition for Meik and co but they were disappointed when falling at the first hurdle to Celtic, by 2-1, and not even a burst ball could help them.

But they were soon back on track and dished out a 4-0 thumping to Hearts at their Tynecastle home. As usual, Rangers were cheered on by a large travelling support, complete with must-have accessory – the ricketty. Not for too much longer, though, as at a meeting of the Association of Brake Clubs (forerunner to the supporters' club), it was suggested that ricketties be banned, to give other supporters a bit of peace and quiet.

The following weekend, a record 26,000 crammed into Pittodrie as Rangers and Aberdeen fought out a 1-1 draw. Rookie boss Struth had marked the contest down as a tough one and took the unusual step of travelling up to the Granite City the night before – and with a squad of 13.

When Rangers edged St Mirren at home, at the beginning of October, it still wasn't enough to shake off a battling Airdrie side who won at Falkirk to remain just two points behind the Light Blues.

A 5-2 win over Dumbarton at Boghead, in which Meiklejohn scored, should have given him the green light to celebrate but he was taken off injured and a newspaper report suggested, 'Meiklejohn was good, but it was only after he went off injured that we saw the best half back on the field. I refer, of course, to James Bowie. Meiklejohn may find his true place in attack – in the inside-right berth.'

The visit of Rangers was obviously as prized then as it is now, as Dumbarton took full advantage of the situation by bumping up prices for a seat in the stand. Rather worryingly, a couple of bottles were thrown on to the field from behind the Rangers goal, and many were calling for the perpetrators to be hit hard in the pocket.

In the midweek leading up to a match against Partick Thistle, the same *Daily Record* correspondent brought us the following news, 'Young Meiklejohn, who distinguished himself by scoring a couple of goals in the reserve cup tie at Ibrox, is given a day off on Saturday. The Rangers directors feel that after the rather strenuous time this clever old Maryhill boy has had recently he is entitled to a rest, and so do I. Too much play makes Jack a dull boy. Against Partick at Ibrox, Bowie operates in the right half-back berth, James's best position nowadays, I reckon.'

Meiklejohn stamped his authority on the Second XI Cup tie at Ibrox, against Clyde. 'As a stop-gap centre forward, Meiklejohn did very well indeed. He made himself extra busy and when, in addition to this industry, a man has a couple of goals to his "ain cheek", you must write him down as a success.'

Meik then turned out in a benefit game for Paddy Allan, the noted Clyde player, at Shawfield. A West Select took on their counterparts from the east and the result was £150 in gate receipts for Allan.

All the talk the following midweek was of the impending Old Firm clash at Parkhead, the first competitive fixture of the new season. Both Rangers and Celtic would enter the match unbeaten and it had all the makings of a cracker. But one young man, it seemed, was again destined to have another Saturday afternoon free of competitive action. All the pre-match talk was of 19-year-old Meiklejohn missing out so he looked on from the stand as Rangers won 2-1 to open up a four-point gap at the top of the table.

But he made his return to the first team for the midweek win over Third Lanark – a match that had its fair share of controversy after the full-time whistle. Thirds goalkeeper James Brownlie refused to accept that Rangers had won the game and said, 'Rangers were the better team, but they didn't beat us. Alan Morton was clearly offside and the goal should not have stood.'

Later in the week referee John Howden rubbished Brownlie's claims and stated that the keeper had touched it last – so therefore, it was a goal.

At the start of November, Billy McCandless made his Rangers debut in a 5-0 rout of Dundee. The former Linfield full-back had a fine game in front of 43,000 but once again it was Meik who stole the show, and after the game one reporter said, 'Meiklejohn is one of the finest players the Rangers have signed in many a day.'

George Henderson was another Ranger in the limelight and his four goals against the Dark Blues had pundits questioning Dundee's decision to 'free' Henderson the previous season. The following weekend, Rangers made the short trip through the Clyde Tunnel to face Clydebank in Yoker and won 4-2 – with Henderson scoring all four. The jury was still out though, and one critic wrote, 'Still not convinced that Henderson is the ideal centre forward for the Rangers. I wish to see him up against sterner opposition!'

The big Forfar-born striker was on the mark again the following Saturday in a 4-0 win over Hamilton Accies. His double made it ten goals in three games, although apparently the feat wasn't as accomplished as Willie Hunter of Airdrie, who managed 'three fours' in as many weeks against Hearts, Morton and Partick Thistle.

It was noted that a Rangers director, Councillor Buchanan, and William Wilton had fancied Henderson when the Ibrox side had travelled up to Dundee the previous season, even though he had been 'stuck out on the wing'. But Henderson had proved his worth and with Celtic losing 2-0 to Clyde on the day Rangers thumped Accies, a seven-point gap opened up at the top of the league table.

As a result of their terrific form, the Rangers players journeyed to Turnberry in Ayrshire to 'escape the Glasgow fog', but Henderson contracted flu and missed the 2-1 win over Albion Rovers. On the same weekend, police put up a notice on Glasgow Green, warning people that football was 'banned on the Green on a Sunday'. Those who ignored the notice were warned of 'dire consequences'. And to think it had been Rangers' first home just 38 years beforehand.

As the season pressed on into December, the Rangers directors announced that as Meiklejohn hadn't yet 'fully matured', he would be rested for the visit of Queen's Park to Ibrox. Simultaneously, referees decided they wanted more money and the Newspaper Proprietors Society suggested to the football authorities that games should start no 'later than 3pm, to give them a fighting chance of getting their copy filed for the next day's papers'. The league declined their 'thoughtful' suggestion.

And as for resting the 'immature' Meiklejohn, he was called up when Cairns withdrew from the game – and scored in a 3-1 win. He was then pushed to right-back when Manderson limped off injured but missed the next match – against Falkirk – when a 2-0 win saw the Gers regain their seven-point advantage. It must have been some consolation that the young right-half was on course to add another medal to his collection.

The week before Christmas, Rangers headed down the coast to tackle Ayr United and required a late goal to eke out a 1-1 draw against the Somerset Park surprise packets. During the match, the Ayr keeper George Nisbet was hit with a couple of cinders, thrown by supporters behind his goal.

Three days before the big Ne'erday clash between Rangers at Celtic at Ibrox, the Light Blues received a triple blow when Jimmy Bowie suffered a broken shoulder, and James Walls, who was 'resident' in the Glasgow Victoria Infirmary, a double leg break. Alan Morton was also struggling to make the game due to a bad cold. It was news Rangers could have done without. What it did do, though, was to open the door for Meiklejohn, and he found himself included in a 13-man squad for the game.

Meanwhile, in light of several unsavoury incidents at recent matches, and a *Daily Record* campaign to cut down on rowdy behaviour, Struth, along with the directors, took the unusual step of banning flags, whistle, bugles and ricketties from Ibrox on the day of the Old Firm game – and until further notice. An advert in the *Daily Record* read, 'Notice is hereby given that on and after Saturday, January 1, 1921, any person found carrying a flag or other paraphernalia will not be admitted to Ibrox Park.' Drivers of supporters' buses (brakes) were required to give police the names and addresses of everyone travelling on their coach. A few days before the game, Struth met up with brake club chiefs to outline his reasons for the flag ban.

Members of the Rangers brake clubs were required to leave their charabancs (coaches) at Fairlie Street and enter by the gates in Copland Road, while Celtic supporters were instructed to enter by Broomloan Road. The match had a 2pm kick-off and admission prices were 1s in the Enclosure, 2s 6d for the Grandstand and 1s in the North Stand.

It was pay at the gate and the 70,000 supporters who filed into Ibrox for the big match behaved impeccably, despite the vast majority being disappointed by the final scoreline of 2-0 to Celtic. The Rangers side was: Robb, Manderson, McCandless, Meiklejohn, Dixon, Muirhead, Archibald, Cunningham, Henderson, Cairns and Morton. Celtic's opening goal arrived when the referee awarded the visitors a free kick for a seemingly innocuous challenge by Meiklejohn on Adam McLean. Joe Cassidy, who notched both goals, scored directly from the kick. Definitely not an Old Firm debut to remember.

Despite the loss, Rangers remained four points clear of their rivals and there was to be no let-up for the Light Blues with Partick Thistle next on the agenda, at Firhill, just 48 hours after the game against Celtic. The trip to Maryhill would see remarkable scenes as a record crowd squeezed into Firhill.

Long before kick-off, the terracing was packed as tight as sardines and eventually the gates had to be closed with thousands unable to gain admission. The crowd, officially returned at 42,000, was a record for Firhill (the record attendance for a Partick Thistle match came in 1922 when 49,838 were present for the visit of Rangers. However, the stadium record remains at 54,728, for a Scotland v Ireland Home International match in 1928), and so greatly was the accommodation taxed that many hundreds, unfortunate to be on the fringes, were unable to see anything of the game.

Among the densely-packed spectators on the terracing, the congestion was severe. Despite the extreme pressure and discomfort resulting from this, the behaviour of the crowd was quite exemplary, with good humour and banter prevailing, although the congestion proved the catalyst for an unfortunate sequel.

Three minutes after the start of the game, the pressure of this great, swaying mass of humanity, packed on the terracing at the city end of the field, broke the crush barriers, and a stream of surging spectators was precipitated down the slope behind the goal.

The increased congestion burst a gap in the fencing round the enclosure and hundreds poured through the opening on to the narrow strip of ground surrounding the playing pitch itself. In the rush down the terracing and the resulting stampede on to the ground, a great number of spectators were trampled upon and at least three were injured, though fortunately not seriously.

Shortly afterwards, the crush barriers near the same end – but on the canal side of the field – gave way and a similar mishap occurred behind the goal at the other end, but again, in both cases, without any injury to person.

Some desperately-inclined enthusiasts succeeded in effecting an opening in the corrugated iron fence surrounding the field on the canal side and, crossing the canal bridge, endeavoured to follow the play from the vantage point of the high ground on the other side of the water. Others, dissatisfied at being unable to see the match, made their way round to the stand side, and clamoured at the turnstiles for the return of their money.

A considerable number made their way home, despairing of seeing anything of the match at all. There was, however, no suggestion of a disturbance of any kind, and even with the spectators almost on the touchline nothing of an untoward nature occurred.

The incident seemed to suggest the necessity of more adequate provision for regulating the admission of crowds to grounds of such limited accommodation as Firhill. Erecting crush barriers in concrete was also discussed in the aftermath of the game.

Astonishingly, within just 24 hours of the match, Thistle directors released plans to increase the capacity of their ground to 60,000, and then made the grand gesture of donating £150 to charity – with Glasgow's three hospitals, the Royal, Western and Victoria, being awarded £50 each. Rangers followed suit by donating £100 to each.

Following their festive exertions, it was back to Turnberry as the players recharged their batteries for the battles ahead. While they were enjoying an evening of music, a directive came through from the football authorities ordering referees to stop poking players in the chest while dishing out a stern lecture.

Rangers travelled back up from South Ayrshire for the Scottish Cup second round tie at home to Morton, but pensioners looking to take advantage of a free admission offer were told they wouldn't be admitted unless in possession of a special permit from hospital confirming that they were indeed of pensionable age. The new measures were put in place due to recent abuse of the scheme.

Rangers won comfortably and it was suggested in some quarters that it was Meiklejohn's finest game to date in the light blue. A crowd of 67,000 watched the Gers move easily into the last 16, and with a healthy six-point lead at the top of the table, everything in the Ibrox garden was rosy.

A trip to Dens Park, Dundee, was next on the agenda and a brake club from Paisley Road West advertised seats on a 'fast and comfy' charabanc, leaving Glasgow at 8.30am on the Saturday, and returning the next day – fare 15 shillings (75p). The Summertown Rangers Brake Club, from Govan, also had spare seats for Dundee, and were five shillings cheaper, but didn't say if they were fast and comfy.

Problems were mounting though for several members of the 'rowdier' brake clubs and in a letter to the Scottish Football Association, the town clerk of Ayr suggested imprisoning offenders – with hard labour. The SFA took the 'lighter' approach of banning flags from all grounds.

Rangers were vastly below strength for the trip and were minus Archibald and Cunningham, who were on international duty for

Scotland against Wales, and Dixon, who was injured. However they still had enough in the tank to edge home 2-1.

There was controversy brewing over Scotland's next fixture though when Rangers became embroiled in a tug-of-war with Northern Ireland over full-backs Manderson and McCandless, both of whom had been chosen to oppose the Scots in Belfast. Rangers decided the pair were required for the Scottish Cup tie against Alloa.

The Wasps had shocked Rangers by drawing 0-0 in the first staging and club directors were taking no chances for the replay. They demanded the withdrawal of Manderson and McCandless from the Irish squad, which prompted a 'play the game' comment from the Northern Irish Football Association. Rangers responded by officially withdrawing the pair, and Cunningham, the national skipper, and Archibald from the Scotland side. The move was unpopular with both international selection committees but it was Rangers paying the wages.

The goalless draw with Alloa had been termed 'the biggest shock in cup football since Arthurlie had beaten Celtic at Barrhead', but it had also produced a flurry of complaints to the SFA, suggesting that perhaps there was foul play at work. With an unusually high number of cup draws that season it was mooted in many circles that it was a deliberate ploy to glean more cash for clubs. In fact, it was shown that replays had raked in more than £10,000 in gate receipts. Dundee Hibs manager Reilly called for half-price admission for replays, while others suggested extra time for first replays.

Regardless, the recall of Rangers' four internationalists had shown how importantly the tie was being viewed on the south side of Glasgow. But there was joy all round as Cairns burst the net with a rocket shot and Rangers won 4-1, while Scotland also achieved a 2-0 success.

The next round of the cup saw the Gers drawn to play at the aptly named Boghead, home of Dumbarton. True to form, the tie took place on a rainy Saturday and the mudheap of a pitch acted as a 'great leveller'. The Dumbarton directors, anticipating a big crowd, were keen for the tie to go ahead and called in volunteers to help whip the ground into shape. The match did take place, there was indeed a big crowd, and Rangers won 3-0 thanks to goals from Bowie, Cunningham and Henderson. Could this finally be the year Rangers would end their 18-year wait for the national trophy?

With the league title all but in the bag, thanks to a thumping 7-2 win over Ayr United, Rangers were drawn against Albion Rovers in the semis of the Scottish Cup – a repeat of the year previous, when the Coatbridge men had sprung the biggest of cup shocks.

No shocks this time though as Rangers swept the wee Rovers aside in a 4-1 win – at Celtic Park. With such a healthy lead in the title race, there was now a realistic opportunity for the Light Blues to land the coveted double.

In the other semi-final, Partick Thistle and Hearts, favourites to progress, were fighting out the second of two drawn games, the second of which took place at Ibrox. Rangers caught the ferry to Belfast to take part in a challenge match against Linfield. Some 15,000 supporters watched the Gers win 2-0 and Meiklejohn was hailed as a 'quality inside right'. The reporter added, 'It was a treat, the Rangers moving like a machine. On play, the score in their favour should have been larger. Archibald treated the crowd to many a great run, while Meiklejohn scored a lightning goal from 20 yards.'

The Rangers party enjoyed their mini break. On arrival in the city they had spent a pleasant couple of hours touring the Belfast sights, including the beautiful County Down countryside. After the match, they were entertained to dinner by Sir Crawford McCullough, a former High Sheriff of Belfast.

The players arrived back in Glasgow to a cup final storm. The match may still have been a fortnight away but a deluge of letters arrived at the offices of the *Daily Record*, protesting over the choice of Celtic Park as venue for the showpiece match. The announcement prompted the 'great cup final scandal'. The year previous, provincial clubs Kilmarnock and Albion Rovers had drawn 95,000 at Celtic Park but with the capacity lowered to around 70,000, supporters and club officials were keen to see the tie moved to Hampden.

One correspondent said, 'With the Rangers in the final we are guaranteed a crowd of at least 100,000 – but not at Celtic Park. There is a great danger to the public if the match goes ahead there. It simply must be moved. It is insane for the game to remain in the east end of Glasgow.'

But while the choice of venue had prompted howls of derision, there was another matter which caused extra consternation – the doubling of admission prices to two shillings (10p). Many people believed this decision had been made to maintain the level of profit at the smaller capacity stadium. Protests continued unabated and increased when Partick Thistle beat Hearts 2-0 in a second replay at Ibrox to join Rangers in the final.

Meanwhile, it was back to the bread and butter of the league, but after picking up a vital away point in Greenock the headlines concentrated not on a fine performance at Cappielow but on 'a game marred by hooliganism'. The rowdy behaviour was perpetrated, according to one commentator, 'by the hordes waving light blue banners and blowing bugles'. Morton were immediately urged to ban brake club paraphernalia.

Thankfully Rangers were back in the news for all the right reasons when the board of directors moved to re-sign their entire first team for the 1921/22 season.

Saturday 9 April 1921 proved something of a watershed weekend as Rangers emerged from a tough contest at Easter Road with a point, despite being without Morton and Cunningham, who both scored in a 3-0 win for Scotland over the Auld Enemy. Meiklejohn was named man of the match in the capital and when it was learned that Celtic had lost 2-0 in Kirkcaldy to Raith Rovers, the Ibrox side required just a point to retain their title. After the match, chairman Sir John Ure Primrose announced that Lord Weir had accepted the honorary presidency of Rangers FC.

Plans were soon afoot to stage an unofficial British championship match between the national cup winners and it was predicted that Rangers would face Tottenham Hotspur. Quite what Partick and Wolverhampton Wanderers had to say about the matter was anyone's guess.

The answer was soon upon us as Rangers and Partick Thistle – both at full strength – arrived at Celtic Park on the morning of Saturday 16 April to prepare for the big match. The SFA had banned flags and ricketties and Rangers lined up with: Robb, Manderson, McCandless, Meiklejohn, Dixon, Bowie, Archibald, Cunningham, Henderson, Cairns and Morton. The pre-match furore over venue and admission prices had taken their toll on the crowd, and less than 30,000 bothered to turn up.

Meiklejohn had two fantastic shots on target early on but it was Thistle who made the breakthrough when John Blair scored midway through the first half. On chances created, Rangers were streets ahead, but the Jags had taken one of the few opportunities they'd had and the Light Blues' long wait for the national trophy would continue.

Just 72 hours later, the disappointment of the cup was forgotten as goals by Henderson, Meik and Archibald saw off a stubborn Clyde to clinch the league title – the only disappointment being that just 10,000 fans were in the ground to see it happen.

The next league match, against St Mirren, was meaningless in terms of the championship but with Love Street under construction, both teams asked the SFA if the fixture could be played at Ibrox. They refused and instead ordered it to be played at Hampden. Just 9,000 saw Meiklejohn score a 'grand goal', the only one of the encounter.

The following midweek, Newcastle United were in town to take part in the Tommy Cairns benefit match. They brought with them stalwarts such as Jamie Lawrence, Billy McCracken and Wilfy Low to honour the Larkhall boy who had played with Bristol City and St Johnstone before joining Rangers. A crowd of 20,000 watched a 0-0 draw but Cairns was the big winner as gate receipts topped £1,000.

The Saturday after, a Muirhead goal in the final league match of the season at Kirkcaldy meant Rangers had won the title by ten points from Celtic – and lost just one of 42 league games. It was a fair reflection of Rangers' domination.

In the Glasgow Charities Cup, successive wins over Queen's Park and Clyde set up an Old Firm final which drew 50,000 to Hampden Park. Unfortunately the season finished on a low note as Celtic posted a 2-0 win.

But as a result of their endeavours over a tough campaign, the Ibrox directors sent the players on a recuperative two-week trip to Denmark – where they would play three matches. The trip was delayed 24 hours though when their liner *Breslin* was held up at Leith Docks. The party eventually set sail and played their first match against Copenhagen Academic. After a comfortable 2-0 win, manager Struth said, 'A great reception and a record gate for an evening match – the trip is a top-hole success.'

Next up was 1903 Jeam and once again the team recorded a victory, this time 2-1, and the attendance eclipsed that of the first match. But the players were far from happy that 'pushing' was allowed in Danish football, something that definitely got their hackles up.

But the team arrived home to a fanfare, unbeaten – after a 2-1 win in their final match over a select side – and to discover that the club had made a substantial increase in revenue during the season just finished. They had taken in £40,000, paid out £12,500 in wages and shown a healthy balance of £14,000, of which £10,000 was set aside for a new grandstand. Happy days.

4

Meik caps a great season

IT WAS a fair cop as Rangers limbered up for the new season by taking part in the five-a-side competition at the Glasgow Police Sports Day at Ibrox – but it would end with Meiklejohn being knocked unconscious by a hooligan supporter in Denmark.

The Light Blues had once again decided to head for the 'tranquillity' of Scandinavia after a hectic season but in the final match of their short tour, against an international select, some poor refereeing led to Gers players contending several awful decisions – something the home fans seemed to take umbrage at, and they invaded the park.

The Scots stars feared for their safety so much that the Danish players were forced to form a ring of steel round their opponents to prevent further injury.

But to the start of the campaign and, as usual, Rangers swept all before them. The fives were a great way for the players to shake off the close-season cobwebs and at the cops' big day, the Light Blues were ably represented by McKenna, Lawson, Meiklejohn, Morton and McDiarmid.

The following Friday there were scenes of pandemonium in Glasgow city centre as the club put their season tickets on sale at sports shop, Lumley's, in Sauchiehall Street. The store, besieged by fans desperate to get their hands on one of the golddust briefs, was forced to open an hour early as upwards of 500 supporters waited impatiently for the chance to secure one of just 200 available tickets. The moment the doors opened, fans surged forward, but in their haste to get upstairs they succeeded only in smashing a glass counter and causing havoc in the store.

That night, between 7pm and 9pm, a further 500 were up for grabs at the Ibrox ticket office. Word quickly spread and by 4pm large crowds had started to form. When the office opened, more than 1,000 people were outside, and within 20 minutes every available membership card had been snapped up. That night, manager Bill Struth, joyful at this ringing endorsement from supporters, signed goalkeeper William Gould from Queen's Park.

Rangers entered a team for the Clyde Sports Day and once again the all-conquering Gers came up trumps. Meiklejohn bagged the only goal of the Old Firm semi-final, and Hamilton Accies were edged in the final. It was a great confidence booster ahead of the new season, and when they repeated the feat a week later at the Ibrox Sports Day, albeit with a single-goal win over Celtic in the final, the set was complete. On this occasion, it was recorded that, 'The Old Firm fought as though the Scottish Cup was at stake.' The winners received the most beautiful ladies' gold watches.

A strange incident took place during the match. Celtic's Joe Cassidy thumped Meiklejohn before scoring, a goal which the referee correctly disallowed, but the injured Ranger was forced to leave the pitch as a consequence. In a true show of sportsmanship, Celtic's Patsy Gallacher offered to go off to even up the numbers but the referee wouldn't allow him.

Late in the second period of extra time, a mistake by a Celtic back proved costly and Sandy Archibald ran off to score the only goal of a game described, the Gallacher incident apart, as the 'most thrilling and needly final of fives ever seen'. The Rangers players were no doubt relieved to hear the full-time gun.

Celtic had an opportunity for revenge when they hosted their own sports day just a couple of days before the opening league fixtures – but somehow it didn't pan out that way. Rangers were represented by McKenna, Meiklejohn, Cunningham, Muirhead and Archibald and after beating Clyde and Partick Thistle, the scene was set for another

Old Firm final. This time though, there was to be no grey area as ruthless Rangers crushed their foes 5-1, thanks to a Cunningham treble and two from Archibald. As a result of their endeavour, the Gers players were presented with 'handsome' clocks.

Rangers were buoyant as they went into the first league game of the season against Third Lanark at Cathkin Park and a 3-1 win was followed by a sound 7-1 thrashing of Clydebank, a game Meiklejohn missed due to the after-effects of a knock suffered in the fives at Celtic Park. 'Jock' Nicholson proved an able deputy. But Meik was in line to return for the visit of Motherwell and took part in a friendly match at Ardencaple Park, against Helensburgh, in the midweek prior to the match.

The players enjoyed a pleasant sail 'doon the watter' before playing a round of golf. Right-back Billy McCandless was forced to miss the Helensburgh trip as his mum took ill in Northern Ireland. Sadly, she passed away while he was en route to the province.

With hardly a ball kicked in anger, Meiklejohn received individual recognition when he was named in the Glasgow team to face Sheffield in the annual inter-city match, scheduled for the Steel City. In the 1920s selectors named their team well in advance, rather than a squad, and subsequent withdrawals were catered for if and when required. Meik was joined in the team by fellow Ger Bob McDiarmid.

Meanwhile, Rangers set yet another new attendance record when they travelled to Paisley to face St Mirren. A crowd of 35,290 squeezed into Love Street to see Rangers win 2-1 but the victory was once again marred by crowd trouble, with the notorious brakesmen battling throughout the match. Squabbling supporters spilled on to the pitch and the game was held up until order was restored.

Saints directors immediately banned brake club paraphernalia. Third Lanark and Queen's Park followed suit as the menace rapidly became a thorny issue for football clubs and the national association. And there was more violence the following weekend when trouble erupted at the Old Firm RESERVE match.

On Monday 13 September, Glasgow travelled down to Sheffield and after the Scots secured a 1-1 draw, the Yorkshire press gushed, 'The best display ever by a Glasgow team in Sheffield. The Scots should have been three or four up at the break.'

Instead they were one down, although Meiklejohn placed a second-half free kick nicely on to the head of Partick Thistle forward Jimmy Kinloch and he nodded home the leveller. Meiklejohn then almost 'uprooted a post' with a thunderous shot, and was afterwards described as the 'top man in the middle of the park'. After the match, the players were treated to an evening at the theatre.

Rangers warmed up for the Glasgow Cup Final against Celtic with a friendly match at Newcastle and even though United edged it 2-1, it was an even game.

The city final was a sparkling affair played out in front of 80,000 passionate supporters, and despite Rangers suffering a pre-match blow when Alan Morton was declared unfit, his replacement McDiarmid didn't let the side down. He played his part in a magnificent 1-0 victory – Rangers' 14th Glasgow Cup win – although it was said they won more easily than the score suggested.

Meiklejohn got a grip of his team early on and didn't let go the entire 90 minutes. Rangers had lots of pressure but the only goal of the game arrived when the ball fell to Meik on the edge of the box and he let fly with a lightning drive. From the moment it left his boot, Celtic keeper Charley Shaw hadn't an earthly of saving it.

Later, referee J.B. Stevenson, of Motherwell, would call the game 'the hardest and hottest he'd ever had to handle'. Mr J. Chalmers, director of the Glasgow FA, said, 'Rangers won on their weight – I never saw a Celtic team so diminutive by comparison with their Ibrox opponents.'

Meiklejohn's dazzling cup final performance had obviously impressed the watching Scottish League selectors and he was chosen, along with team-mate Tommy Muirhead, to represent his country against the Irish at Clyde's Shawfield Stadium in November. *Daily Record* columnist 'Waverley' said, 'Great to see the Rangers wing half backs getting recognition. They have the ability but are they possessed of the indefinable national temperament?'

By the time the inter-league match came around, Meiklejohn and Muirhead were joined by a third Ranger, Andy Cunningham, and the Light Blue trio played their part in a 3-0 win. Some 14,000 looked on as the match was held up when a dog ran on the pitch and no one could catch it. Another bonus arrived when the directors of Rangers decided to revive their annual dance at the Grosvenor Cafe. 'A real terpsichorean treat,' offered one commentator.

The beginning of November 1921 also brought Meiklejohn and co a new team-mate, someone they had first crossed paths with while touring Denmark. Carl Hansen was over in Glasgow on business but turned up at Ibrox for a trial, although it's likely that was organised while Struth and the squad had been in Copenhagen. He was a skilful centre-forward with pace to burn, and 'tried out' in a Scottish Alliance League fixture against Hamilton Accies. By all accounts his examination was a success and he excelled in a 2-0 win. His name was soon added to the list of signed Ibrox players.

The injured Meiklejohn missed a league match against Dumbarton at Ibrox, but what was simply a run-of-the-mill game turned to tragedy afterwards when the Sons' keeper, Joseph Wilkinson, took ill. The former Rangers custodian, who was just 22, had complained to the Ibrox trainer of feeling unwell before the game. After getting showered and changed he was conveyed to his home by motor car but took a turn for the worse and was rushed to the Western Infirmary where peritonitis was diagnosed.

Struth was one of the first to visit Wilkinson and after holding a conversation he lost consciousness, which he never regained. Wilkinson had been studying for an honours degree at university and had served three years at sea during the First World War, being twice torpedoed. Struth and several first-team players attended Wilkinson's funeral at Dumbarton Crematorium.

Meiklejohn returned to the first team and played his part in a win at Morton before 100 couples enjoyed the annual bash at the Grosvenor. Soft drinks were the order of the day as the players had a match against Queen's Park the following day, in Lord Provost Paxton's Unemployed Cup. Hansen was down to play but was reminded by Struth that straight after the match he would start the process of becoming more fluent in English.

Cunningham, Cairns and Dixon were all doubtful, although Struth moved quickly to remind the press that their lack of fitness had nothing to do with the previous night's dance. The match, played at Hampden, soon morphed into the 'Carl Hansen show' as the tricky little Dane smashed in a stunning hat-trick. 'Waverley' suggested that his second goal was 'the best seen in a long time'.

In the next round of the Unemployed Cup against Partick Thistle there was no Meiklejohn, who had been feeling unwell and groggy. Hansen started again though and came up with a 'sublime chip' to clinch the win for the Gers in front of 10,000 fans at Ibrox. The following Tuesday, 25,000 watched Rangers dump Celtic 2-0 at Hampden with Hansen once again on the scoresheet. Rangers had relaxed at Turnberry prior to the game with a round of golf at the famous course.

The Light Blues entered the festive period with a table-topping three-point advantage over Celtic after a 2-1 win over Dundee, in which Hansen had netted. It was a busy period for the team and they welcomed Meiklejohn back for the match against St Mirren at Ibrox on Hogmanay. In one of their best performances of the season they slammed four goals past the beleaguered Saints, and two days later drew 0-0 with Celtic.

No rest for the wicked and they were in action just 24 hours later at home to Partick. The game finished all square, but only after goals from Cairns and Meiklejohn had hauled Rangers back from two goals down. At the close of a busy festive period, the Gers were still three points to the good.

So how did the players relax after such a busy spell? They played another match the following night, this time a benefit for Clyde stalwart Tommy Shingleton. Some 3,000 spectators watched a 2-2 draw at Shawfield and once again Hansen found the net, but the game was notable for the Light Blues' keeper Willie Robb playing outfield – and dislocating a hand.

Afterwards, he told the press, 'There is no chance of me missing Saturday's league match at Ayr.' And true to his word, he was back between the sticks less than 72 hours later – and kept a clean sheet. Hansen hit the post three times but Archibald popped up to nab the game's only goal.

It was Scottish Cup time and Rangers found themselves facing a lengthy trek to Inverness to face Highland League side Clachnacuddin. The Light Blues were naturally overwhelming favourites to progress but the logistical issues involved in a January trip north led to the club making Clach officials a monetary offer in return for switching the game to Ibrox. It seemed a win-win situation all round – Rangers wouldn't have to travel and Clach would secure one heck of a pay day.

The Highlanders knocked back the offer, calling it 'wholly unacceptable', and Rangers were forced to head north. They negotiated the potential banana skin tie, romping to a 5-0 win, and also took home a cheque for £70, their share of the gate.

A mini blip in the league saw Rangers lose at home to Raith Rovers and draw at Hamilton in mid-January, leaving Celtic to top the table on goal difference, but the Light Blues' indifferent form didn't prevent Meik being called up for Scotland for the Home International match against Wales in Wrexham the following weekend. It would be his first full cap and was a belated 21st birthday present for the popular Govan man. He was joined by team-mates Alec Archibald and Alan Morton.

And so began the build-up to one of the biggest weeks of Meik's career. The Scotland squad left Central Station on the 10.10am train bound for Liverpool, where they stayed the night, before catching another train to Wrexham the following morning. They arrived in the largest town in North Wales a little under three hours before kick-off, and Archibald scored for the Scots in a 2-1 defeat.

Meiklejohn, though, was reported to have played well. One sour note, though, was the refusal by the SFA to allow Rangers' proposed league game at Motherwell to be postponed, despite three of their top players representing their country in Wales. A 2-0 defeat at Fir Park helped Celtic edge a point clear at the top.

Back to domestic action and Meiklejohn, still on a high from making his Scotland debut, opened the scoring in a Scottish Cup second round replay at Ibrox as Rangers thumped Albion Rovers 4-0. It was a sweet 30-yard drive that slipped under the Rovers keeper.

When the third round draw was made, Rangers would face either Hearts or non-league Broxburn. The sides drew 2-2 at Tynecastle but Hearts won the replay 2-0 and in the crowd was a small posse of Ibrox 'spies', including manager Struth and director Bailie Buchanan.

While Hearts were beating Broxburn in the replay, Rangers had come through the 'Battle of Firhill' anything but unscathed. Several top players were injured in a match watched by almost 50,000, although the Light Blues still had enough in the tank to register a 4-0 win in Gorgie, thanks to goals from Cunningham (two), Muirhead and Morton. It was a tricky hurdle safely negotiated.

But their stuttering league form was becoming a real concern for Struth and an opportunity to regain pole position in the title race was missed when they could only draw 0-0 at home to Falkirk on the last day of February – the day of the royal wedding between Princess Mary (daughter of King George) and Viscount Lascelles. It was a public holiday but 18,000 supporters went home frustrated at a lack of action in a dour match. The following night, Celtic trounced Hamilton 4-0 to open up a two-point gap at the summit.

Rangers were without three players against Morton – thanks to the Scotland v Ireland international at Celtic Park – but managed to beat the Greenock side handsomely and with Third Lanark holding Celtic at Cathkin, the points deficit was halved.

But there was a storm brewing and it was one that would rumble on for many weeks. Rangers had five players picked for the Scottish League's match against the English, on the same day they were due to face Aberdeen in an important league tussle at Pittodrie. With the title race so tight, naturally Rangers asked for a postponement (the rule stated that a club having three or more players in an international squad was entitled to have a domestic match postponed). The request fell on deaf ears and Rangers appealed what appeared to be a harsh decision. The SFA, not for the first time, buried their head in the sand, although the Light Blues refused to accept the decision.

Meanwhile, the club had a Scottish Cup quarter-final replay with St Mirren to negotiate after the first match, in front of 67,700 at Ibrox, had ended 1-1. A 2-0 victory in Paisley saw the Light Blues through to the last four of the competition. A crowd of 37,000 spectators, a new record for Love Street, turned up for the match, which drew £1,700 in gate receipts.

As a reward for their gallant victory, Struth took his players to Portobello 24 hours later for a relaxing day at the seaside. The draw for the semi-finals pitted Rangers with Partick Thistle, the side that had beaten them in the previous year's final.

The row over Rangers' forthcoming match at Aberdeen intensified and the sporting integrity of the Scottish Football Association was once again called into question. Directors of the Ibrox side insisted that the championship was far more important than gate receipts – but several Scottish clubs disagreed. Regardless, the SFA were forced into an embarrassing U-turn and Muirhead, Cairns, Cunningham, Archibald and Morton played for Scotland, who crashed to a 3-0 defeat at the hands of the Auld Enemy at Ibrox. With Rangers inactive, Celtic went six points clear, by gaining a point at Falkirk, although the Light Blues had three games in hand.

Rangers gained some consolation for their Scottish Cup Final defeat 12 months earlier by dumping Partick Thistle 2-0 to book their place in the final. Some 55,000 turned up for the match, but the action wasn't just confined to the field of play. At one point the pavilion chimney caught fire and there was talk of abandoning the game. Curiously, Rangers played in white and Partick in blue.

Rangers were playing catch-up in the title race but wins over Hibs, Ayr United and Raith Rovers – within six days – put them right back in the frame.

The international games were also coming thick and fast and Scotland included Archibald, Cairns and Morton in their team to face England at Birmingham. On the same day, Rangers travelled to muddy Boghead for yet another must-win match. The game remained goalless for the first 70 minutes before Meik fired the Light Blues ahead with a 'rocket shot', and three more put Dumbarton to the sword.

Scotland managed a 1-0 win over England with Archibald supplying the cross for Andy Wilson, of Middlesbrough, to nod past Jerry Dawson, the keeper who would provide the moniker 'Jerry' for the future Rangers custodian James Dawson.

In the race for the title, Celtic had shown a greater consistency and led by three points, and despite playing one game more they were still red-hot favourites to land the crown. Meanwhile, tickets went on sale at the Sportsman's Emporium, in Sauchiehall Street for the Scottish Cup Final between Rangers and Morton, priced at 7/6 (37p) for the Centre Stand, and 5/- for the East and West Stands. It would be manager Bill Struth's fourth Scottish Cup Final, two with Clyde and his second at Ibrox.

It had been 19 years since Rangers last won the cup and the responsibility this year would lie with Robb, Manderson, McCandless,

Meiklejohn, Dixon, Muirhead, Archibald, Cunningham, Henderson, Cairns and Morton. The Gers were red-hot favourites to win but in the build-up to the match, several reporters questioned whether or not Rangers were cursed, as they always seemed to bottle it in the later stages.

A crowd of 70,000 saw Alec Archibald taken off after just 26 minutes with a fractured jaw, and with no substitutes permitted, Rangers were forced to continue with just ten men. Meiklejohn then injured a leg but while he stayed on, he was barely able to play any part in the game. As a consequence of Gers keeper Robb carrying the ball outside the box, Morton were awarded a free kick and Jamie Gourlay scored the only goal of the game. It was a bad day all round as Celtic won 2-0 at Albion Rovers to stretch their lead to five points, with Rangers having just two games in hand.

Rangers had to beat Queen's Park 48 hours later to keep alive their slender title hopes. The match was evenly poised at 1-1 with 75 minutes on the clock when Newton, the Queen's keeper, carried the ball outside the box. Referee Campbell, of Dundee, awarded Rangers a free kick which Carl Hansen took quickly and fired into the back of the net – his second of the match.

It was the strangest of goals as the Queen's keeper, and his defenders, moved out the way and left a clear path to goal – believing the free kick was indirect. Campbell signalled for a goal kick and was at once surrounded by fuming Rangers players, who claimed a goal. They told the ref that the same thing had happened to them in the Scottish Cup Final and that the goal had stood. After consulting his linesman, Campbell changed his mind and awarded a goal. The Queen's Park players were furious and refused to restart the game.

Following lengthy mediation the game was eventually played to a finish, with no more scoring, and the following day Campbell defended his decision, insisting it had been the correct one. The matter caused uproar in the press and Queen's insisted they had been misled by the referee into believing the free kick was indirect. The Hampden club wrote to the Scottish League demanding a replay but their appeal was dismissed.

Hansen smashed home a stunning hat-trick in a 3-0 win against Airdrie and was instantly compared to the great R.S. McColl after the match. He was offered a contract for the following season, which he duly signed. Celtic had just one game to play and Rangers two.

Next up for Rangers was a trip to Kilmarnock where Hansen was once again on target in treacherous conditions. Cairns scored a late goal to give the Gers a 2-1 win with Meiklejohn outstanding. Both halves of the Old Firm had just a single match to play and the destination of the title would come down to the last day.

Before that though, there was the small matter of a benefit match for Andy Cunningham, Rangers' international forward, and Newcastle United arrived in Glasgow near the end of April. Cunningham – an Ayr-shireman who had played for Newmilns and Kilmarnock – was injured and called on the services of a great rival to take his place in the match. A crowd of 20,000 supporters turned up at Ibrox and couldn't believe their eyes when they saw Patsy Gallacher of Celtic in a Rangers shirt. They cheered wildly when Gallacher scored Rangers' equaliser with a cheeky lob after working a clever one-two with George Henderson.

But 'sell-out Saturday', and the league title head-to-head, arrived and the outcome of Clyde v Rangers and Morton v Celtic would determine the destination of the flag. Clyde bosses warned Rangers 'brakesmen' to leave their flags and ricketties at home while at Cappielow, Celtic fans were promised regular 'bulletins' from Shawfield.

It was termed the most strenuous league title ever and in Greenock, Alfy Brown scored for Morton after 35 minutes to throw Rangers a lifeline. At half-time Celtic fans rioted and threw stones at the police. Over in Rutherglen, Alan Morton hit the post for Rangers in a first period of very few chances. After the break, Tommy Cairns missed the 'chance of the century' when the ball rolled across the line and he somehow managed to scoop it over the bar – after it had run up his leg. Back at Cappielow, Andy McAtee scored for Celtic with six minutes remaining to deny Rangers a dead heat, and the prospect of a championship play-off.

It was a bitter pill to swallow but Rangers had a modicum of revenge the following Saturday when they edged Celtic in the semi-finals of the Glasgow Merchant's Charity Cup at Hampden. Some 33,000 watched the teams fight out a 0-0 draw but Rangers progressed to the final courtesy of accumulating four corners more.

Prior to the final, Struth knocked back a transfer bid by Raith Rovers for centre-forward J.R. Smith, and included the Battlefield lad against Queen's Park. However, one correspondent suggested that the players refused to pass to 'JR', and it was left to a Sandy Archibald hat-trick to give Rangers the trophy.

Once again, Rangers chose to head off to Denmark at the end of another tiring campaign – although this time the tour would be mired in controversy. The first-team party, plus Great Dane Carl Hansen and J.R. Smith, left Queen Street Station on 25 May, bound for Copenhagen, where they would play three matches. Rangers started off by beating a Copenhagen Select 1-0, with fringe player Smith getting the only goal in front of 15,000 spectators.

The second game, a 3-0 win over Copenhagen Athletic, a select team comprised of players from the 1903 Club, the Academicals and Frem, was played in damp conditions in front of around 10,000. Hansen was given a tremendous ovation when the teams took to the park and repaid his compatriots by putting on a first-class exhibition of football, scoring two fantastic goals in the opening half. Tommy Muirhead grabbed a third.

Struth said, 'The scoring ended at three and our boys treated the natives to a real entertaining exhibition of spectacular football. The Danes were outplayed, and goals were there for the scoring, even with our own Dane limping throughout the second half. Carl, who was the victim of a rather hefty "block", also suffered from a painful foot as the result of getting a heavy ball too much on his toes.

'I have been told that the international team we face on Monday will be quite a different proposition. I hope so. Up until now, the teams we have met have been a good bit behind those we played a year ago. Last Saturday we were in Sweden – at Malmo, whose club ground we visited. The enclosure, which is well appointed and equipped, is run without municipal or State aid; the club members pay the piper.'

Hansen missed the final game of the tour, but Cairns and Jock Nicholson scored for Rangers. However, regrettable scenes took place at the end of the match when fans invaded the pitch and Meiklejohn was knocked unconscious by a hooligan supporter.

In the second half, Smith was sent off, a decision which the Rangers players deemed grossly unfair. With just two minutes remaining, a free kick was awarded to the home side, and again Rangers took the referee to task over the decision. This seemed to incense the home support and when the final whistle sounded several of them invaded the park. A major scuffle broke out and Meiklejohn was hurt so badly that he was completely KOd.

The incident was so serious that the Danish players had to form a human chain around the Rangers players until police managed to restore order. Meiklejohn was then stretchered from the field where he regained consciousness in the quiet of the pavilion. Later that night, and to show no hard feelings, the official Rangers party dined with their Danish hosts, and the following evening, Rangers were guests of the Danish FA at a festival in the Palace Theatre, and later to the Tivoli, where both parties enjoyed a relaxing supper.

It was a somewhat harrowing end to a great season for the young player.

5

Three out of four ain't bad

T HE players had little time for rest after their Danish excursion and enjoyed just a few days off before heading through to Edinburgh for the Hibs Sports Day, and Jamieson, Meiklejohn, Walls, Lawson and Archibald maintained the Light Blues' impressive record in five-a-side competitions by taking top spot at Easter Road. Single-goal wins over Alloa and Celtic ensured the gold medals would arrive at Ibrox.

Next up was the Partick Thistle fives and the players who descended on Maryhill were Robb, Meiklejohn, Lawson, Cairns and Laird. An impressive 3-0 victory over the hosts in the final saw Rangers take first place. On the same day, Rangers season tickets sold out in just 45 minutes.

Meiklejohn and co then headed for Shawfield, where they once again annexed Clyde's top prize with Meik in great scoring form before the final fives competition of the close-season came, the big Ibrox day out. Meiklejohn carried on where he had left off in Rutherglen by bagging a brace in a 3-0 success over Partick Thistle. A 4-0 semi-final romp over Queen's Park set up a final against old foes Celtic – and that's when things started to go wrong.

It took three periods of extra time to separate both teams, and it was the Parkhead side who registered the win as they collected one goal and three points. Points were accrued by scoring through a small set of goals AND a larger set behind them. Rangers also registered two points – both bagged by Meiklejohn – but lost out narrowly in the final analysis.

No-nonsense Alloa visited Ibrox on the opening day of the season and J.R. Smith – who scored his first league goal for the club in a 2-0 home win – and Meik were injured in a rough match. There was further bad news in the next game – a 5-1 victory over Third Lanark – when Hansen was in the wars. The talented little Dane scored twice but in his haste to net a third, bounced straight off goalkeeper Brownlie and thumped into the post. The result was a broken tibia and Hansen was a 'guest' of the Western Infirmary for a fortnight.

Rangers faced Burnley and Preston North End in a mini tour of north-west England in September but Meiklejohn missed both games, a 3-0 defeat and 1-1 draw respectively, due to yet another injury, but returned for a league match at Brockville where a surprise 2-0 win for Falkirk was the catalyst for ugly scenes on the terracing.

Rangers fans rioted after Falkirk scored their second goal and many spectators were arrested. Two policemen were taken to hospital as a minority of the 8,000 crowd vented their anger at a poor display on the park. Falkirk star William Moore would later describe the trouble as a 'real Irish Donnybrook'. But the trouble didn't end there as members of a Rangers brake club were involved in fighting on the way home when their charabanc stopped in Kilsyth for 'chips'.

The hooliganism witnessed at the match prompted calls for brake clubs to be regulated and for clubs to inaugurate a registration system whereby each member would supply their name and address to the club they followed. It was also mooted that Rangers should use stewards to help monitor fans during away games. Those involved in any trouble would have tickets for future road trips withdrawn. It was the boldest step yet to rid the game of ruffianism.

A break from the darker side arrived in the shape of a well-deserved benefit match for Gers star Alec 'Sandy' Archibald. Burnley travelled north for the 25-year-old Scotland international and included the likes of former Thornliebank ace Joe Anderson and R. Kelly, 'the best inside forward in the English league'. The match finished 2-0 to Rangers with Smith scoring twice.

Next up for Rangers was a Glasgow Cup tie with Third Lanark, and in an unprecedented move, law-abiding brake club members offered to assist the police in rooting out the hooligan element. The club's loyal followers were fed up with their reputation being tarnished by a small minority. Chief constable A.D. Smith also placed a notice in all Glasgow papers warning of the consequences for those bent on causing disorder. Smith put checkpoints in place en route to Cathkin, where officers would randomly stop and search those travelling to the match by charabanc. A crowd of 47,000 watched a 2-2 draw and the draconian measures seemed to work to good effect as the afternoon passed off peacefully.

Another great Rangers player, Tommy Muirhead, received his benefit match late in September when Preston provided the opposition. Muirhead had been injured during the match at Cathkin but an able replacement in Doc Paterson, formerly of the Light Blues and now of Arsenal, took to the field and proved popular in the 1-0 defeat in front of 5,000.

Meiklejohn missed the game due to a recurring leg injury but was back in his rightful place for the Glasgow Cup semi-final replay against Third Lanark which ended in a 2-1 win for Rangers, to set up a final the following Saturday against Clyde at Celtic Park. That match finished goalless, and once again the ability of Rangers to sparkle on the big occasion was called into question. Rangers edged the replay and afterwards the players were treated to the second house at the Pavilion.

Manager Struth obviously felt that his players were in need of a rest – due to 'too much football' – and whisked them off to Turnberry for a few days. The break had the desired effect and on their return, they registered a 3-1 win at Parkhead. A match report suggested, 'Meiklejohn had a good grip of Celtic's Patsy Gallacher.' The points moved Rangers up to third in the table, two points behind Dundee and Aberdeen, but with a couple of precious games in hand.

Following a 0-0 draw at Pittodrie, Dons boss Jamie Philip tried to sign Smith but the striker decided to remain at Ibrox and fight for his place. At the beginning of November, the Govan Silver Prize band – who played before all Rangers' home games – inspired the team to a resounding 4-1 win over Partick Thistle to edge them closer to the top.

A breaking story that Smith had signed for Bolton Wanderers drew a strong rebuke from the Rangers man, who said, 'I wish these busybodies would leave me alone. Take it from me, I have not signed for any English club.' Struth backed up the story by saying, 'There is no deal – he is a Rangers player.'

The following day, Smith did indeed sign for Bolton and his short association with Rangers was over. He had shown great promise in his early days at Ibrox but had found it nigh on impossible to dislodge George Henderson from the number nine jersey. Smith, a Scottish Cup winner with Kilmarnock, would go on to become one of the few players to win the cup on both sides of the border when he played a pivotal role in the (in)famous FA Cup win at the end of the season as Wanderers beat West Ham 2-0.

An estimated 100,000 spectators rushed the barriers and gained entry to the ground. It is believed that close on 200,000 people were present when the game eventually kicked off. One thousand people were injured when a stampede took place, and shortly afterwards, Smith received his winners' medal from His Majesty the King.

Back at home, Rangers were making heavy weather of their title charge and a loss to St Mirren was followed by a must-win match at home to high-flying Airdrie. The Diamonds led after 20 minutes but a Rangers revival, led by a Henderson hat-trick, brought a 4-1 victory, and after a similar win over Dundee the Light Blues were back on top, which allowed the players to enjoy their annual dance at the Grosvenor.

In the middle of December, Rangers strengthened their squad with the double signing of James Kilpatrick from Renfrew Juniors and Murdoch McDonald, who had been forced out at Cowdenbeath for refusing to act as a linesman during a match. It was a busy week off the park as both Bert Manderson and Carl Hansen were also married.

The Christmas weekend was a good one for Rangers. A 2-0 win at Alloa, coupled with defeats for both Dundee and Celtic, opened up a two-point gap at the summit, with Rangers having three games in hand over the Dark Blues, and Celtic a further four points back. The traditional New Year clash with Celtic was literally shrouded in mystery as a thick fog developed over Ibrox, which meant many in the 30,000 crowd couldn't see a thing. Referee Tom Dougary decided to press on with the game but a large section of the crowd began fighting and many demanded their money back.

Struth insisted it was impossible to offer refunds as almost 10,000 had paid for 'half-time admission'. He described the trouble as 'infinitesimal'. Goals from Hansen and Archibald gave Rangers a 2-0 win.

Four days later, Meiklejohn was the star turn as Rangers edged Motherwell 2-1 at Ibrox. It was reported that he had played a 'delightful game' and 'coolly flashed the winning goal past Rundell'.

Rangers' search for the Holy Grail, the Scottish Cup, started with the short trip to Shawfield where they easily disposed of Clyde 4-0. The second round saw them up against Ayr United at Somerset Park, which meant they missed out on a visit by royalty. The Duke of York was scheduled to be in Glasgow on Saturday 27 January, the day of the match, and was said to be keen to take in a game. In light of this, Rangers made the Ayr board a financial offer to switch the game, but they declined. The Gers had better news when they received permission from the SFA to give Hansen and Manderson wedding presents.

Rangers headed down the coast to Ayr on cup day but all the attention was on the match at Hampden between Queen's Park and Bathgate, as the Duke of York took up his seat in the stand. It was a bad day all round as Rangers lost 2-0.

The following weekend, the cup defeat was a distant memory as Rangers thumped Hibs 3-0 with the second goal described as a 'typical Hansonian strike from the Great Dane, Carl'. Meiklejohn had cause to celebrate three days after Valentine's Day when he was called up to play for the Scottish League against England at Newcastle's St James' Park. Scotland lost 2-1, and Meik's Rangers team-mate Tommy Muirhead was carried off, but the Govan lad received tremendous praise in the press following the match.

England's opening goal, scored by Tunstall, went in off Meiklejohn but he had a good game and, according to one paper, his forward passes were exceptional. It added, 'Doesn't he know how to tackle! He watches, waits and invariably wins.'

The afternoon was not free of controversy though as, due to having four players called up for international duty, Rangers had exercised their right to have the day's league game at Ayr called off. Councillor

Alexander Stirling, of Ayr, took it upon himself to criticise the Light Blues in a letter to the club, which accused them of 'stooping to the low manoeuvre of taking advantage of the rules'.

Rangers were loath to take on such an important league match minus four of their top players and had initially been happy to play when just three of their players – Meiklejohn, Cairns and Morton – had been selected, but it was only when Muirhead was added that they asked for the cancellation. Days later, the Scotland team for the match against Ireland was named and *Daily Record* correspondent 'Waverley' was outraged that Meiklejohn had been omitted from the side. Selectors had instead plumped for Davie Steel of Huddersfield.

But Meik was called up for the Home Scots v Anglo Scots trial match at Cathkin and played well in a 1-1 draw before starring in a re-run of the controversial match at Ayr, which earned Rangers another two points courtesy of a George Henderson double. Wins over Dundee and Falkirk meant the club needed just two more points for the title, but a defeat and a draw in their next two games left them requiring a point from a nervy trip to Easter Road at the beginning of April.

Three days beforehand, Rangers honoured a promise to travel over to Belfast for a match against Linfield in aid of Blues player John Campbell. A crowd of 10,000 watched Rangers win 1-0, but they made the most of their whistle-stop visit to enjoy a motor trip up the coast to the famous Glens of Antrim before being guests of honour at a banquet, at which they were presented with handsome gold medals for their narrow win.

Back in Scotland, Rangers travelled through to the capital with just one thing in minds – the Scottish First Division title. Should the Gers fail in their quest to beat Hibs, there was still a chance they could lift the championship if Third Lanark beat nearest challengers Airdrie. Following 90 minutes of tense, nervy football, the scores read Hibs 2 Rangers 0, and Third Lanark 1 Airdrie 2. Both clubs were locked on 51 points with two games remaining. It was that tight, but players and staff refused to let the disappointment get to them and donned their black suits and 'dicky-bow' ties for a night of dancing at the F&Fs, a famous Glasgow eaterie, to celebrate the club's Silver Jubilee.

The following weekend's fixtures saw the Light Blues entertain Kilmarnock while Falkirk were the visitors to Broomfield Park,

Airdrie. Beforehand, though, Struth sent strong sides to Arthurlie, for a friendly match, and to Kirkintilloch Rob Roy to play a benefit match for Dan Michie. When Killie came to Ibrox the Gers were in tip-top shape and a Henderson goal was enough to secure victory. Airdrie's 5-1 mauling of Falkirk proved immaterial and Rangers were champions once more.

Meanwhile, Celtic had won the Scottish Cup for the tenth time, equalling Queen's Park's record and held their social in the Bank Restaurant – with Mr Gray of Rangers presenting their medals.

There was still the Charity Cup to play for and Rangers beat Celtic in the semi-finals before thumping Queen's Park 4-0 in front of 35,000 at Ibrox. Later that night, the players received their medals from the Lord Provost Sir Thomas Paxton at a civic function in the City Chambers, and the club signed Tom 'Tully' Craig from Alloa – a former Celtic player.

Craig was included in a Rangers squad of 15 that left St Enoch Station on the morning of Tuesday 22 May, bound for France and Switzerland, where a number of challenge matches had been arranged. A game against C.A.P. Paris Gallia at the Olympique Stadium would open the tour before the party moved on to Switzerland, where matches had been fixed against the likes of St Gallen, Basle and Geneva. Somewhere in the middle of the trip, the players found time for a break in Lucerne, before taking in the Epsom Derby on their arrival back in the UK.

The first game ended in a resounding 6-1 win for Rangers, for whom Henderson and Hansen both scored twice to complement strikes by Cunningham and Archibald. It was said that the French side showed some clever play but lacked the experience to cope with the Scottish champions. Rangers really put on a show and Struth reported that while the French had little ball control, they were definitely improving, and their fans cheered every time a Rangers player back-heeled the ball. 'This tickled their fancy,' admitted Struth.

Henderson then scored five times as St Gallen were brushed aside 7-0, and Basle were soundly beaten 3-0. Swiss champions Berne were also slain 7-0 while Chauxdefords fared little better against the superior Scots. Struth admitted the trip had been 'highly satisfactory'.

6

A new challenger emerges

IT may have been five years since the end of the First World War but tensions were still running high in central Europe. The Ruhr region of defeated Germany was still in dispute between the Allies of Britain, France and Belgium, and the situation was exasperated when a train carrying Belgian soldiers was blown up by German militants in Duisburg with the loss of nine lives. But while Prime Minister Stanley Baldwin had a real dilemma on his hands, the feelgood factor was back amongst Gers fans and season tickets were selling like hot cakes.

The new campaign started with the annual Glasgow Police Sports Day at Ibrox, and in the five-a-side competition Rangers again prevailed, beating Celtic by a single goal in the final. Meiklejohn missed a penalty but Alan Morton came up trumps with the only counter of the short-sided game.

The following Saturday, 7 July, Rangers entered teams into two different sports days, one at Lochwinnoch and the other at Firhill Stadium, home of Partick Thistle. Robb, Meiklejohn, Cairns, Archibald and Muirhead, who was still unsigned, headed for Maryhill, while Hamilton, Rollo, McDonald, Hansen and Roberts made the short trip to Renfrewshire.

At Firhill, Meiklejohn and co crashed out of the competition in the first round to Celtic, while at Lochwinnoch a Carl Hansen-inspired five went all the way, beating Celtic, Ayr and Morton without the loss of a goal. In doing so, the players won handsome easy chairs, while the Morton players received oak smoker's cabinets.

Tommy Muirhead signed on for another season at Ibrox and upstairs in the boardroom, William Craig succeeded Sir John Ure Primrose as chairman. Craig had been vice-president of the SFA for 15 years.

Next up was the Rangers Jubilee Sports Day, the biggest and best in the country, and expertly run by Struth. The star attraction was Olympic champion Eric Liddell, who was competing in the 100- and 200-yard sprints. Struth had signed up the Olympian after watching him in action at the Chelsea Sports Day in London the previous month. But 30,000 spectators watched the great athlete trail in third behind W.P. Nichol and T. Matthewman.

In the fives, Cairns, Meiklejohn, Muirhead, Archibald and Morton secured a one-goal victory over Celtic, a game which was played with all the hostility and tempo of a Scottish Cup tie. In the final, a Muirhead goal was enough to land five gold watch bracelets for the players, and silver equivalents for their partners. During the final there was a melee in the Partick Thistle box and Meiklejohn was knocked out cold. After lengthy treatment by the Rangers medic, Dr Shearer, from St Kilda, he was able to carry on.

With the sports days out of the way the players set about preparing in earnest for retaining their title. First up was a practice match between the first 11 and the reserves, proceeds of which were earmarked for Elder Cottage Hospital in Govan.

The Light Blues opened with a comprehensive 3-0 win at Motherwell before 14,000 fans watched Mrs Craig, wife of chairman Bill, unfurl the championship flag at Ibrox on the afternoon of the match against Falkirk. Disappointingly, Rangers let a two-goal lead slip – and a precious league point, but made amends by thrashing St Mirren 5-0 in their next match.

Early in September 1923 Rangers sent a strong squad to Haugh Park, Kilsyth, for a match against Kilsyth Rangers in aid of the tragic victims of the Gartshore Colliery disaster in which eight people lost their lives after a massive explosion. Rangers won 4-0 in a match that attracted a crowd of just over 1,000.

Just two days after a tough 1-0 win at Morton, Liverpool travelled north to Ibrox for a benefit match for gritty Oldham man 'Lil' Arthur Dixon. The match, billed as the 'unofficial championship of Great Britain', ended 1-1 with Hansen scoring for Rangers. Celtic favourite Patsy Gallacher acted as linesman.

Rangers should have won the match when Henderson scored in the dying minutes but it was getting dark and the referee, Rangers trainer George Livingstone, decided an infringement had taken place and disallowed it. No one complained as they couldn't see. All 22 players were awarded silver cigarette cases, a present from the Rangers directors.

The following Saturday was Glasgow Cup semi-final day and as Rangers and Celtic prepared to do battle at Ibrox, Glasgow Police announced that they were at war with the hooligan element of the brake clubs. Thankfully the match passed off peacefully and a Henderson goal was enough to send Rangers through to the final.

Airdrie were emerging as a real force in Scottish football and began to challenge Rangers for domestic honours, pushing Celtic aside in the process. Saturday 22 September saw Rangers beat Aberdeen 2-0 but it was the Diamonds who led the way in the race for the title, a point ahead of Rangers – and 12 in front of Celtic.

During the match against the Dons, Meiklejohn took umbrage with a linesman's decision, something frowned upon in the early part of the 20th century, although Struth announced after the game that his player would face no disciplinary action.

On the September weekend holiday, Rangers beat Clyde 2-1, courtesy of goals by Cairns and Craig, which saw them move ahead of Airdrie at the top of the pile. Six days later, Rangers staged the Glasgow Cup Final against Third Lanark at Ibrox, a move that drew criticism from certain quarters of the Cathkin side. Many believed the game should be played at a neutral venue but Bailie Crerar, on behalf of Thirds, answered, 'We have been criticised for going to Ibrox for the final but in these hard times it was our duty to conserve our finances.'

Rangers won 3-1 and were presented with the handsome trophy in the boardroom by Hugh Logan, of Queen's Park. A crowd of 25,000 had watched Third Lanark take the lead in the 19th minute but second-half goals from Muirhead, Archibald and Henderson kept the trophy at Ibrox. On the same day, Airdrie thumped Clyde 6-1 to regain their advantage at the top of the league.

Followers of the Light Blues could buy a copy of the new book, *The Story of The Rangers*, written by John Allan, and available in two different formats; cloth-bound, which cost four shillings (20p), and leather-bound for an extra 4s 6d.

Rangers turned up the heat in the league championship by comprehensively winning their next three games on successive Saturdays. Dundee, Ayr and Hibs were taken care of with 12 goals registered. Meiklejohn chipped in with a couple of unstoppable drives against the latter two.

Near the end of October, Meik and club skipper Tommy Cairns were named in the West side to face their eastern counterparts at Ibrox in a trial match, from which the Scottish League team to face the Irish League at Halloween would be chosen. Proceeds from the match were pledged to the Royal Samaritan Hospital in Glasgow. The Rangers half-back was favourite to be chosen ahead of Steel, of Hamilton.

A Glasgow gentleman had put up attractive eight-guinea wristlet watches for the winners – so the match was keenly contested. Meiklejohn, injured in the warm-up, was forced to withdraw from the West side, as was Cairns. Carl Hansen deputised for Cairns and scored but couldn't prevent his team losing 4-2. The weather was wretched but the game still drew gate receipts of £600, which would have been well received by the hospital. Afterwards, both sets of players enjoyed the first house at the Metropole Theatre, but the injured Meiklejohn was an injury doubt for the Old Firm match just four days later.

In the pre-match build-up to the 'big one', Rangers were regarded as hot favourites as it was suggested in the press that they were 'far superior' to their city rivals. Meik won his race against the clock but in front of a 38,000 crowd, neither side could find the net. The draw, however, was enough to move Rangers two points clear. The following Saturday, an Alan Morton hat-trick inspired Rangers to a 6-0 win at Partick Thistle, a result which doubled their advantage in the title race.

And it wasn't long before the West had a chance to avenge their defeat against a Hearts/Hibs select at Tynecastle. This time the gate receipts would go to the Capital Unemployment Fund, and Bailie Sleigh, an Edinburgh magistrate, put up a set of silver cigarette cases for the winners. Rangers were represented by Reid, Meiklejohn and Cairns, and the trio played their part in a 4-2 win. Celtic's Patsy Gallacher turned in an 'imperious' display for the West, while Meiklejohn was next best. It was as though they had played together all their days.

The Govan-born star was playing at the top of his game and scored in a 2-0 league win over Third Lanark but when the players travelled to Falkirk the following week, they were met by a blizzard on arrival at Brockville. It continued to snow throughout the match, which made it difficult for the Light Blues to pick out a team-mate, as they were wearing their all-white kit, 'à la Corinthians'.

Sadly, Meiklejohn picked up an injury in the 'Battle of Falkirk' and was forced to withdraw from a match against Partick Thistle in aid of the St Andrews Ambulance Association Building Fund. Hansen was on the mark twice as the sides fought out a thrilling 4-4 draw at Firhill.

After the match, news filtered through that Rangers chairman Bill Craig had died suddenly of a heart attack. The successful Justice of the Peace had been a keen sailor in his earlier days and had taken part in the America's Cup on board the yacht, *The Thistle*. Craig had first joined Rangers' committee in 1897 and became a director six years later. More than 300 people, including the entire Rangers squad, attended his funeral at Cathcart Cemetery.

December, traditionally a profitable month for a title-chasing Gers side, was so once again, and wins over Clydebank, Queen's Park, in which Meiklejohn scored the only goal of the game with a header, Raith Rovers and Hamilton Accies followed. The club also appointed a new chairman, Joseph Buchanan, who was introduced to the players during 'a lazy weekend' at Turnberry.

The Gers travelled to Celtic Park for the traditional Ne'erday game, and both sets of players were hailed for putting on a first-class show of skill in front of a 60,000 crowd. The teams shared four goals, and twice Rangers were forced to come from behind. Dixon and Meiklejohn were named as the best in blue.

But the team slipped up at Ayr, losing 2-1 at their bogey ground, although a collection taken to aid children without shoes proved a big success. Another away trip, this time at Hamilton, looked like ending in similar fashion as the Accies carved out a 2-0 half-time lead. But back came Rangers and second-half goals by Cairns and a couple from ex-Celt Tully Craig – the first of which the Accies players claimed hadn't crossed the line – was sufficient to take both points back to the south side of Glasgow. It was a vital win as Airdrie had also emerged victorious. It was thrills and spills all the way in the mud of Douglas Park and the win was described as a 'title-winning performance' in the Monday papers.

Lochgelly United travelled to Ibrox for a Scottish Cup first round tie at the end of January, and the stubborn Fifers put on quite a show before going down 4-1, thanks largely to a George Henderson hat-trick. The victory set up a second round tie with St Mirren.

A few days later, selectors were due to announce the team for the forthcoming international against Wales and *Daily Record* correspondent 'Waverley' insisted that Meiklejohn and his team-mate Tommy Muirhead just had to be included. He added, 'Davie is not such a spectacular half as his brother Ranger, but he's as solid as a rock, a grim tackler, and can keep his forwards going. He often shoots a goal, and when least expected.'

And 'Waverley' got his wish as Meiklejohn was named in the side for the match in Cardiff. Fellow Light Blues Archibald, Muirhead, Cunningham and Morton were also called up. The Scotland party left Central Station the day before the match and took ten hours to get to the Welsh capital. According to match reports, Meiklejohn failed to live up to his normal Rangers form in the 2-0 loss and it was an early start for the four Gers players (Cunningham had withdrawn) as they had a midweek match against Kilmarnock to prepare for.

The players, along with Struth, joined the press gang on the 7.20pm train to Crewe, where they picked up the sleeper to Glasgow. They arrived in Glasgow bright and breezy the following day while the rest of the party enjoyed a motor trip to Porthcawl and travelled home on the Monday.

The extra time in Glasgow obviously helped as Rangers beat Kilmarnock 2-0 just five days after the international, Meiklejohn was selected to face Ireland at Celtic Park, but 'not on his Cardiff form', said 'Waverley'. 'He is one of our most promising half backs, and he has to show that on the big stage.'

But joy turned to despair when Rangers' Scottish Cup dream was once again brought to a shuddering halt against Hibs at Ibrox. The home side had enjoyed the lion's share of possession and taken the lead courtesy of a Meiklejohn thunderbolt, but some sloppy defending by McCandless allowed the visitors to nick an equaliser, and they grabbed the winner in the dying minutes.

Rangers got back on track 72 hours later with a 3-0 win over Clydebank but Meiklejohn picked up a knock and had to withdraw from the Scotland team. The season was entering a crucial phase, and Struth was forced to travel to Kilmarnock minus five first team players, but still came away with a point.

The following midweek, Rangers went into another key league game minus three stars but this time it was through choice as Struth rested the players due to the representative international between the Scottish and English leagues on the Saturday. A late George Henderson goal – in front of a disappointing 5,000 crowd – was enough to see off Hearts and sent Rangers nine points clear of Airdrie with just seven matches remaining.

The international match took place at Ibrox but once again Meiklejohn failed to reproduce his club form in the 1-1 draw. Alan Morton scored for the Scots in front of 65,000 fervent spectators.

Rangers' title hopes suffered a minor setback when they lost 1-0 to Albion Rovers but Meiklejohn, Muirhead, Cairns, Cunningham and Morton had the consolation of being named in the international trial squad for the forthcoming match against England at Wembley. Three days later though, a comprehensive 3-1 win at Third Lanark pushed Gers ten points clear at the top of the table.

On the day of the international trial, SFA bosses met to ratify a pay retention rate of £4 per week for players called up for international duty. This amounted to £208 per year. Almost 10,000 people watched 'one of the best trial matches seen in years' and while Meiklejohn played well, and was tipped for the side to face the English, he would be disappointed. Cunningham, Morton and Archibald were named in the team.

Meik had a quick opportunity to make amends when he lined up for Rangers in a league match against Hibs at Ibrox, where a home win would see the Light Blues retain the title. It was a nervy performance, though, and Hibs led 1-0 at the break. Meik levelled from the spot before Cunningham grabbed the winner. It was the Gers' fifth title win in seven years, a real model of consistency that the others simply couldn't match. In the 267 matches played in those seven seasons, just 22 had been lost, and the 1923/24 title had been secured with three games still to play.

Just a couple of days after winning the league, Rangers took the trophy north for a friendly match with Forfar Athletic. It was a tough night but before winning 3-2, the players were taken on a charabanc trip around town before heading to Cortachy Castle, seat of the Earl of Airlie. After strolling through the extensive grounds, they journeyed to Kirriemuir, where they saw the play *A Window in Thrums*.

It was then on to nearby Glamis Castle, where they were received by the Earl of Strathmore and shown around what was believed to be Scotland's most beautiful castle. His Lordship entertained officials and players to tea, before taking his seat at Station Park alongside 3,000 supporters for the match. Goals by Cairns, Craig and Morton did the trick and then it was off to Redholm, the splendid home of Sir John Ure Primrose, where the players were once again treated like royalty. There was no rest for the wicked though as Rangers were scheduled to travel to Liverpool a few days later, where back-to-back matches against the Anfield side and Manchester United had been fixed up.

A crowd of 38,000 watched Rangers beat Liverpool and the visiting players were cheered from the field by home fans dazzled by 'an exhibition of football seldom seen nowadays'. Alan Morton created both goals, scored by Henderson and Cairns, and was the chief architect of Liverpool's downfall.

But 72 hours later the players arrived at Old Trafford amid a torrential downpour, and it remained a constant throughout an evenly-balanced match which ended 1-1. A crowd of 4,000 saw Archibald equalise for the Light Blues.

At the beginning of May, the big news coming out of Ibrox was that Davie Meiklejohn, now one of the first names on manager Struth's Saturday team lines, had failed to sign for the following season, but it didn't prevent the big right-half turning in a five-star display in the 3-0 Charity Cup win at Shawfield on the first Saturday in May.

Four days later, a Tommy Craig header secured another charity win against Partick Thistle, but the Light Blues lost 2-1 in the final to Celtic.

After the game, Meiklejohn put pen to paper and declared that there was never any doubt that he would commit his future to the Gers. The delay was down to idle gossip that the club were preventing Meik from being awarded a benefit match, a fact that Struth vehemently denied.

But one Ranger who wouldn't be a part of the squad the following season was Tommy Muirhead. The scheming midfielder was named as the manager of American side Brooklyn, a club newly formed in Boston, and after a presentation night in the City Café, West Nile Street, in which Muirhead was presented with a handsome Masonic apron, together with a wallet of treasury notes, he set sail on the *Cameronia* for a new life in the United States. On the morning of his departure, from St Enoch Station, he was handed a lucky horseshoe by supporters who had turned out to bid farewell to one of their favourites.

During the close-season a benefit match was held in aid of struggling Busby Cartvale. The old club were in danger of going bust, and fellow juniors Pollok agreed to play the match. Meiklejohn was referee for the night, and Arthur Dixon ran one of the lines. One wonders how Meik felt being on the 'other side of the fence'.

Aside from their short excursion to the north-west of England, Rangers had refrained from going on a European tour so the players were anxious to get back to playing and the Rangers Sports Day gave at least five of them – Meiklejohn, Dixon, Cairns, Archibald and Morton – the chance to lift some silverware, which they duly did. Without doubt the best five-a-side team in the country beat Partick Thistle 3-0, with goals from Archibald, who scored twice, and Meiklejohn, before an Alan Morton double ensured victory over Celtic in the final, but the players were rocked the following day by the death of Sir John Ure Primrose.

The popular Rangers director passed away at his home in Dumbreck, just a mile or so from Ibrox Stadium. Sir John had been appointed president in 1912, following the death of Bailie James Henderson, and had been a member of the Rangers since 1887, in the month in which the first Ibrox was opened by Preston North End. He was elected honorary president at the annual meeting in 1888 and eventually vacated that office to become chairman.

Of Sir John, *Daily Record* chief sports writer 'Waverley' said, 'A man of culture and high ideals, Sir John brought into football an influence that was cleansing and elevating. He had fine social skills and possessed the faculty for saying the right thing at the right time. His genial presence will be missed.'

7

League champs, but 'Scottish' remains elusive

FRESH season, fresh challenge for Bill Struth's side and it was one that the experienced Ibrox players were relishing. It may have been five years since Meiklejohn had signed for the Light Blues but he was still proud as punch every time he pulled on the famous jersey, be that in a cup final or eve-of-season five-a-side competition.

On the first Saturday in August, Meiklejohn and co annexed the Rangers Fives by winning all three games 3-0, but once again the star attraction was Olympic hero Eric Liddell who won the quarter-mile race.

It was then time for the annual trial match at Ibrox, with the Blues thumping the Whites 5-1, and Meiklejohn was none too pleased at being on the receiving end of a pre-season thumping. He made amends by teaming up with Archibald, Morton, Dixon and Cunningham to bag a winners' medal at Celtic Park. The Parkhead club had decided to ditch their annual sports day in favour of a bigger and more inclusive five-a-side competition. It was a gamble that paid off as 15,000 watched a sprint race with a difference that saw players having to run with a ball and dribble in between cones.

Meik got Rangers off to a flying start in their quest to cement yet another First Division title by scoring the only goal of the game at Aberdeen early in the season, but the preparations for the match were far from ideal. A delay en route to the Granite City meant the partially-stripped players didn't arrive at Aberdeen train station until 2.35pm. They were herded straight into waiting cars and whisked off to the ground, pulling up outside Pittodrie at 2.46pm. After lacing up their boots, they were out on the park and ready to play at 3.03pm, and the game kicked off within 60 seconds.

Three minutes later, Meiklejohn got hold of the ball at the pavilion end of the ground and one swish of his cultured right foot later the ball was nestling in the back of the net. There the scoring ended. After the final whistle, the players got showered and changed and were on the 5.30pm train back to Glasgow, making their total stay in Aberdeen less than three hours. The following day a match report said, 'If you want anyone on the end of a shot, it's Meiklejohn, as he very rarely misses.'

The win at Aberdeen, Rangers' third on the trot, made for the perfect start to the new season, but supporters were saddened when stylish centre-forward Carl Hansen announced he was heading home to Denmark. The *Daily Record*'s 'Waverley' said, 'The boy has been badly knocked in Scottish football. He was so keen on the game itself that he forgot to look after himself.'

Hansen had been a breath of fresh air on arrival from Copenhagen, but while appearing to be a natural goalscorer never quite managed to dislodge Henderson from the first team and appearances were confined mainly to challenge matches and the Alliance team.

The Rangers bandwagon rolled on and Meiklejohn and Morton were named in the Scottish League team to face their English foes at Hampden, with one newspaper columnist reporting, 'There is no finer half back in the country than Davie Meiklejohn.'

The talented Ranger celebrated by helping his club crush Partick Thistle 6-1 in a match staged to mark the opening of the Glasgow Tramways Recreation Club's new grounds. The Duke of York performed the opening ceremony before being introduced to the players by Struth. He then hilariously took centre and knocked a photographer's hat off. The victorious Rangers players were presented with silver cigarette cases.

Despite their fantastic start to the new campaign, the Light Blues were again matched all the way by Airdrie and after six games both sides had amassed 11 points, although the Diamonds led by a solitary goal. Meanwhile, on the other side of the pond, 3,000 fans watched Tommy Muirhead's new club Brooklyn beat the Bethlehem Steel Works 3-1.

Rangers and Thistle were then engaged in a bruising Glasgow Cup semi-final encounter at Ibrox and Meiklejohn suffered strained muscles, but played on to ensure his side weren't at a numerical disadvantage. Several players were injured in the 'fight' but Rangers had sufficient resources to win the replay 2-0.

The following Saturday, the Light Blues were involved in another rough encounter, this time in a top-of-the-table clash at Broomfield Park, Airdrie. Skipper Tommy Cairns was sent off and Billy McCandless was carried off as the home side edged it. Later, Rangers appealed Cairns's dismissal but that was thrown out, and it would be almost two months before the Scotland international was allowed to play again. Overall it was a bad day at the office with the defeat leaving Rangers trailing both Airdrie and Hibs in the flag race.

Just 48 hours after the 'Battle of Airdrie', Rangers showed great character to beat Hearts 4-1, a match in which Meiklejohn scored and the referee, Mr Campbell of Dundee, was knocked unconscious when he got in the way of a stinging drive.

The defeat at Broomfield had galvanised Rangers and they rallied to thump Celtic 4-1 in the Glasgow Cup Final at Parkhead, where 74,000 turned up, the vast majority no doubt on cloud nine when Celtic opened the scoring on 19 minutes. Enter the big guns though, and Henderson, with a brace, Morton and Cunningham scored to make sure the trophy was bound for the other side of the city. It was thought that Meiklejohn had broken his nose while challenging Adam McLean at the Celtic goal but hospital x-rays later gave him the all-clear.

The following Saturday, Rangers slipped to fourth in the table after a 2-2 draw at Cowdenbeath but the players bounced back magnificently with a 1-0 win over Celtic thanks to an own goal by Hilley, although Alan Morton was given the credit after supplying the cross which the unfortunate Celt turned past his own keeper.

Rangers were tucked in behind Airdrie at the top of the league and received further good news when Tommy Muirhead arrived back in

Glasgow from the US following the expiry of his six-month visa. He was expected to re-sign for the club.

Six wins from their next seven league games would have been sufficient to shake off most teams but Airdrie proved a dogged rival and, ably led by bullish striker Hughie Gallacher, the country's top marksman, maintained their challenge. At Christmas, the top three scorers in the division were Gallacher and Devlin (Cowdenbeath) with 19 goals, and Henderson of Rangers just one behind.

However, New Year proved a purple period for Rangers and they managed to open up a three-point gap on Airdrie. As a storm swept through Glasgow, Rangers provided their own whirlwind start to 1925 by thumping Celtic 4-1 – thanks to a brace from Henderson and singles by Cunningham and Archibald. Watched by 34,000 hardy souls, the Light Blues streaked into a 3-0 lead with just 25 minutes on the clock, but as the weather worsened, the ball began to stick in the mud. The referee played the match to a finish, much to the chagrin of Celtic, who slipped 14 points behind after the latest Old Firm defeat.

The hectic early-January programme saw further wins for both Rangers and Airdrie but a Diamonds win over Celtic put the once-mighty Parkhead club out of the title race once and for all.

The beginning of January brought a new Scottish Cup challenge although the big question was, 'The real deal, or just another false dawn?' Rangers started off their campaign with a 3-1 win at East Fife. The second round brought a trip to Links Park, Angus, to oppose the minnows of Montrose. To try and avoid a round trip of 450 miles, Rangers offered an 'incentive' to the Gable Endies – a £250 lump sum and half the gate over £550. The offer was rejected, which one columnist suggested was down to greed rather than a desire to avoid travelling to Glasgow. The tie proved a relatively easy affair for Rangers, who won 2-0.

The following weekend, Hamilton beat Rangers to cut their lead over the Diamonds to a single point, but Meik comforted himself with a call-up to the Scotland team for the match against Wales at Tynecastle. He was also named in the 'A' team for the trial match to find a team to oppose the English League at Goodison Park, Liverpool.

In a fall-out from the Accies game at Douglas Park, Rangers captain Tommy Cairns reported the referee for something he 'shouldn't have said'. He fired off a letter to the Scottish Football League describing his displeasure over the incident.

Saturday 14 February – Scotland 3 Wales 1. It was to be a sweet Valentine's Day for Meiklejohn as he rattled in the opening goal against the Welsh at Tynecastle. The conditions underfoot were difficult with heavy rain before the match leaving the playing surface like a quagmire, but following great interplay by Rangers duo Morton and Cairns, after which the former let fly with a shot, keeper Gray could only parry and Meik followed up with a thunderous and unstoppable drive. The Ranger was described as a 'sixth forward' at times and was praised for his overall performance in the victory.

Some 12,000 spectators – including several Airdrie players – then turned up to see Falkirk host Rangers in a vital league match. With the visitors trailing 1-0, Meiklejohn and Morton combined to set up Henderson for the equaliser and it remained that way until full time.

The following day, Scotland selectors named a 'same again' side to face Ireland in Belfast – and the draw for the second round of the Scottish Alliance Cup was made, with Rangers down to face either Aberdeen, Raith Rovers, Falkirk, Hearts or Cowdenbeath.

The 'big' team made progress in their Scottish Cup tie at Ibrox, eventually defeating plucky Arbroath 5-3, and then it was on to the league decider – in February. Rangers hosted Airdrie and 40,000 turned up at Ibrox to watch Rangers pound the Diamonds rearguard only for the plucky Broomfield side to 'escape' with a point.

The match had been played midweek as both sides had players involved in the Ireland–Scotland match at Belfast on the Saturday. In a comprehensive 3-0 win for the Scots, Meiklejohn again scored for his country AND was named man of the match. He fired home the opening goal of the game after just four minutes – with another unstoppable shot – and generally got the better of his Rangers team-mates Billy McCandless and Bert Manderson in the Irish rearguard.

A severe cold forced Meiklejohn to withdraw from the Scottish League trials but he was still named in the team – along with club-mates Archibald, Cunningham, Cairns and Morton – which was announced while the Light Blues were playing golf at Turnberry. The break had the desired effect and the Rangers players in the side turned in impressive performances, but it wasn't enough to prevent the

English winning by the odd goal in seven. Meiklejohn was then named in the full Scotland side to face the Auld Enemy at Hampden Park.

Before that, though, there was a tricky Scottish Cup quarter-final at Kilmarnock and a couple of league matches to negotiate. Killie led 1-0 at the break but goals by Henderson, who suffered a knee injury in the process, and Cunningham sent Rangers through to the last four of their bogey competition.

But they suffered a real setback to their title hopes when they lost 4-1 to Hibs in the capital. On the same evening Airdrie thumped Third Lanark with Hughie Gallacher scoring four times, to edge ahead at the top of the pile. With their win at Easter Road, Hibs had also overtaken Rangers.

And then the Scottish Cup final before the final – a last-four clash with arch-rivals Celtic. A staggering crowd of 101,714 packed out Hampden for the long-awaited tie, but it was the green hordes who were left celebrating.

Trailing 1-0 at the break, a rejuvenated Rangers emerged for the second half. Meiklejohn rattled the upright with a fierce drive and Cairns had a header brilliantly saved – but the floodgates opened and Celtic ran out 5-0 winners. It was a humiliating experience for all in light blue and Struth urged his played to respond in a positive manner when they faced Raith Rovers in a league match at Ibrox. This they did by winning 4-0, although Airdrie were still one point clear with just five matches to play.

Unlike today, when a light fall of snow is usually sufficient to have a game postponed, the players of the 1920s were hardy lads and it took more than three or four inches of the white stuff to have a game cancelled. On the evening of Wednesday 1 April, Rangers hosted Cowdenbeath and a single goal from a McCandless spot-kick was enough to seal the points. Heavy snowfall had taken its toll on conditions but both sets of players muddled through the 90 minutes and the result was that Rangers forged a point ahead of Airdrie, although they had played a game more.

On the Saturday afternoon, Meiklejohn, making his debut against England, turned in a quiet and effective performance as Scotland beat the Auld Enemy 2-0 in front of 92,000. Airdrie's Gallacher scored both goals but Alan Morton was named man of the match. For the first goal Meiklejohn played an inch-perfect pass to Cairns, who found Gallacher in space, and the prolific centre found the net.

The following midweek, a Cairns double was enough to see off Aberdeen while St Mirren edged Airdrie 1-0 to leave the Light Blues three points clear at the top of the league. And when the Irish named their side to face Wales, there was no McCandless or Manderson. An Irish official said, 'Due to the Airdrie league menace, Glasgow Rangers could not release Billy or Bert.'

Rangers were hitting form at the right time and in their next game, at home to Third Lanark, they romped into a four-goal lead but looked on in horror as the Cathkin side pulled a couple of goals back. However, Meiklejohn and Cairns showed great leadership to steady the ship, and the former set up Archibald to score a fifth and decisive goal. Airdrie won 2-0 at Raith Rovers to keep the pressure on but the ball was firmly in Rangers' court with just a couple of matches remaining. If Rangers could win their last two games they would be champions.

But that all changed on the next matchday when Motherwell drew at Ibrox – and Airdrie beat third-placed Hibs 2-0. Rangers were two points clear but the Diamonds had a game in hand, which they fulfilled against Dundee the following midweek. With the scores tied at 1-1 and time ticking away the normally proficient Gallacher missed a penalty kick.

It all came down to the final day of the season. Rangers were to host Ayr United, who needed a win to avoid relegation, while Airdrie travelled to Perth. As it transpired, a Billy McCandless free kick was enough to give Rangers the narrowest of wins while St Johnstone beat Airdrie. Newspaper correspondents called it 'the most satisfying title race ever', and by losing just three matches, Rangers were once again crowned kings of Scotland.

Just 48 hours after clinching the title, Newcastle United travelled north for James 'Fister' Walls's benefit game and 4,000 saw Meiklejohn set up George Henderson for the only goal.

Next up for the Light Blues was a Glasgow Charity Cup tie against Third Lanark. Meik opened the scoring with a trademark howitzer as Rangers blitzed the Jags 4-1, but he suffered a twisted knee late on. He was passed fit for the semi-final clash with Partick Thistle the following weekend and played a pivotal role in a 2-1 win to set up a final tie with surprise packet Clyde at Ibrox. A 1-0 win gave Gers their 12th victory in the competition and they were invited to the City Chambers to receive the magnificent trophy from Lord Provost Montgomery.

The players were due a break and, courtesy of the club, they headed south to take in the Epsom Derby. They plundered Manna and were celebrating again when jockey Steve Donoghue romped home to set up another big pay day for the Ibrox stars.

On his return from England, Struth signed Morton centre-forward Bob McKay and, following the previous year's crush in a city centre shop, it was decided that season tickets would only go on sale, priced 30 shillings, at Ibrox.

8

An injury-ravaged campaign

THE summer of 1925 saw Glasgow's night skies aglow as a number of blazes kept the city's fire departments on call 24/7. The most high profile of these saw the £65,000 Kelvin Hall completely gutted and tenants of nearby Blantyre Street were forced to flee for their lives as the flames, fanned by a strong breeze, headed in their direction.

Nearby, College and Kelvingrove United Free Church was also ravaged by fire when sparks from the Kelvin Hall blew across the road and set it ablaze, while adjacent tenements were also affected. These fires came just 24 hours after a large malt whisky barn at Port Dundas suffered around £50,000 of damage after being set alight.

The city responded by holding collections for those affected by the blazes, although football fans were soon gripped by the start of the new campaign – but for one Rangers player it would be a pre-season to forget.

Alan Morton was involved in a sickening incident during a match against Partick Thistle in the Glasgow Tramways Sports Fives. He collided with a Jags player during the 1-0 loss and had four teeth knocked out.

Ironically, the Partick Thistle Sports Day was next on the pre-season agenda and Morton was replaced by Steel of Hamilton Accies.

Meik was on target in an opening 3-0 win over Hibs, and after a 'corners' victory over Partick in the semis, Cunningham and McKay made sure the Rangers maintained their reputation as the fives 'kings' by scoring the only goals against Clyde.

Next up was the Millport Fives and over 5,000 people looked on as Rangers won the competition without conceding a goal. Normally Willie Reid would have been in goal for the Gers but he played outfield and scored in all three games, including the final against Cowdenbeath.

But the big one was the Rangers Sports, and 32,000 turned up to watch a high-profile mix of field sports, with athletes from as far afield as New York and Illinois, and football. Cunningham, Archibald, Meiklejohn, Craig and McKay represented the hosts and thumped St Mirren 3-0 in the final. Supporters were then treated to the beautiful sight of the league flag being unfurled by Mrs Buchanan, wife of the Rangers chairman, who was presented with a manicure set by Struth for her troubles.

A new Scottish football rule was put in place just in time for the Celtic Fives. When taking a throw-in, the player didn't need to be flat-footed any more. Standing on one's tip toes was now allowed. At the Celtic tournament, young McKay was in startling form and outshone the great Jimmy McGrory to score three times and help Rangers to yet another triumph. Bring on the new season, was the cry, although perhaps that was a shade premature as the campaign ahead would prove to be one of the most frustrating in the club's 53-year history.

The champions broke with tradition and warmed up for the start of the new season in a rather different fashion – by playing cricket. As the previous campaign had come to a satisfactory end, Struth accepted an invitation from the West of Scotland Cricket Club for Rangers to play in a fundraising match at their Hamilton Crescent field. It was hoped that the proceeds would help pay for a new boundary wall.

The Rangers players were taking the match very seriously indeed. In fact, so intensely had they been preparing for the challenge they had been chucked off the Ibrox pitch by a furious head groundsman for setting up a makeshift wicket on the hallowed turf. Rangers also had an ace up their sleeve, Oldham-born Arthur Dixon. The centre-half was a dab hand with a bat, but there was a real concern over how Meiklejohn and co would fare.

When the match started, a good crowd was present to see the Light Blues make a real fist of it, so much so that the final outcome was in the balance until close of play. The West batsmen 'kindly' allowed the footballers to get in a good night's training, especially Morton and Henderson, who were often seen sprinting after some well-hit balls. The latter, a fine centre-forward, could have done with some lengthier spikes in his boots as he continuously slid in his pursuit of the leather but his sliding and gliding antics did not go amiss.

Jamie Bowie, however, was the star turn in the footballers' team, with his lightning catch from the bat of Mair as fine a thing as had been taken at Partick all season. Rangers didn't begin well but Morton and Dixon soon showed that the bad start would not unnerve them.

Wee Alan assumed a characteristic pose at the wicket but even a footballer could be pardoned for 'swanking' after hitting a six. Arthur did not have to swank, although it was a pity that he just missed out on his half century. Meiklejohn, a natural all-round sportsman, could also hold his head up high. He may not have played a straight bat all night, but he hit the ball with 'gusto'.

The scorecard:

West of Scotland

C.T. Mannes	lbw	bowled Russell	11
J.S. Mitchley	lbw	bowled McDonald	20
P.C.S. Hengler	retired		54
E.C. Caldwell		bowled Dixon	21
G.B. Mair		c & b Bowie	4
K.I.G. Mathieson	caught Bowie	bowled Dixon	22
C.C. Downie	lbw	bowled Henderson	7
J.P. Mahaffy		bowled Dixon	9
H. Davison	caught Russell	bowled Henderson	2
G.S. Milne	not out		3
Extras			18
Total	(innings declared)		171

Rangers

J. McDonald		bowled Mair	3
G. Henderson	caught Mair	bowled Davison	8
A.L. Morton		bowled Mair	21
A. Dixon		c & b Mahaffy	45
J. Bowie		bowled Davison	13
D. Meiklejohn		bowled Milne	21
R. Russell	caught Mair	bowled Milne	0
T. Muirhead		bowled Milne	0
W. Chalmers		not out	9
J. Marshall		bowled Mannes	10
D. Gray	caught Downie	bowled Mannes	0
Extras			4
Total	(all out)		134

And so to the football, which saw Rangers head to the Fair City for an opening-day match against St Johnstone. The Light Blues were suitably kitted out for their first challenge – and trotted out the tunnel in new white tops and black 'sateen' shorts. The material resembled normal satin, with the only difference being that cotton was used in the manufacture of sateen. The material still gave off a high sheen and the players looked resplendent in their new kit, which had a positive effect as they headed back down the road to Glasgow with a 3-0 win and two points safely in the bag.

Meiklejohn came down with flu after the game and missed the next match but was back in his usual place for a 4-1 win at Greenock, in which Alan Morton was badly injured.

On the last day of August 1925, Real Madrid became the first Spanish club side to visit England but were thumped 6-1 by Newcastle United at St James' Park. Forty-eight hours later Rangers headed for Tyneside to tackle the Geordies by way of a thank-you for Newcastle providing the opposition for 'Fister' Walls's benefit match. Ten thousand fans were present to see Rangers take Newcastle apart with goals by Archibald and Muirhead. Perhaps it's just as well they didn't let Meik and co loose on Real Madrid.

Back in Scotland, the Ibrox side suffered something of a mini slump by losing 2-1 at Airdrie, in front of a record Broomfield crowd of

25,000, and suffering another road loss at Aberdeen. The common denominator was the absence of Morton. The defeat at Pittodrie saw Rangers fall to seventh in the league table but they made up some ground with wins over St Mirren, in which young Bob McKay made his league debut, and Hibs at Easter Road two days later.

Unfortunately, Meiklejohn suffered a nasty ankle knock in the latter match and was unavailable for his own benefit game, against Huddersfield Town at Ibrox the following night. Despite the games being separated by just 24 hours the entire first-team squad were keen to play against one of the leading English sides of their day. However, Struth erred on the side of caution and plumped for: Robb, Gray, Hamilton, Ireland, A. Kirkwood, Muirhead, Archibald, D. Kirkwood, Dick, McKay and Chalmers.

The match took place amid dreadful conditions and just 2,000 spectators defied the rain on a cold and miserable night. Meiklejohn was such a popular player that he would surely have drawn ten times that crowd had the match taken place on a pleasant evening.

Those who did turn up, though, were treated to a first-class exhibition of football – by Huddersfield Town. The Yorkshire side ran out 5-1 winners and one can only assume that had Rangers turned out their regular first team they would surely have triumphed.

The match report stated, 'Rangers, with but three of their regulars, were certainly not inferior to Huddersfield, who, nevertheless, thoroughly deserved their victory.' Scottish international Alec Jackson scored twice, as did George Cook, while George Brown netted a single. D. Kirkwood replied for Rangers.

The report continued, 'A feature of the match was the display of Gray and Hamilton. The ex-St Mirren man was ever in the picture, tackling and clearing soundly. As a result, Jackson, apart from scoring his two goals, was seldom seen. Young Gray excelled against an elusive left wing.'

Whether or not it was the humiliating defeat, or other reasons, it would be the last benefit match awarded to a Rangers player for more than 50 years. John Greig would be the next Ibrox recipient.

Meiklejohn's ankle injury kept him out for a few weeks and he missed a cracking Glasgow Cup semi-final tie at Celtic Park as Rangers secured a 2-2 draw against Celtic in front of 65,000 spectators. The following weekend the Light Blues, minus five top-team stars, beat Kilmarnock 3-0 while Airdrie thumped Celtic 5-1.

There was a real anticipation ahead of the Glasgow Cup replay that Rangers, despite their troubles, could win the game. Despite the match taking place on a Tuesday afternoon, 50,000 watched Rangers struggle on without Meiklejohn, Cairns and Morton.

Special police officers were on duty outside Ibrox to prevent fans entering the ground with ricketties and flags. Anyone waving a flag outside the ground or inside would be deemed to be creating a misdemeanour and would be arrested on the authority of the Chief Constable, but when Celtic scored after just 15 seconds, fighting erupted in the grandstand of all places and several arrests were made. Cunningham equalised for Rangers and a second replay was set for the Thursday. Sadly, there were several fights outside the ground as spectators made their way home. For the replay, five first-team players were absent for Rangers and, somewhat inevitably, they lost 2-0.

As a result of so many injuries, inconsistency plagued the team in many of their ensuing games. A 2-0 loss at Partick Thistle was followed by a 1-0 win over Celtic in a league game at Ibrox, as Chalmers notched the only goal. No doubt a little recuperation therapy at Turnberry did the trick.

In a bid to ease their growing injury problems, Rangers signed Jamie Fleming from St Johnstone. It was hailed as the biggest transfer of the season and he arrived in Govan with a first-class reputation having notched 19 goals for the Perth side in the previous campaign. He must have been quite something as THREE Rangers players – the brothers Kirkwood, and Jamieson – were used as 'deal makeweights' and travelled in the opposite direction. Fleming scored on his debut against Dundee at Ibrox but Rangers lost 2-1.

Meiklejohn made his comeback against Raith Rovers in Kirkcaldy but the Fifers won 1-0, which saw Rangers slump to eighth in the table. The following week saw the most bizarre of games when the Light Blues played Queen's Park at Hampden. Rangers defied gale-force winds to romp into a 6-1 half-time lead. Just before the break, though, Meiklejohn suffered a nasty fall and sprained his knee in the process. He was carried off in great pain and spent the entire second half receiving treatment in the dressing room.

Barr scored twice in the second half to complete his hat-trick but Rangers won 6-3, with Fleming – who scored four times – the star of the show. A couple of days later, it was announced that Meiklejohn would be out for 'a considerable period of time'.

And there would be no 'jigging' for the Ranger at the club's annual dance in the Grosvenor. In fact, several of the players battled their way through dense fog just to get there. A couple of days later fog led to an abandonment at Motherwell nine minutes after half-time. The Light Blues were 45 minutes late in arriving at Fir Park and had to fight their way through a large section of the 12,000 crowd who, at that time, were clamouring to get their money back.

The match, played at the end of November, was actually stopped due to darkness. In the replayed fixture the following midweek Rangers won 3-1, but the big talking point was the ordering-off of Well skipper Willie Frame, who received his marching orders for grabbing the referee by the scruff of the neck.

The team was constantly crippled by injuries and when they travelled down to Ayrshire, to face Kilmarnock, Rangers were without Manderson, Robb, Meiklejohn, McCandless and Cairns, but still eked out a 2-2 draw.

Meiklejohn remained on the sidelines when Hibs visited Ibrox in a game which yielded a 3-1 win. Coincidentally, Hibs had prepared for the match on the sands of Gullane, a full half-century before Gers boss Jock Wallace would inflict 'murder hill' on his reluctant stars.

Nine days before Christmas, the Rangers players were treated to a day's golf at Turnberry, in which goalkeeper Willie Robb reportedly recorded the longest drive witnessed at the Ayrshire course. The new record failed to inspire the side though, and they lost 2-1 to Dundee United.

It was then announced that Struth was to give Meiklejohn a run out with the reserves up at Perth – on Christmas Day. The pitch was as hard as iron and the second XI recorded a 2-1 victory, but sadly the 'big' team couldn't emulate their success on Boxing Day and lost 1-0 at home to the Saints.

Since signing for Rangers some six years previous, Meiklejohn had never known the club to be struggling so badly and was well aware that anything other than victory in the Ne'erday Old Firm clash at Celtic

Park would see the title heading elsewhere. It was a tall order because Celtic, after a bad start to the season, had been on a great run and had taken over as league leaders from long-time front-runners St Mirren. They wouldn't be in the mood to give up top spot easily.

Almost 60,000 filed into Parkhead and saw Celtic race into a two-goal lead by the break. Jimmy McGrory scored the first while the second, claimed by McInally, took a wicked deflection off Meiklejohn before ending up in the net. What a difference a year had made. In the previous Ne'erday clash Rangers had simply toyed with their foe and ran out easy 4-1 winners, but their spectacular fall from grace was down to a prolonged injury crisis and not a loss of form. In fact, Celtic had started the day as hottest favourites since the league began.

Meiklejohn's injured knee gave way in the fifth minute and with no substitutes allowed, he was moved out to the left wing with Morton and Cairns taking turns at left-half. In the second half, Rangers roared back from the dead and goals by Cunningham and Muirhead, which deflected in off Morton, earned the visitors a well-deserved draw. It perhaps didn't do them many favours in terms of league position but dignity had been restored.

In the next six games, four of which were won with two draws, Rangers were without many recognised top-team players and Cunningham and Cairns joined the ever-growing injury list, the likes of which had never before been witnessed at Ibrox.

Meiklejohn was reduced to a mere spectator as Lochgelly United were despatched in the first round of the Scottish Cup. In the second round Rangers were drawn away to Stenhousemuir but the Second Division leaders agreed to switch the tie from Ochilview to Ibrox in order to bag a bigger cheque. It was a strange afternoon as Rangers played in light blue in the first half before changing to 'white blouses and black velveteen knickers' after the break. George Henderson scored the only goal of the match and was injured in the process.

Meiklejohn attempted another comeback against high-flying Airdrie at the beginning of February but Rangers lost 2-1 and Archibald suffered a serious groin injury. The knee injury again plagued Meik in the following match but he played through the pain barrier in the Scottish Cup win at Falkirk. With the side short of fully-fit, experienced players he agreed to play in a midweek league game against Falkirk, but that was the last supporters would see of him that season. The team continued to blow hot and cold, although Fleming put a smile on the faces of travelling supporters when he scored the lot in a 5-1 win at Dundee.

And that good form continued in the Scottish Cup quarter-final tie at Cappielow when rampant Rangers won 4-0 in a match sadly marred by serious crowd trouble. Rangers supporters had entered a section of the ground known as 'Little Dublin', a local stronghold, and on two occasions trouble had broken out with surrounding barriers broken in the melee. Morton supporters had taken exception to these 'foreign invaders' and forced the Rangers fans on to the field.

A large number of police officers quickly restored order but it kicked off again and the Rangers fans, swelled by a batch of supporters who had just arrived on one of the many special trains, used bottles and bricks as ammunition and cops struggled to contain the violence. There were charges by groups of fans wielding sticks from the broken barricades. The Glasgow fans were still in the minority though, and were again forced through the perimeter fence. This time they made their way across the pitch and into a section reserved for those paying three shillings extra. A few supporters were taken to Greenock Infirmary where they were treated for minor cuts and bruises.

After the game, it was announced that Meiklejohn would be entering a nursing home to undergo an operation on his troublesome knee. More bad news followed when skipper Tommy Cairns was also ruled out for the rest of the season, suffering from acute neuralgia. The talented forward had been unwell during a visit to Turnberry and a dentist was called to remove a problem tooth. It was exactly what the club didn't need with a Scottish Cup semi-final clash against St Mirren looming.

A vastly understrength Rangers were still regarded as favourites to dispose of Saints in the last four at Hampden but things didn't quite go according to plan. Rangers were searching for their first national cup success in 23 years but despite dominating for large periods, St Mirren scored the only goal of the game. The wait would go on.

The same teams met again seven days later in a league match in Paisley and Rangers, without Liverpool-born Tommy Malone, who had injured an ankle in the cup clash, lost 3-2. It was their 12th league defeat of the season, the most they had lost since records began. And the 13th duly followed at home to Aberdeen with Tommy Craig missing out due to flu, while Muirhead was injured during the game. Rangers followed up a win at Morton by edging Dundee United at Ibrox in a fixture watched by Meik, who had just undergone knee surgery. One reporter said, 'Davie Meiklejohn is walking about as if he'd never had an op!'

During the course of the season Rangers had lost 12 top-team players to injury with Meik suffering on four different occasions. But the reserves fared better and won the Scottish Alliance Cup with a 7-2 aggregate win over Clydebank. The destination of the trophy had never been in doubt after 10,000 witnessed a 4-0 demolition job at Ibrox in the first leg.

With the league programme over, and a disappointing fifth place secured, Rangers turned their attention to the Glasgow Charity Cup but their woes continued when they were dumped 4-3 at Ibrox by Clyde. It had been a difficult season, but despite a lack of success on the field they still showed a healthy profit of more than £3,500. The bulk of this went on a major project to build a new grandstand, which still stands proudly today. The building included new dressing rooms, baths and all mod-cons for the players. The new stand would have seating for 10,000 people while the enclosure in front could comfortably accommodate a further 16,000. When finished, it was hoped that Ibrox Stadium would have a capacity of 125,000.

The season ended with controversy surrounding the future of Tommy Muirhead, who had been offered the secretary/manager's job at Raith Rovers. He was keen to take it but had just signed a new contract with Rangers – and the club were determined to hold him to it. He had been offered £500 a year to manage Raith but finally agreed to honour his agreement with the Gers.

9

Meik survives horror bus crash

MEIKLEJOHN'S pre-season began in the middle of June, at the Glasgow Police Sports Day at Ibrox. Normally the five-a-side event wouldn't have raised too many eyebrows but for the Ibrox star it was the day he made his comeback after an injury-ravaged campaign. There was to be no cigar though as Celtic beat Rangers 3-1 in the opening match.

Three new players had been acquired for the new season. William Moyes, a goalkeeper from Bridgeton Waverley, and Hugh Shaw, a half-back from Hibs, had joined Jimmy Smith, the former Clydebank player. Big things were also expected of Jimmy Marshall, a fearless centre-forward who had arrived near the end of the previous season. Many felt Struth had acquired a good blend of youth and experience, although the key to a successful campaign was keeping everyone fit. Some pundits, though, were saying that Rangers had too many old ones.

Participation at the Clyde Sports Day was marred by the death of Rangers director John 'Jock' McPherson, formerly a successful player with the club. Jock had won three Scottish Cups with the Light Blues and had been a great servant for 12 years. Sadly he collapsed and died in the directors' box at Shawfield.

As usual, the start to the league campaign involved two games in four days and it was deemed too much for the returning Meik. He missed the opening-day win over Dundee United but was back in situ for the victory over a Dunfermline side making their first top-flight visit to Ibrox.

Despite three games in just eight days, Rangers were still keen to do their bit for the greater good of Scottish football and played benefit matches for Bridgeton Waverley and Johnstone FC before seeing off Partick Thistle in a league encounter at Ibrox. The team had made such a positive start to the new season and sat proudly at the top of the league with seven points from just four games.

What a difference a week makes though. A 2-1 defeat at St Johnstone left many correspondents questioning their ability to go all the way, with one scribe saying, 'A shake-up is required at Ibrox. The directors must act now – because Rangers are NOT potential champions.'

They responded by beating Motherwell 2-0 in a game where 'Meiklejohn played like his old self until he seemed to tire of his old injury'. Struth then took his team to Yorkshire to face English First Division champions Huddersfield Town in a benefit match for a local infirmary. A crowd of 15,000 watched Rangers indulge in some 'sparkling football' on their way to a 2-1 win – which doubled as revenge for the thumping defeat in Meik's testimonial. Each player received a mini replica of the Hospital Cup, valued at £6.

A turning point in the season arrived at Ibrox during the traditional September weekend holiday. Rangers were up against league leaders Aberdeen and the situation looked bad for the Light Blues when the Dons raced into a 2-0 lead, with Meiklejohn at fault for the second. But back roared the home side to clinch a dramatic 3-2 win, and a return to the top of the table.

However, while all seemed rosy in the Rangers garden, the downside was a damning critique in a popular Glasgow newspaper which read, 'Rangers' half-back line did not impress me too favourably – and I'm not sure Meiklejohn is well adapted for the central position. Either that or he has lost some of his "fire", which he had before meeting with the accident which troubled him for a time.'

Meiklejohn poured scorn on the criticism and responded by helping his side put seven past Scottish Cup holders St Mirren in their own backyard, with Henderson grabbing a treble, but inconsistency dogged the Light Blues and after losing 1-0 at home to Queen's Park, Jamie Marshall scored five in an 8-2 rout of Morton at Cappielow. More importantly, though, they were back where they belonged – on top of the table.

But just as Meiklejohn was enjoying a run of games and making the critics eat their words, disaster struck. He was returning from a night out in Glasgow city centre with team-mate Willie Hair when the bus he was travelling in was involved in a serious smash, leaving the Ibrox player among seven injured.

The crash happened just after midnight and a stone's throw from his Copland Road home. The bus was approaching the junction of Eaglesham Street and Paisley Road when it was forced to swerve to avoid an oncoming vehicle. In his pursuit of safety, the driver could do little more than guide the bus straight through the front window of a local grocer's shop, R&J Templeton. The shop window caved in immediately and goods were scattered all over the pavement. The main door of the bus was ripped off in the accident, with the front window smashed and bumper badly broken up.

The scene resembled that of a disaster movie and the screaming and wailing of the injured could be heard long before the distant sirens of the emergency services. Many of those caught up in the smash suffered bruised and cut knees, although one passenger received horrific cuts to his face.

Meiklejohn was taken to nearby Plantation Police Station where he awaited the arrival of a casualty surgeon to examine an injury to his left knee. When asked by a reporter how he was feeling, the 25-year-old answered, nonchalantly, 'In the pink,' which implied he wasn't badly hurt. He added, 'I'm hopeful the injury won't interfere with my football.'

Forty-eight hours later the Rangers players converged on the Grosvenor for their annual dance, but we can take it as read that Meik steered well clear of the dance floor. The impact of the crash kept him out of the team for the best part of a month but he returned to play his part in a thrilling 2-2 draw at Easter Road before picking up win bonuses against Falkirk and Clyde. The team was moving along nicely – until unfancied Hamilton Accies left Ibrox with a shock, but deserved, 4-1 victory.

December's Scottish Cup draw paired Rangers with Leith Athletic and the Edinburgh club refused to switch the tie to Ibrox, especially with Hearts and Hibs being drawn away from home. Athletic's Powderhall ground was classed as one of the best stadiums in the country and a gushing report added, 'There is no finer expanse of turf to be found in the whole of Scotland.'

But by Christmas Rangers had slipped to third in the league, behind Motherwell and Celtic, and the Ne'erday clash against Celtic at Ibrox became a must-win fixture. The bulk of the 63,000 crowd were decked out in red, white and blue but it was Celtic who scored first, although Archibald equalised and Marshall scored the winner in the dying minutes of the game.

The two points drew Rangers level with Celtic with both trailing Motherwell by three. The first half of the campaign had produced an interesting race for the title but could Rangers sustain their challenge?

On Monday 3 January further progress was made. Rangers made light work of Partick Thistle at Firhill while Queen's Park completed a grand Old Firm away double by edging Celtic 3-2 at Parkhead. One reporter reckoned that 'nothing could've stood up to the Rangers forwards in the opening 20 minutes – as they were like storm troopers'. Motherwell drew 3-3 with Falkirk so Rangers tucked in just two points behind, but with a crucial game in hand.

A virtual full-strength Rangers travelled to Motherwell a fortnight later in a first versus second clash and walked off with their heads held high, and a 4-1 win. Goals by Fleming, Archibald, Cunningham and Meiklejohn put the Light Blues joint-top of the table with the Steelmen while Celtic handed out a 7-0 thrashing to Clyde, thanks to five-goal Jimmy McGrory.

Just days after Andy Cunningham had helped Rangers back to the top of the table he was linked with the vacant manager's job at Tottenham Hotspur. Rangers boss Bill Struth insisted he wanted to keep Cunningham, a bank clerk before taking up football, at Ibrox, but also intimated that he would not stand in the way of a man who had been a great servant to the club. The position was eventually offered to W.H. Minter, who had been six years at White Hart Lane as trainer.

It was Scottish Cup time again and it was announced that 24 turnstiles would be in operation at Powderhall for the tie between

Leith and Rangers, but there was a shock in store for the Glasgow side when the Edinburgh minnows took an early lead. Rangers eventually won 4-1, but supporters were stunned when the news broke that prolific centre-forward George Henderson had been transferred to Darlington.

In the second round Rangers played host to St Mirren, and a stirring performance saw the home side run out 6-0 winners. A win seven days later against the same side, this time by 4-0, left Rangers just a point behind Motherwell in the title race.

Struth was obviously keen to embellish his striking options and had been tracking the progress of Airdrie's Bob McPhail, a young Barrhead man with a real eye for goal. When Everton agreed a fee with the Diamonds, McPhail looked Merseyside-bound, but he refused to sign for the Toffees and told Airdrie he would go only to Rangers.

Meanwhile, the Light Blues disposed of Hamilton Accies in the third round of the Scottish Cup as McPhail was scoring a brace for Airdrie in their 5-0 romp over Queen's Park.

With Motherwell continuing to impress, Rangers had to keep winning, and they maintained their end of the deal with a 3-1 midweek victory at Dunfermline. Fleming hit a hat-trick but Meiklejohn was outstanding and set up the second goal before thumping the bar late on, from which Fleming sealed his treble. The win saw Rangers leapfrog Motherwell. Both sides were on 41 points but Rangers had played three games less.

A Patsy Gallacher-inspired Falkirk gave Rangers a real fright in the fourth round of the Scottish Cup at a packed Brockville. In a thrilling tie, the Bairns led 2-1 with just seven minutes remaining when Meiklejohn unleashed a thunderbolt. It looked like flying past the post until striking the arm of McIlwaine, and Billy McCandless made no mistake from the resultant penalty.

A record crowd of 80,000 filed into Ibrox for the replay but just one goal was scored on the night, deep into extra time, and it went to Mason of Falkirk. Collecting a pass from Gallacher, he appeared to send in a cross but it flew straight over the head of Hamilton in the Rangers goal and into the back of the net. Rangers had been on top throughout the statutory 90 minutes but did everything bar score. The club had harboured high hopes of winning their first Scottish

Cup since 1903, but would have to wait 12 months for another opportunity.

Dropped points against Airdrie and Cowdenbeath saw Motherwell regain the advantage in the title race, and then a battle royal at Brockville – when Rangers seemingly had the points in the bag – provided another dagger to the heart. Marshall and Meiklejohn, with a 25-yard drive, had the Gers on easy street and although the Bairns pulled one back, Meiklejohn played in George McMillan to restore their two-goal advantage.

However a Gallacher double – coupled with a 6-0 Motherwell win over Dundee United – saw both clubs locked on 49 points, although Rangers had a vital game in hand. Motherwell had just four games to play and when Celtic lost 4-1 at Brockville, the championship became a two-horse race.

Rangers fans were crying in their beer when their favourites slipped up at third-bottom Clyde, only to be rejoicing again when news filtered through from Firhill that Partick Thistle had beaten Motherwell. A striker crisis meant Meiklejohn was pushed up front for the match at Hamilton but the Light Blues could only draw, and all eyes switched to the Old Firm game on Monday 18 April. Rangers desperately needed the win but hadn't captured the league points from Celtic Park in 12 years. Regardless, they were on top of their game and, superbly prompted by makeshift inside-right Meiklejohn, the Gers forwards ran the Celtic defence ragged and despite only having a Fleming goal to show for their efforts, it was enough to snatch the win.

The following day, Bob McPhail put pen to paper for Rangers, which was a crushing blow to Everton manager Tom McIntosh who had been a frequent visitor to Broomfield. McIntosh had been quoted as saying he would 'pay anything' but McPhail's heart lay at Ibrox and the Toffees boss recognised a losing battle when he saw one. The former Pollok forward would go on to become one of Rangers' greatest ever players but just 48 hours after the Old Firm victory, McPhail made an inauspicious debut at Ardencaple Park, Helensburgh, in an Alliance League match.

To the first team, though, and Rangers needed just one point from their two remaining league matches to win the title. They duly got it at home to Dundee, although in a bit of a damp-squib ending the match finished goalless. It was still sufficient to secure a 15th league flag.

Just four days later, TWELVE Rangers players were in action in benefit matches up and down the country – and scored all ten goals between them. A crowd of 20,000 looked on as Meiklejohn, Cunningham, Muirhead and Fleming took part in the Burns Memorial Cup for the Scots against the Anglos at Newcastle. Cunningham scored twice and Jamie Fleming a single in a 3-1 win.

A bit further down the road, at Bradford City's Valley Parade, Manderson, Archibald, Cairns, Morton and Hair helped out Willie Watson in his benefit. The Rangers players were part of Jock Ewart's Select, and the scorers in a 3-2 win for the Scots were Morton, Archibald and Hair.

A bit closer to home, at Somerset Park, Ayr, 1,000 fans gathered for the Tom Kilpatrick benefit. Rangers won 4-1 and on target were Chalmers, with a double, Hair and Ireland.

The following Saturday, a Fleming goal in the last league game of the season at home to Kilmarnock put the seal on another remarkable campaign, and meant Rangers had won the league by five points.

Fleming was in fine form and scored four times in an 8-1 rout of Queen's Park in the first round of the Glasgow Merchant's Charity Cup, while Meiklejohn was 'immense' in the midweek semi-final with Celtic as Rangers won 4-1 at Parkhead. Bradford City sent a representative to watch Manderson and signed the Northern Irish defender, who had been a loyal servant to the Light Blues for 12 years, four days later.

With a final against Partick Thistle looming, Friday 13 April proved unlucky for the Gers when five players – Tom Hamilton, Craig, Muirhead, Archibald and Cunningham – sailed off on the good ship *Melita* as part of the touring Scotland squad bound for Canada. Despite the obvious handicap, Rangers still held Thistle to a 3-3 draw after 90 minutes but capitulated during extra time and lost another three. Sandy Hair was on top form for the Jags with five goals.

There was no rest for the wicked and Rangers took part in a number of post-season benefit matches as well as winning five-a-side competitions at several sports days. At the Glasgow Police Open Day, held at Ibrox, Tommy McInally of Celtic incurred the wrath of the home crowd when, during a first-round match against Partick Thistle, he stood on the ball and invited the opposition players to try and take it off him. No one took him up on his 'offer', and play was all but suspended for a minute or two. *Daily Record* correspondent 'Waverley' condemned McInally's actions and said, 'It could have led to serious crowd trouble.'

In the end, Partick had the last laugh by winning 2-1. Just as the crowd had jeered McInally, they cheered Hair when he scored the winner. But the day belonged to Rangers as Meiklejohn gave the perfect exhibition of how to play five-a-side football, and after beating Partick in the final, the players were presented with a tea set and tray.

So if June was the month for five-a-sides, July was reserved for Meiklejohn's other passion, golf. The brothers Morton, Alan and Jack, teamed up to play Meiklejohn and official starter Jamie Alexander at the Old Course, St Andrews. Alan Morton served his intentions early on when he hit a beauty of a drive off the first tee and straight down the middle. After several hours, Alan stepped off the 18th with a round of 78 under his belt and Meiklejohn was right on his tail. After the golf the Ranger spent some time indulging in his other passion, sea swimming.

10

Season has a silver lining

NEW season, new broom. Bert Manderson and Tommy Cairns had moved to Bradford City and Arthur Dixon was on the hunt for a new club after being freed. Rangers entered the 1927/28 campaign with a first-team squad of 25 players and just Cunningham, Archibald and Muirhead had been resident at Ibrox longer than Meiklejohn.

As storms ripped through Glasgow and nearby Paisley, the Scottish First Division flag was unfurled at Rangers' 41st annual sports day and the club had extra cause for celebration when Meiklejohn, Craig, McPhail, Fleming and Morton won the keenly-contested short game. For their efforts, the Famous Five carried off a case of sterling silver military hat and coat brushes.

On day one of the new season, Rangers travelled to Pittodrie and took an early lead – 15 seconds to be precise – without an Aberdeen player touching the ball.

Fleming kicked off and played it short to Cunningham, who found Archibald with a crossfield pass then Fleming got on the end of a centre to prod home. Fleming, with a second, and Morton made sure Rangers started the season in winning fashion, but most of the plaudits were reserved for the Light Blues' 'outstanding' half-back trio of Meiklejohn, Muirhead and Craig.

Wins over Hearts and Cowdenbeath once again put Rangers in the driving seat for a second successive title but the latter of the two games saw Meiklejohn sent off for the first, and only, time in his career. With 15 minutes remaining he 'raised a hand' to Willie Wilson and was promptly despatched from the field.

Afterwards, the player refused to speak about the dismissal, although he did privately admit to regretting the incident. His team-mates insisted he had been provoked by Wilson and lamented the fact that the guilty party had got off scot-free.

Meiklejohn played in the next match – a 5-1 win over St Johnstone – before facing the SFA Referees' Disciplinary Committee. The meeting didn't last long and the player was severely censured for his actions at Central Park – a mere slap on the wrist.

A 6-0 victory at Firhill was followed up by a narrow win over Airdrie at Ibrox – a sixth straight league win – but despite Meik's man-of-the-match performance at Motherwell, the Gers dropped a point in a 1-1 draw.

Rangers were rampant, though, and merely underlined their superiority by thrashing Clyde 7-0 at Ibrox in the first round of the Glasgow Cup. The undoubted star of the show was Fleming, who scored six times. He became just the fourth player to perform the double hat-trick but had missed a sitter which would have seen him in seventh heaven.

On the Saturday prior to the final against Celtic, Rangers thumped St Mirren 4-2 but skipper Tommy Muirhead, arguably the finest player of his generation, suffered a nasty shoulder injury and was withdrawn at half-time. The remainder of the players warmed up for the big match against Celtic by partaking in a night at the dogs. They joined 10,000 spectators at Carntyne as Glaswegians got their first glimpse of the 'new sport of the electric hare and bounding hounds'. Former Ger Arthur Dixon had a smile on his face when his dog Cleena won the second race.

Just short of 85,000 were present at Hampden Park for the Glasgow Cup Final and despite another herculean performance from Meiklejohn, Rangers lost 2-1. It was said that the Gers missed the craft and guile of Muirhead, and the disruption his absence brought to the half-back line.

The teams met seven days later in a league match at Ibrox and 60,000 saw Fleming score the only goal of the match to end Celtic's unbeaten record and move Rangers clear at the top of the table. Celtic complained vehemently that Fleming was offside when he scored and McInally was sent off for questioning the referee's decision. The return of Muirhead allowed Meiklejohn to slot into the centre-back position, where he was a tower of strength and kept Jimmy McGrory in check.

Rangers continued their impressive start to the season with a 7-0 demolition of Raith Rovers – and another Fleming hat-trick – but Tully Craig was sent off for a flippant comment made to the referee. The visitors were awarded a rather dubious penalty and after they had missed it, Craig, trotting by the match official, said, 'That was a bonny penalty, but they missed it anyway!'

The weekend was complete when Meiklejohn was named in the Scotland team to face Wales in Wrexham – and the *Daily Record* reported that Rangers had signed a player named Archie McPherson from Alva Albion Rangers. Surely not *the* Archie!

Following the Raith game, the Light Blues showed their liking for a smaller ball when they took on the rugby players of Watsonians at golf at Mortonhall Golf Club in Edinburgh. Just 48 hours later Meiklejohn had packed away his clubs and boarded a train at Central Station to take him and his Scotland team-mates to Liverpool, where they spent the night before moving on to Wrexham for the Home International clash with the Welsh and secured a 2-2 draw. Meiklejohn did himself no harm whatsoever with a sterling performance at centre-half.

November proved an extra-special month for the Light Blues as they clocked up four successive league wins, but they still found an impressive Motherwell side hanging on to their coat-tails. The month ended with a night of dancing as the Rangers players – including Meiklejohn, Gray and Morton – and directors tripped the light fantastic at the Grosvenor. In the presence of Lord Provost Mason, the players indulged in the waltz, foxtrot and the more boisterous 'Paul Jones'.

Mixed form in the lead-up to Christmas saw the Gers drop a couple of points to Hamilton and Kilmarnock, in games where the crowd was down quite considerably due, it was believed, to the popularity of the wireless, but the team secured wins over Dundee and Aberdeen – the latter a stunning 5-0 victory thanks to another Fleming hat-trick. The day before the win over the Dons, Rangers signed Jock Buchanan from Morton – and then it was off to Turnberry for rest and golf.

The New Year's Day clash of 1928 looked like finishing goalless until McGrory popped up to score the only goal of the game. It was reported that Meiklejohn had the little striker in his pocket but in stretching to stop a sure goal had twisted his knee in the process and McGrory had taken advantage to fire home. The defeat left Motherwell top of the pile by just a single point, although they had played one game more.

In the middle of January, Rangers were desperate for a win over Airdrie at Broomfield, following a disappointing start to the year in which just three points had been yielded from a possible six. A stunning performance – in blue and white stripes – brought a tantalising 7-2 win, but even such an incredible victory against one of Rangers' main title rivals was hidden in the small print as one individual claimed all the headlines the next day. During Celtic's 9-0 mauling of Dunfermline, McGrory scored eight.

The Light Blues had drawn East Stirling in the first round of the Scottish Cup with the tie scheduled to take place at Shire's ramshackle Bainsford ground. Rangers had initially offered to host the game – with no cash incentive put forward – but Shire directors knocked it back. The Bainsford pitch clearly wasn't up to scratch but club officials worked hard to rectify the situation and the game went ahead as planned, with Fleming scoring three times in a 6-0 victory.

A 3-1 win over Bo'ness the following Saturday eased Rangers four points clear of Motherwell, with a game in hand. The second round of the Scottish brought Cowdenbeath to Ibrox and this time it was Bob McPhail who bagged a hat-trick as Rangers won 4-2, but the team was still dogged by inconsistency into February and lost a key battle against title rivals Motherwell at Ibrox a couple of days before letting a 3-2 lead slip against St Mirren at Love Street.

Rangers marched on in the Scottish Cup and after switching their third-round tie with King's Park from Stirling to Ibrox, they overcame a first-half scare when the minnows took the lead to win 3-1 in front of 20,000.

Next up for half the Rangers side was the Scotland v Ireland international at Firhill. Meiklejohn was joined in dark blue by Muirhead, Gray and Morton, while Bob Hamilton played for the Irish. The visitors won by a single goal but Meiklejohn went close to equalising and only a brilliant stop by Liverpool keeper Elisha Scott ensured Irish eyes were smiling at the end of the 90 minutes.

Rangers' league game against Raith Rovers had been postponed, which allowed Celtic to go one point clear at the top, although they had played two games more.

On the eve of the Scottish Cup quarter-final tie with Albion Rovers at Cliftonhill, Meiklejohn was named in the Scottish League side to face their English counterparts at Ibrox and a Cunningham goal, after good work by McPhail, eased Rangers through to the last four.

The Light Blues regained their rightful position at the top of the league despite playing out a goalless draw at Tynecastle, but Meiklejohn picked up a leg injury which ruled him out of the league international – and denied him the chance to captain his country for the first time. He had been keen to play but failed a late fitness test. As it turned out, a strong English side crushed the Scots 6-2.

On the Monday after the game, Rangers were drawn to face Hibs in the semi-finals of the Scottish Cup – and a telegram arrived from Canada confirming that Rangers would take part in their first trans-atlantic tour of North America during the forthcoming close-season.

In a dress rehearsal for the Scottish Cup tie, Hibs beat Rangers 2-1 at Easter Road, a result which saw the Gers slip to third place behind both Celtic and Motherwell but, more importantly, six players were placed in the doubtful category after picking up knocks in the capital.

Rangers manager Bill Struth changed his team's approach to the tie against Hibs and plumped for what was described in the popular press as 'storm tactics', but it did the trick and goals by Archibald, McPhail and Simpson saw Rangers run out comfortable 3-0 winners. After the game, Meik said, 'The tactics were spot on. I must admit that's my favourite way to play the game, because it doesn't give your opponents much of a chance to get into their rhythm.'

'Waverley' said in the *Daily Record*, 'Big Davie was the Goliath of the party, he totally neutralised the threat of centre forward Jamie McColl.'

Rangers may have been impressive but the biggest cheer of the afternoon was reserved for the half-time scoreboard which read, 'Queen's Park 2 Celtic 0', although sadly the chap responsible had blundered and Celtic won 2-1. But Rangers were in the final of the Scottish Cup and their followers were convinced this would be the year they finally laid that hoodoo to rest.

The first Saturday in April saw the lead change hands at the top of the first division. Rangers eased past Hamilton, with Meik back in the side after a 'chill', and with Motherwell beating Celtic 3-1 at Fir Park the Light Blues held a slender advantage.

Monday 9 April was a red-letter day for Rangers as they cruised past Dunfermline, and with Airdrie beating Celtic the Light Blues had opened up a three-point gap at the top with just three games remaining – and three days later the entire Rangers squad offered supporters a pre-Scottish Cup Final boost by signing on for the next season. On the same day, the club put their old grandstand up for sale. 'Five thousand top quality seats at a reasonable price!'

There was nothing else for it but to instantly forget the thrills and excitement of the Scottish Cup Final for Rangers were back in action just four days later, in a vital league match up at Dundee. The 13th minute proved lucky for Gers as the Dundee defence expected Meik to shoot directly from a free kick but he cunningly slipped it to McPhail, who almost burst the rigging with a spectacular drive. Despite Celtic winning at home against St Johnstone, it was enough to bring the league flag back to Ibrox.

The following midweek, Meiklejohn joined Gray, Cunningham and McPhail in Newcastle for the fourth annual Burns Memorial match, which drew a crowd of 15,000, and just three days later a staggering crowd of 20,000 turned up at Ibrox to see Rangers reserves beat Ayr 1-0 to clinch the Second XI Cup to go with their Alliance League title – making it a double/double achievement for Scotland's most successful club.

Sadly, though, as players from both Rangers teams danced the night away at their annual social evening at the Grosvenor, and the first-team players were presented with brand new Angus gold watches, vandals were causing damage worth hundreds of pounds to the new Ibrox grandstand, smashing windows and breaking what they could.

Regardless, the triumphant Gers added the Glasgow Merchant's Charity Cup to their already impressive haul of silverware by beating Queen's Park 3-1 in the final at Celtic Park. One correspondent described Davie Meiklejohn as a 'man of might'.

It had been a long and arduous campaign but the pot of gold at the end of the rainbow came in the form of a close-season tour of the United States and Canada, and it was a happy Rangers party that departed on their month-long adventure of a lifetime.

Before leaving though, there was the small matter of the Scottish Cup Final against Celtic.

11

The wait is finally over

WHILE preparing for a European Cup Final, former Barcelona manager Pep Guardiola said, 'In cup finals it is fear, or holding something back in reserve, which can defeat you. The worst that can happen in a match like this is that nobody wants to have a shot, score the goals or assume responsibility for winning because nerves dominate their choices. We need to be brave, show what we are made of, and how good we are.'

These very words could have been scripted for Davie Meiklejohn many generations before flowing from the mouth of the Catalan genius. The 1928 Scottish Cup Final gave Rangers players the perfect opportunity to become legends in the eyes of their supporters. It had been 25 years since the Light Blues had lifted the national trophy: a national disgrace as some fans put it. On that occasion, Hearts had been defeated. This time, though, Celtic stood between Rangers and immortality. Meiklejohn and co were determined to right a very serious wrong.

For a quarter of a century the club had been the butt of many a music hall joke, with a string of funnymen promising audience members 'boundless wealth when the Rangers finally win the cup', or that Celtic favourites Patsy Gallacher and Willie McStay had more Scottish Cup badges than they had room for on their waistcoats, and that if the Rangers players asked nicely, Patsy or Willie would give them one.

It was the 50th cup final and, despite previous shortcomings, there was a real air of optimism in the Ibrox camp as they made their way to Hampden for the showdown meeting with their great rivals. When they arrived at the national stadium supporters of both sides were milling around in their thousands. By kick-off time there would be 118,115 people inside the ground, half decked out in blue and white and the other half in green.

As captains Meiklejohn – deputising for the absent Tommy Muirhead – and McStay shook hands, and the referee tossed the coin, excitement in the crowd was at fever pitch. McStay called correctly and elected to shoot with the wind, no doubt hoping to conjure up a healthy enough lead to give the Parkhead side the upper hand in the second period.

Going into the match, Celtic had been red-hot favourites to pile on Rangers' Scottish Cup woes and they were first to carve out an opportunity but Tom Hamilton saved Adam McLean's effort. The Ibrox goal had several further narrow escapes as Celtic used a howling gale to their advantage. A five-minute spell before half-time constituted Rangers' most trying time of the afternoon, and Hamilton played a starring role. It was a delighted Light Blues that reached the break with their goal intact.

It was a different story early in the second half as Rangers took command and Cunningham, Morton, Buchanan and Fleming went close. There were 56 minutes on the clock when the game's pivotal moment arrived. From a Morton cross the ball was fired in by Fleming – and John Thomson was beaten. McStay stuck out a hand and referee Willie Bell had no hesitation in pointing to the spot.

Many spectators at that end of the ground believed the ball had already crossed the line. Bell had doubt in his mind though and a penalty kick it was – but there were no takers. Not a single Ranger stepped forward to assume responsibility from 12 yards. Regular penalty man Bob McPhail turned his back on the ball. Sensing a lack of confidence among his team-mates, Meiklejohn played a true captain's part. The ground fell silent. Twenty-five years of hurt rested on this single kick. Score, and the Light Blues would surely go on to lift the elusive trophy. Miss, and the consequences could be fatal.

As if operating in slow motion, the 27-year-old half-back placed the ball on the penalty spot, took one look at Thomson in the Celtic goal, turned and walked away from the ball. He turned again, eyed the referee, who sounded his whistle, and began his run-up to the leather, which he kicked with total precision beyond the reach of the Prince of Goalies. It was 1-0 to Rangers, and up in the air went 60,000 bunnets.

With their tails up, Rangers rattled into their opponents and an Archibald shot shook the bar before Fleming flashed one narrowly past. Ten minutes after Meik's opener, McPhail was in the right place at the right time to thump the ball past Thomson. Game over?

Two minutes later it was and when Archibald let fly from 25 yards, the agonising wait was over. Thomson had misjudged the flight of the ball and it was soon nestling in the back of the net. But 'Sandy' didn't finish there and with ten minutes remaining, McStay cleared straight to the feet of the Rangers star, who controlled it in a flash, steadied for a fraction of a second, and drove it like a rocket past the dumbfounded keeper. It was time to celebrate.

Full-backs Dougie Gray and 'Newry' Bob Hamilton were stand-outs for Rangers in the first half while Meik was solid in the middle line. The Ibrox skipper was a tower of strength and ensured Jimmy McGrory had a quiet afternoon.

Striker Jamie Fleming was a worrier with a punch, as was McPhail, after a rather disappointing start. This pair of strong-going, fearless forwards did much to harry the almost-always worried, and later overwrought Parkhead back six. Archibald, his two goals apart, did a power of running and, with a lively Alan Morton, contributed his quota to this glorious Ibrox victory.

Afterwards, Meik said, 'I am too pleased to be able to express my true feelings. When we were awarded the penalty, and I stepped up to take it, I have never felt so anxious in all my life. It was the most terrible one minute of my football career. I had time to think what it might mean if I missed, and I can tell you I was glad when I saw the ball lying in the back of the net.'

Asked why regular 'spot man' McPhail didn't take the penalty, Meiklejohn said, 'Bob told me he wasn't taking it because he had been missing them. He had missed two and when a man does that, his confidence is shaken.'

But McPhail was at his captain's elbow just before the kick and one could have been forgiven for thinking that he, and not Meiklejohn, was taking it. That, apparently, was the plan.

In the Hampden reading room, Rangers chairman Joseph Buchanan was presented with the cup and made it known that he was glad that at long last the spell had been broken. However he was at pains to say that at no time during the 25 barren years had anyone at the club ever become downhearted or pessimistic.

He was particularly pleased that when it finally came along, it was Celtic who had been defeated in the final, as that was the long-held ambition. He added, 'No matter how long or tortuous the road, it was bound to have a turning. The cup is fuller because we have beaten the Celtic. It was a grand game and a determined struggle between giants; a struggle worthy of the reputation of the clubs and the magnificent patronage. These Rangers–Celtic encounters do much to popularise the game – long may the friendly rivalry continue.

'Celtic were unfortunate to get our boys on their toes, and everyone must agree that on play we deserved to win. When Celtic's time comes again we will congratulate them as heartily and sincerely as they have done us.'

Tom White, replying for Celtic, was, as usual, short, humorous and to the point. With a merry twinkle in his eye he said, 'I am glad to have lived to see the day Bailie Buchanan has taken custody of the Scottish Cup.' The comment drew a laugh, as did, 'After seeing this latest performance of the Rangers, I begin to wonder if Celtic will ever win it again!

'Rangers won very well indeed, but I was worried that in the last ten minutes we could see an avalanche. I hoped and prayed that the fifth goal wouldn't go in.'

The heroes of the hour then dressed in their finest attire and took to the field to be photographed with the cup. Afterwards, a triumphal return to Ferguson & Forrester's where, in a gaily bedecked room – blue and white flags, Union Jacks, and Royal Standards – directors, managers and players dined together, with Bailie Buchanan in the chair.

Getting to the restaurant proved a pleasant problem for the Rangers party as a constant stream of Gers fans filled the route from Hampden to Buchanan Street. And when they spotted the cup in captain Meiklejohn's car it was the signal for a massed raid, hands through the opened window and shakes galore. At Gorbals Cross hundreds surrounded the car, and stopped its progress for some minutes. The hoodoo had finally been laid to rest and it was a day to remember for all connected with the Rangers.

But the evening was just beginning as for the previous 18 weeks or so at the Glasgow Princess's Theatre, George West had been bringing on a replica Scottish Cup 'to show the Rangers what it looked like!' Well the real article was on stage that Saturday. Rather fittingly, it was the last night of the King o' Clubs pantomime. It was a real impromptu happening and when the Rangers players arrived with the cup, West tipped his cap and paid great homage to the 'boys who had brought home the bacon', while lamenting the passing of 'a great gag'.

Over 50 cables and telegrams arrived at Ibrox from well-wishers looking to congratulate the players and directors on their grand achievement. Old Rangers supporters in Pennsylvania and Toronto cabled congratulations on the great victory while Henderson's the Jeweller presented gleaming Angus watches to the victorious Rangers 11.

It had been a long day, but an even longer wait was over – Rangers had taken charge of the Scottish Cup again.

12

Gers go Stateside

THE first World Cup was still two years away when Rangers headed off on their maiden transatlantic adventure – destination North America. The USA would finish third at the inaugural competition in Uruguay and it's perhaps a little indulgent to think that the Rangers might just have taught them a thing or two about the game, and set them on the road to glory in Montevideo.

But back to reality, and the official Rangers party set sail on the good ship *California* from Yorkhill Quay on the morning of Saturday 19 May 1928. The travelling group comprised of 17 players, nine of whom were full internationals, manager Bill Struth, and directors Duncan Graham and James Bowie. Some 600 passengers were also on board the vessel. New York would welcome the weary tourists nine days later with the Knickerbocker Hotel in Times Square their plush headquarters. It was proposed to play nine matches in 24 days but that quickly became ten when an extra fixture was added to the itinerary.

On leaving Scotland the players and officials had received the most rapturous of send-offs and as the ship slowly snaked its way down the River Clyde, thousands of supporters and well-wishers turned out to bid farewell to the Scottish Cup holders. While the tugs were taking charge of the ship, those on the banks of the Clyde broke into song and gave a hearty rendition of an old Rangers classic, while on board the *California* a band named the Three Oxford Boys, from the Hamilton Hippodrome, entertained passengers for over an hour with a less rousing form of music. When they had finished their set, they were rewarded with the presentation of Rangers badges by Struth. Was it because they had finally finished?

Passing vessels displayed the red, white and blue of Rangers, and work in the various shipyards was suspended until the men in overalls had given a loud cheerio to their favourites lining the ship's side. Rangers 6 New York 0 read a banner prominently displayed by two Fairfield workers as a squad of riveters pointed proudly to one of their colleagues who was wearing a light blue jersey.

As the ship sailed past Clydebank, the waiting crowds cheered for trainer Jimmy Kerr, while at Renfrew, a special reception awaited goalkeeper and resident Tom Hamilton. His namesake Bob, the left-back, quipped, 'Man, I wish this boat was sailing past Belfast, then there would be a special cheer for Billy McCandless and I.'

Once the *California*'s bow was pointing out to the open seas, out came the deck billiards and quoits. Before Alan Morton and Sandy Archibald had proved their right to the title of billiards champions of the upper deck the hilarity was so boisterous that the chief engineer came up to enquire if the ship had struck an iceberg. For dinner in the evening, Dick McMillan, of the Anchor Line, their chaperone-in-chief, had provided a nice surprise for the travelling Gers. The tables were decked in blue and white and there was a souvenir menu card on which was inscribed, 'Farewell Dinner in honour of Rangers Football Club: Good Luck and Bon Voyage'.

With the repast over, a round of snappy speeches ensued. McMillan welcomed his esteemed guests and said, 'If there is anything better in the United States, then they must be quite a team.' The Rangers directors thanked McMillan and his staff for their generous hospitality and the club chairman insisted that they had a reputation to defend because they had never before been defeated outwith the shores of Great Britain, and he predicted that enviable stat would remain untarnished.

Skipper Tommy Muirhead then lived up to his reputation as a top after-dinner orator by insisting that the players were going to America not to let the folk there see the football that won the cups, but the football that won the league championship. There would be no kick and hustle.

The last stop for the *California*, before nosing out once again to the open sea, was Moville, at the northern tip of Donegal, where a party of football people had congregated to say their farewells. It was here, also, that many who had accompanied the players and officials on the first stage of their voyage, departed to join the SS *Cameronia* for the trip back to Glasgow.

Two days into the journey the players took part in an organised fancy dress ball and, it was said, they were so made up that their partners would not have recognised them. One quick change later and members of the squad were entertaining fellow guests with a song or two. Looking sharp in suits and bow ties, the group called themselves the Twenty Apostles and the bo'sun's mate remarked that if they had to give up football they would do just fine in the music halls.

The party arrived safe and well in the land of Uncle Sam and were welcomed ashore in Boston by the McLean Pipe Band, where the blood thickened with the skirl of the pipes and a demonstration of Highland dancing. Mr J.C. Creagh, chief of the Lindsay Clan, welcomed the team to the city and invited them for dinner when they were scheduled to play against the city footballers later in their trip.

Next stop New York, and Mr McInnes, royal chief of the Scottish Clans, was awaiting their arrival with similar fervour. The pipes were once again in evidence and the players were treated to some traditional Scottish music before making their way to the Knickerbocker Hotel where they would prepare for their opening challenge against Philadelphia, at which it was hoped Bill Struth would field the side that won the Scottish Cup.

Before the match, the Rangers party was introduced to Captain Pomfrey, British Consul at Baltimore, who had travelled quite a distance with his wife to see the match.

And what a grand opening to the tour for Rangers thumped their hosts 8-1. The ground was hard but the players soon mastered the conditions and went on to produce a first-class display of football. Their passing game offered little hope to the home side and Rangers were four clear at the break. Local spectators appeared to enjoy a fine display of football, even if their favourites were being somewhat overrun.

The match did throw up one topic of real conversation and that was the use of the 'substitute' by the host team. Struth said, 'The Philadelphia team used some 14 players during the game by means of substitution. We are having some lively arguments over this. On the subject of Prohibition, let's just say we can "get one before bed" if we wish!'

The team that took part in Rangers' first historic game on the other side of the pond was: T. Hamilton, Gray, R. Hamilton, Buchanan, Meiklejohn, Craig, Archibald, Cunningham, Fleming, McPhail and Morton. Scorers in Philadelphia were McPhail (two), Fleming (two), Buchanan, Cunningham, Craig and Morton.

Next to fall were Brooklyn Wanderers. Some 20,000 spectators turned up to watch the same Rangers side win 4-0 with Fleming getting a hat-trick and McPhail a single, but the American fans were left to drool over a superb performance by Andy Cunningham who teased and tormented the home players throughout a one-sided encounter. And when the Brooklyn forwards did break free from midfield, they found Meiklejohn and co a hurdle too high and never seriously tested Tom Hamilton in the Rangers goal. At times the Yankee crowds marvelled at the clever combination play of the Light Blue forwards.

The players had a couple of days' rest before their next match, at Fall River in Massachusetts – and there was a shock in store for Rangers when they fought out a scoreless draw with the local side. Manager Struth made just a single change with Muirhead replacing McPhail. But for the brilliance, however, of the Fall River goalkeeper Douglas the tourists would certainly have made it three wins from three games. Each of the five forwards, as well as Meiklejohn, Craig and Buchanan, had great attempts on goal but simply couldn't get past the talented young stopper.

Next on the touring Scots' itinerary was a trek of nearly 600 miles to Pittsburgh, where the players and directors were welcomed by the mayor at the local municipal building. Struth, Ex-Bailie Graham and James Bowie were presented with a golden key to the city, the highest honour available for visitors. In the evening they were guests of the Clan Grant, all 150 of them, and were wined and dined until the 'wee sma' hours'.

In return for their superb hospitality, Rangers hammered the locals 9-0 and produced a display of scintillating football in front of the 8,000 crowd. McPhail scored a hat-trick and there were a couple for Marshall and Morton, with Craig and Fleming completing the scoring.

The party were soon on the move again, this time heading north to Detroit via the picturesque trail around Lake Erie. In all, the journey took around seven hours and Meiklejohn, Archibald and Gray were given a further rest, sitting out the game to allow McCandless, Jamie Simpson and Willie Hair to make their first appearances of the tour. And for the second Sunday in succession, Rangers were held to a draw.

The stalemate was once again largely as a result of the spectacular form shown by the home goalkeeper Sprott, the Detroit number one. In fact, his display was so good that he was 'chaired' from the field at the end of the game. Some 15,000 people watched the action on a firm but rather small pitch, and saw Jock Buchanan turn the ball past his own keeper before Hair scored the equaliser. A Glasgow man, Mr D. Evans, was the referee, and one should remember that the game was played in 80-degree heat.

After an overnight stay in what had just become the Motor City the players were on the move again, this time to Toronto, where their reception outshone even that of Pittsburgh, which was really something. In an emotional ceremony, the players were accompanied to the town hall by the Pipe Band of the 48th Highlanders. On the way to the building a stop was made at the Cenotaph, where the party laid a wreath for the fallen of the Great War. A speech by Mayor McBride ended with each player being awarded the Freedom of the City.

Then it was time to take to the football field, and in front of 19,000 fervent supporters, Rangers produced a sparkling display of football to beat Ulster United 7-0. Before the match, though, yet another honour was bestowed upon the visitors when a representative of the Scottish Citizens Group presented Ex-Bailie Graham with a handsome scroll framed in beautiful oak. At the ground, scores of expat Scots had awaited the arrival of Rangers with great enthusiasm. People originally from Govan, Partick and all over Caledonia had turned up to see the Rangers in action. And they weren't disappointed as McPhail slammed in four goals to add to strikes by Cunningham and a Fleming double.

At the close of play there were rousing cheers for another great exhibition of delightful football. Struth said, 'This was the best team we had come up against so far on the tour, so it says much for the standard of our performance. Although the margin was so big, the Ulster combine showed real ability – they were quite a clever side.'

And Struth revealed how the tour of the US and Canada had captured the imagination of so many people. He said, 'From the moment we get up in the morning until 12 o'clock midnight we are kept busy with callers at our hotel. Everybody who is Scotch wants to drop in and talk about the old country and football. Very nice, too, but it is an extra job we did not have on the itinerary.

'Our game against Brooklyn Wanderers was a pleasant affair. Their goalkeeper, Smith, who is an old Aberdeen player, put up a magnificent game and was responsible for making the match something of a contest. It was only in the second half that our boys wore him down. The Wanderers showed a good conception of the game. Their team work was excellent. You will see from the *New York Times* that Brooklyn are regarded as the equal of any team in America. Though we won 4-0, they came out of the match with great credit.

'The conditions we are experiencing are more like cricket weather, and are exhausting to the players. We found ourselves up against it when we met Fall River the day after Brooklyn. We boarded a train on the Saturday night in Brooklyn at 11.30, and arrived at Fall River at 7.30 the next morning, feeling very tired. It was a case of making for the field almost straight away. There was a great gathering of Scots and Yanks and we received a wonderful reception.

'We received another when the game began. The Fall River team were not long in letting us know what was what. They slipped it across Tom Hamilton in the first few minutes, and when he was knocked out the crowd thought it was great fun. Naturally, our fellows did not take it all lying down, but the effect was that the game was spoiled as an exhibition. We were glad to get away with a few skinned legs and no fractures. I don't think there will be any Fall River in our next – if there is a next – American programme. There was just one thing we regretted and that was our inability to accept the proffered hospitality of the Caledonian Scots of Fall River.

'Back to New York, the boys got a fine pick-me-up at the Turkish Baths. They are all in good fettle now. The New York Nationals club are chasing us for a game at the finish of our tour. Up until the present, nothing has been settled, but I expect we shall play them before we sail on the 27th. I am now switching off for an ice-cream soda. Say, guys, what do you think of that?'

When the party arrived in Montreal, they found a large assembly of passionate Scots excitedly awaiting their arrival. Struth said, 'There is just the danger should we strike a city or a town where the inhabitants don't fall over the top of one another to extend the glad hand we will feel badly done by. Never surely was such hospitality extended to a touring "soccer" party.

'After lunch with the St George's Snowshoe Club, we spent the afternoon on the bowling green, and thoroughly enjoyed the "old man's game". There was then a sad parting of the ways as Morton and Fleming need to go home for work reasons. We don't want to lose them but they simply had to go, and we showed our grief at their departure by giving them a rousing send-off. Bon voyage, boys.

'We have fixed up an extra game. We play at Chicago on June 20, and are all well and enjoying every minute – the players are in the pink!'

Rangers played Montreal on the Saturday night and came away with a 5-1 victory, despite the playing field resembling Glasgow Green in many respects. McCandless replaced fellow Irishman Bob Hamilton while Marshall and Muirhead deputised for the departed Morton and Fleming. Doubles from Cunningham and Marshall were supplemented with a single from McPhail. Rangers were three ahead at half-time and in Struth's mind, 'Montreal emerged after the break looking as if they meant business!' They showed lots of dash and swarmed around the Light Blues' goal and looked very like scoring – but didn't.

After McPhail had notched the fifth and final goal, Rangers displayed their brilliant brand of fast and free-flowing football and gave an exhibition of the quality that had made them champions of the Scottish League for three years running. All kinds of shots rained down on Noseworthy but the Canadian goalkeeper was equal to the task. A breakaway gave opposition striker Duguid, the former Queen's Park centre-forward, his chance and he took it with aplomb.

Next on Rangers' Yankee itinerary was a trip to Boston to take on the city's first XI. The home side didn't let down their supporters in the 12,000 crowd and earned a 2-2 draw, the Gers' third 'check' of the tour. Boston took the lead in the tenth minute when forward John Ballantyne shot past Hamilton. Goals either side of the break, by

Marshall and Cunningham, gave Rangers the lead but with just five minutes remaining Ballantyne fired home a fine equaliser.

Tom Hamilton, Cunningham and Marshall were best for Rangers while the brothers Ballantyne, John and Robert, both of whom at one time played for Partick Thistle, stood out for Boston.

Players and management were able to sample some fine Boston hospitality before catching a train for Chicago, where they would play their next match against Illinois. On arrival in the city the players were entertained to lunch by the St Andrews Society before gaining the freedom of the city in a ceremony performed by the mayor, Big Bill Thompson. He expressed himself as being keenly interested in the Rangers tour and demonstrated that he could say nice things – even to the Scots. The party spent a pleasant few hours with the mayor and other civic leaders.

The players then visited an old people's home before getting to the Illinois football stadium in time for a 6.45pm kick-off in very wet weather. In the circumstances it wasn't surprising that only a moderate attendance was present, but those who turned out witnessed a most frenetic opening five minutes when, first of all, Cunningham scored for Rangers, a goal which was equalised soon after by Cuthbert, Chicago's inside-left. McPhail edged Rangers in front minutes before the interval but the hosts made a real game of it in the second period and it was only the brilliance of Rangers' play, and further goals by Marshall and McPhail, with a superb solo effort, which secured the win.

It was a terrific performance and result, considering the Light Blues had travelled more than 1,000 miles to get there and had only arrived a little over three hours before kick-off. Julius Hjulian, the former Celtic goalkeeper and the USA custodian at the 1934 World Cup, was a standout for Chicago's all-star side, but Clem Cuthbert was their star turn.

Alan Morton and Jamie Fleming arrived home aboard the good ship *Athenia* just as their colleagues were preparing to play their final game in Brooklyn. Morton said, 'It was a wonderful trip and we thoroughly enjoyed it, but we're glad to be home.

'Football was taken seriously in the States, but the conditions were difficult, especially on the bare grounds, and with the humid atmosphere. Only in the palatial baseball enclosures did they have any grass pitches to play on.'

Regarding the 'roughing up' at Fall River, Fleming smiled, 'I'm saying nothing to anybody about that match,' before Morton chipped in, 'It was tough!' When told that many in Montreal were saddened by the early departure of the duo, Morton insisted that he couldn't have played anyway, having been injured in the draw at Detroit, but he said his injury had healed during the crossing, and added, 'I proved my fitness by challenging for the deck tennis championships!'

He continued, 'On both sides of the border [Canada and the USA], the crowds were exceptionally well behaved, and of course a big percentage were Scots. I think our appearance excited a lot of people, but also made them homesick to a certain degree.'

On the other side of the Atlantic, Rangers brought a most satisfactory tour of North America to a close with a resounding victory over an American Select in Brooklyn. A crowd of 18,000 watched the travellers win 6-0 with goals from Archibald, Buchanan, Marshall and McPhail, not to mention a double from Cunningham.

Everyone had been keener than ever to see how the Scottish champions would fare against the best the Americans had to offer and the answer was there for all to see – Rangers were simply the best, despite travelling the best part of 3,000 miles in just eight days to show off their soccer skills in as many different cities as possible.

The match in Brooklyn was an afternoon affair, getting started at 4.10pm and in the middle of a thunderous downpour, but despite a terrific first-half performance only an Archibald goal separated the teams.

The teams turned round almost immediately and that was when the Rangers produced their magic. Goals galore rained down on the Brooklyn stadium and locals gasped at the sparkling skills of the tourists. When McPhail walked number six into the net a fan was heard to say, 'This is the finest exhibition of football we have ever witnessed in these parts.' Uncle Sam's best had been no match for the famous Light Blues.

After the match, Struth said, 'We are finished and remain unbeaten on foreign soil. The ovation we received before returning to the dressing rooms was so incredible that I cannot find the words to describe it, but let me say that some of the more enthusiastic carried Cunningham shoulder high.

'And so a most successful American tour may be said to have entered its final stage. We board the SS *Berengaria* in New York on Wednesday, and touch Southampton on the Monday of the following week, before arriving in Glasgow a day later.'

So, on a tour which brought 46 goals and nine different scorers, our man Meiklejohn was one of the few who didn't manage to find the net on Yankee soil – but he had still played a massive role in making Rangers' inaugural transatlantic trip a huge success.

As a footnote, Austrian player Ernie Schwartz had turned out against Rangers for the Nationals side in New York and spoke with Struth after the game about the possibility of joining the Light Blues at some point during the season, a prospect that the talented player was more than keen on – providing immigration difficulties could be overcome. Sadly, for Rangers and the player, the issues proved too high a hurdle to negotiate.

However one lad who would go on to make his mark with Rangers was central defender Bob McDonald, who Gers fans would soon be hearing a lot more about. And he would have the perfect partner to show him the Scottish ropes.

Rangers' complete tour record:

30 May: At Philadelphia – beat National League Select 8-2
2 June: At New York – beat Brooklyn Wanderers 4-0
3 June: At New Bedford – drew with Fall River 0-0
9 June: At Pittsburgh – beat Pittsburgh 9-0
10 June: At Detroit – drew with Detroit Select 1-1
13 June: At Toronto – beat Ulster United 7-0
16 June: At Montreal – beat Montreal 5-1
18 June: At Boston – drew with Boston 2-2
20 June: At Chicago – beat Illinois All Stars 4-1
23 June: At Brooklyn – beat American Select 6-0

Goalscorers: Bob McPhail 14, Jamie Fleming 9, Andy Cunningham 8, Jamie Marshall 7, Alan Morton 3, Jock Buchanan 2, Tully Craig 1, Willie Hair 1, Sandy Archibald 1.

13

Wing king Alan is very much alive

THE beginning of 1929 brought the news that 17 arrests had been made when a riot broke out at a meeting of the Labour party in Shettleston. Among those 'taken away in Black Marias' was a well-known Glasgow Communist, four women and a blind man. King George V was in the 50th day of a serious illness, and Rangers star Alan Morton was still alive.

The last item of news made the front page of the *Daily Record* and came as a relief to the man himself – as well as thousands of Rangers supporters. A nasty rumour that the talented winger had died in a car accident had spread like wildfire, so much so that a reporter telephoned the Morton household only to be told by the man himself, 'Well, as you can hear I'm very much alive. I have just got home in my car and I hear that people have been ringing the house from all over the place.'

Just a week after returning from their tour of the United States, several Gers players took to the greens and fairways of Scotland's golf courses. Meiklejohn teamed up with an old adversary, John McFarlane of Celtic, on the Old Course at St Andrews. They were joined by Dave Ayton, the well-known American professional, and Jamie Alexander, official course starter. The Old Firm combination put up a stout resistance, eventually losing out only on the 16th green. Morton was fit and well enough to play at Prestwick, and Tommy Muirhead and Sandy Archibald hit a few balls at Aberdour.

Due to their American adventure the players were given extra time off to enjoy their close-season break, and just days after reporting back from training they won the invitational five-a-side tournament at the Ibrox Sports Day in front of 33,000.

Rangers started off the new season in style, thumping Kilmarnock, St Mirren and Cowdenbeath, and in the match against the Saints, Meik was described by one correspondent thus, 'As safe as a fort. The Ibrox centre half back is an almost wonderful compote of ability, grit and power.'

Dundee were next up at Dens Park and the Ibrox cornerstone almost grabbed a sensational hat-trick. Dundee were 2-0 up but Morton pulled one back before Meik scored twice to put Rangers ahead. He then hit the truest shot imaginable which Robertson, the Dundee goalkeeper, somehow managed to fingertip over the bar.

Rangers were then pushed to the limits at Tynecastle before a Jamie Fleming strike gave them victory. Meiklejohn won a key midfield battle against Hearts' speedy John Johnstone, which helped tip the balance in Gers' favour.

Following a 7-1 league win over Raith Rovers, Motherwell visited Ibrox, put up the shutters and left with a point – the first Rangers had dropped in seven games.

Five goals at Third Lanark were followed by eight at home to St Johnstone as the unstoppable Light Blues threatened to run away with the league. Their stunning early-season form was recognised at national level when Gray, Meiklejohn, Muirhead, McPhail and Morton were picked to represent Scotland against Wales at Ibrox.

Before the international, though, there was the not-so-insignificant matter of an Old Firm match at Parkhead. By all accounts it was a thrilling encounter and goals by McMillan and Archibald saw Rangers cancel out an earlier McGrory counter to win 2-1. Meiklejohn was injured on the hour when he overstretched a muscle while making a tackle, but heroically played on and cleared certain danger on a number of occasions – as well as playing McGrory out of the game. In fact, when McGrory scored early on, one lone voice in the Rangers end cheered – and lived to tell the tale.

Sadly the injury sustained at Parkhead forced Meik to withdraw from the Scotland team, and he also missed away league victories at Hibs and Falkirk, but he was present at the celebratory tea in the North British Hotel on Princes Street as a reward for the win over Hibs.

As we motored towards the end of 1928, successive wins over Hamilton, Clyde and Ayr put the Light Blues firmly in the driving seat for yet another title success. Hearts and Aberdeen emerged as the likely challengers with Celtic a distant fourth.

A couple of weeks before Christmas, Meiklejohn had a new defensive partner – Bob McDonald, a lad the Gers had picked up on their tour of the United States. He made his debut in a 6-0 rout of Clyde in the semi-finals of the Dental Cup. Later that evening, Bill Struth did a sterling bit of business with East Stirlingshire when he snapped up 17-year-old centre-forward Jimmy Smith, who would go on to become one of Rangers' greatest ever goalscorers. The following midweek, Rangers lost the final of the Dental Cup 2-0 to Partick Thistle on an afternoon when the Gers attack was described as 'feckless'.

Just to prove he was human, Meiklejohn gifted Airdrie two goals in a 5-2 win for the Light Blues at Broomfield. For the hosts' first he was caught napping and the second was deflected off his thigh but a Fleming hat-trick helped pull him out of a hole. Rangers were seven points clear of second-placed Hearts and also had a couple of games in hand. Fleming, with 23, was just one goal short of Hearts' Barney Battles and Evelyn Morrison, of Falkirk, in the race to be crowned top scorer.

On New Year's Day 1929, Glasgow's Lord Provost, Sir David Mason, declared Rangers' magnificent new grandstand open then sat back and watched the hosts turn on an electrifying display of football as they comprehensively beat Celtic 3-0 with Archibald and a Fleming brace doing the damage in front of 60,000. The game might have been played in dense fog and on a snowy pitch, but at least the result was perfect.

The victory re-wrote the history books as for the first time since the league was instituted in 1890, the Light Blues took the lead over Celtic in the matter of victories gained in league matches between the two clubs. Both had been members since the competition started and had met 78 times. The 3-0 victory was the 26th time Gers had won the fixture while Celtic had 25 wins to their credit. The remaining 27 games had ended in draws.

Rangers had a real look of champions about them and on 2 January at Firhill, a Meiklejohn penalty was all that separated the sides as once again the match was played in slippery conditions. A 2-0 win at Cowdenbeath ended the perfect holiday period.

Then came the news that Morton was safe and well, and hadn't died in a car crash, and thankfully the Wee Blue Devil was fit to take his place against his former club Queen's Park at Hampden as Rangers extended their lead at the top of the table with a 4-0 win. An outbreak of flu at Ibrox forced several players – including Meik – to miss the game but Struth booked golf and brine baths at Turnberry, and the players headed south after the game.

Meiklejohn missed the following Saturday's Scottish Cup first round mauling of Edinburgh City at Ibrox. The rampant Gers were 8-0 up at half-time and, after easing off, ran out 11-1 winners. A correspondent said, 'Rangers were very charitable with their scoring in the second half, or it could have been a record.'

The influential half-back returned to the team for a league encounter at Airdrie – but missed a penalty with the scores level. No doubt he was put off by referee Joe Rowe, who time after time insisted that Meik hadn't placed the ball properly on the penalty spot. A lengthy debate ensued and Meik eventually missed the kick. The incident, however, prompted calls for a goal to be awarded when a player deliberately used his hands to prevent the ball crossing the line. Regardless, a 2-0 victory put Rangers eight points clear of Hearts and with three matches in hand. Hapless Celtic were a distant 17 points behind their great rivals.

The end of January constituted the end of an era for Gers when Andy Cunningham, who had signed for Rangers 14 years previously, moved south of the border to join Newcastle United. He shed tears when collecting his boots from his locker but while Cunningham's infectious personality was missed in the Ibrox dressing room, the players made light work of Partick Thistle in the second round of the Scottish Cup by winning 5-1 in front of 67,000. The only problem was that the teams were wearing virtually identical kits – Rangers in light blue and Thistle in a slightly darker shade – and many passes were said to have 'gone astray'.

After the game, Rangers skipper Tommy Muirhead was forced to come out in the press and dismiss stories of 'civil war' in the dressing room. He said, 'As captain of Rangers, I take violent exception to the scurrilous story about discontent amongst the players at Ibrox. It is a lie, and that is as strong as I can put it.'

Rangers pressed on relentlessly in their quest for league glory and beat Raith Rovers and Clyde away from home. Third Lanark were next up, but with six players being called up for the international match between Scotland and Ireland in Belfast – Gray, Muirhead, Meiklejohn, Craig and Morton, as well as Ireland's Hamilton – they asked for a postponement. It was duly granted and Scotland thumped the Irish 7-3, with five goals by the legendary Hughie Gallacher a highlight.

Meik received a knock on the head but played on and did a sterling job. Afterwards, he said, 'If you take it on goals scored, it was a fine international. But we were the better team in what was a real test of stamina.'

After the game, the Rangers players rushed off to catch the 6.25pm train to Turnberry, via Larne, Stranraer and Girvan, to prepare for the game against Thirds, which had been rescheduled for the Tuesday night. Rangers romped it 5-1 – after a large covering of snow had been cleared from the pitch – before Dundee United were beaten in a Scottish Cup quarter-final tie at Ibrox. Wins over St Johnstone and Hibs followed and by the beginning of March, Rangers led the table by a staggering ten points from Hearts, and had four games in hand.

After a 2-0 win over the Tynecastle side, in which Meik 'shackled' Barney Battles, the Scottish Football Association met to discuss league reconstruction – and the possible formation of four leagues of ten.

On Saturday 16 March Rangers stumbled to a 1-1 draw with Falkirk at Ibrox, but it was sufficient to win the title as Celtic had taken a point off Aberdeen at Parkhead. Incredibly, Rangers had won the league with eight games to play.

All eyes were now fully focussed on the Scottish Cup and after a battling 3-2 semi-final victory over St Mirren, Kilmarnock stood between Rangers and a second successive double, following a 1-0 win against Celtic. On the eve of the cup final Scotland's selectors 'staggered the football public' by including three uncapped players in their team to face England. Rangers' Jock Buchanan was one of them, and would join Meik, Muirhead and Morton for the match against the Auld Enemy at Hampden.

The weekend before, though, Rangers were on cup final duty at the national stadium, and with 114,780 in attendance were forced to play second fiddle to the Ayrshiremen. It was a controversial match with Killie taking both their chances and Rangers squandering several. However, there was uproar on the terraces when Buchanan was hauled down in the box and referee Tom Dougray awarded Rangers a penalty. It was 0-0 at the time, and Killie protested. The under-pressure ref consulted his linesman and changed his mind.

That was the cue for Meik to lead a counter protest by Rangers and, after consulting his linesman, Dougray changed his mind again. After the furore had died down, Tully Craig stepped forward and took the kick – but the keeper saved it. Despite Meiklejohn being described in the papers as a 'colossus', he was the most disappointed of the lot as the players trudged off the pitch having just lost the cup final. Another downside was a serious facial injury sustained by Muirhead, which affected his breathing and forced him to miss the Scotland–England match.

The night before the international at Hampden, several of the players attended the dog racing at White City. There was an added attraction for everyone as one of the races featured greyhounds owned by Meiklejohn and the legendary England centre-forward Dixie Dean.

Meiklejohn's Spartan Mercury, and Dean's self-titled dog, were racing for ten sovereigns and a handsome cup. As you can imagine, it was a titanic struggle between the hounds but the Everton player was celebrating after his dog romped home in a record time of 30.49 seconds. The upper hand for the Englishman?

But the following day the Rangers player got his revenge thanks to a last-gasp strike by Alec Cheyne straight from a corner kick. It was an eventful match for Meiklejohn, who was winning his second cap against England in front of 110,000 passionate spectators. Midway through the second half a shot struck him on the hand inside the

Scotland box, but despite vehement protests by the English, referee Mr Josephs of South Shields waved away all appeals for a penalty.

One newspaper report insisted that Meiklejohn was 'undoubtedly the best and strongest middleman afield. He shackled Dixie Dean and found the time to help out his forwards. He proved beyond doubt that he is Scotland's number one centre half back.' Jacky Robertson, the former Scotland international half-back, praised Meiklejohn's performance and brilliant positional sense.

The following midweek, Alan Morton scored Rangers' 100th league goal of a more than satisfying campaign as the Gers thumped Motherwell 4-2. Three days later Rangers travelled to Aberdeen and carved out a 2-2 draw and, on the train home, the entire squad – save for Muirhead – signed on the dotted line for the next season.

Meiklejohn was injured in the match but despite pluckily carrying on, he paid the small price of missing out on the final two games of the season as Rangers equalled Celtic's record of 67 points from a 38-game league campaign. By netting 107 goals they were the top scorers in the league while just 32 against represented the meanest defence. They eventually won the championship by 16 points from Celtic.

Meiklejohn was back in time for a tilt at the Glasgow Merchant's Cup where wins over Partick and Third Lanark set up yet another Old Firm final. McGrory scored an early goal for Celtic before spending the remainder of the afternoon in Meik's back pocket. Doubles from Muirhead and Marshall helped Rangers win 4-2. It was a fitting end to a tremendous campaign.

14

Four-midable Gers sweep the boards

THE 1929/30 season began with in excess of 100 Scottish players desperately searching for a club. It was the worst scenario possible for the out-of-work footballers, although the surplus didn't affect Rangers as they had long signed on those they wanted for the new campaign.

The season opened in the traditional manner with lots of five-a-side football. Meiklejohn and co took part in the Glasgow Police Sports Fives at Ibrox but were dumped out in the semi-finals by Partick Thistle. Next up was the Glasgow Tramways tournament at Parkhead and despite beating Celtic 2-0 in the last four, Partick once again usurped the Light Blues, this time in the final.

But it was a case of third time lucky and revenge, when it came, was sweet. Meiklejohn, Gray, Fleming, Marshall and McMillan represented Rangers in the Partick Thistle Sports at Firhill and a Jamie Fleming goal prevented a hat-trick of unwanted losses to the Maryhill team.

In the final, a McMillan shot hit the Partick bar and Simpson, of Thistle, broke free but Meiklejohn, who was guarding the Rangers goal at that moment, effected a daring save.

Just days after his goal won the fives for Rangers, Fleming passed his intermediate physiology and anatomy examinations at university and his certificate sat proudly next to the honours he had accrued with the Light Blues.

For the golf lovers at Ibrox it was time to hit the fairways, and Meik and Tommy Muirhead headed for the sanctuary of Fife where they played almost non-stop for a week. Pro golfer Dave Ayton and good friend Jamie Alexander were undefeated throughout the week but were tested most severely by Meik and Muirhead, who had been playing some 'hot stuff' in the Kingdom of Fife. The match, played on the 'neutral' Hill of Tarvit course, near Cupar, was keenly contested, with the pros eventually winning a tight match by 2&1. Manager Bill Struth joined his players for a round or two.

Another Ranger making the headlines was Sandy Archibald who, attending a fete at Aberdour Golf Club, won a competition to register the longest drive, but it wasn't just length that decided the winner. Three drives had to be placed in a narrow fairway, or the competitor was disqualified. Sandy's prize was a nice silver spoon.

Eager for revenge after their narrow defeat at Hill of Tarvit, Meik and Muirhead threw down the gauntlet to Ayton. This time the affair was decided on the Old Course at St Andrews with Ayton playing the best ball of the Rangers men.

The two Ms were playing good golf, both breaking 80, but Ayton was out for blood and after shooting a 73 he won the contest with a bit to spare. The bye was played and the Rangers pair won it, Meiklejohn taking the hole in the perfect three. Ayton's score had only one blemish – a six at the long fifth.

The following day, the players were back for more – and finally had their day. Getting six strokes from Ayton and J.B. Thomson, the local 'scratch' man, Meiklejohn and Muirhead won by 2&1. The best ball score of the Ibrox duo was an impressive 74. It was a case of saving face for the footballers after they had earlier lost a putting match to Jamie Alexander – and his wife.

From the golf course it was straight on with the serious nature of the Scottish football season – once everyone had gotten their head round an edict from the Scottish Football Association ordering all referees to wear khaki blazers during matches.

But normal service was resumed when the Light Blues visited Fir Park, Motherwell, on the opening day of the new campaign.

Archibald and Fleming made sure the Gers got off to a flying start but one newspaper reported, 'Meiklejohn towered above all others as a spoiling middleman and his policing of Cameron was a big factor in keeping the Motherwell forwards at arm's length of Hamilton's goal.'

The following Saturday saw Rangers host Hibernian but amid a routine 3-0 home win, Meiklejohn received a severe blow to the kidneys from visiting centre-forward McColl. He wasn't the only Ranger on the treatment table come Monday morning as Alan Morton was still the main occupant, having suffered a leg injury after tripping over a hurdle at Rangers Sports.

Meiklejohn's regular replacement, Joe McDonald, left Ibrox to return to the US and signed for emerging club Bethlehem Steel. But how the Light Blues could have done with his services as during a home match against Falkirk, Meik sprained a knee in a tackle and staved some fingers. After the 4-0 win, he somewhat cryptically told the press, 'Gadzooks! This is a scurvy age. I shall want an infirmary to myself if this goes on!'

The beginning of September saw Rangers make the trip north to Aberdeen and custodian Tom Hamilton conceded his first goal in seven matches as Rangers dropped their first point of the season. A record crowd of 30,600 – which didn't include the 'touring' Duke and Duchess of York, who had declined an invitation to attend – saw Rangers eke out a 1-1 draw. The weather was so foul that most of the players caught a heavy cold, although one reporter said of Hamilton, 'Tom is on a diet. Over one stone of what was once Hamilton is no longer there!'

A 2-0 defeat at Tynecastle saw Rangers deposed as league leaders for the first time that season but Meik was once again in the wars, although it didn't prevent him from going along to the Kelvin Hall to help team-mate Tommy Muirhead judge a typewriting contest. The winner, who had a speed of 88 words per minute, was presented with a new typewriter by the players.

Next up was the small matter of an Old Firm Glasgow Cup Final and more than 77,000 filed in to Hampden to watch an exhilarating game. Despite it finishing goalless, supporters left convinced they had received their money's worth. And one young man who was also feeling jolly was Celtic keeper John Thomson, who recouped a little bit of revenge from the 1928 Scottish Cup Final when he saved a penalty from Meiklejohn.

It was one of the first matches to incorporate the new penalty rule which stated that goalkeepers could only move from the ankles up. The penalty was awarded in the 71st minute when Archibald shot for goal and it was missed by Thomson, but up popped Denis McCallum on the line to fist it clear, an offence punishable by a simple ticking off in those days.

But despite failing to score from 12 yards, the big Ranger was named man of the match with one report reading, 'Meiklejohn played brilliantly. Davie dominated play and held McGrory in check.' Rather controversially, ex-Rangers and Scotland star Jacky Robertson declared after the match, 'Anyone who misses a penalty should go straight to jail.'

Thankfully Meiklejohn managed to avoid prison and was available for the replay, a match which a rampant Rangers won 4-0, to lift the Glasgow Cup for the 18th time. There was a spell in the match when, after a number of fouls had been committed, referee Tom Small called together both captains, Meiklejohn and Celtic's Jamie McStay, and told them that the next player to commit an offence would be sent off. Meik relayed this information to his players but just moments later, he committed a foul on a Celtic player and, with no sign of him being sent off, McStay rushed over to the referee to call his attention to the matter. Small waved away the protestations of McStay, however, and allowed play to continue.

Scotland's selectors watched the match with interest and, later that night, announced their team for the forthcoming international in Wales. It included Gray, Meiklejohn who would captain the side, Muirhead, Craig and Morton, while Buchanan and Archibald were named as reserves. Later, Bill Struth announced that Rangers' proposed league match with Celtic, scheduled for the same day, would go ahead. The only Celt called up was keeper Thomson, who was a reserve.

In a match against Partick Thistle at Firhill a Jamie Fleming goal was enough to give the Light Blues the points, although they had Meik to thank for a spectacular goal-line clearance. Sadly, though, he was injured while effecting the manoeuvre and was forced off due to being 'lame', as one reporter described it. However he made a startling return to the fray, which allowed Bob McPhail to resume his role as a striker, and Meiklejohn used his right foot to clear several moments of danger.

Inevitably, Meiklejohn withdrew from the Scotland team and missed a month's worth of action with a groin strain. In his absence the SFA sent a letter to Sunderland, requesting the services of Jacky McDougall as Meik's replacement, but the Black Cats refused and John Johnston of Hearts was drafted in to cover.

Scotland won 4-2 in Wales with Muirhead taking over the captain's armband from Meiklejohn, but, more surprisingly, Rangers beat Celtic 1-0 at Ibrox on the same day, minus the international contingent along with Jock Buchanan and Bob Hamilton, who had both gone down with flu on the morning of the game.

Struth put his faith in an all-Alliance half-back line and they didn't let him down. Maybe it was the soothing tones of 'Carmen', played by the Govan Burgh Band prior to the game, that calmed the nerves.

With Rangers and Aberdeen in charge of proceedings at the top of the Scottish League table, and the winter months approaching, the Light Blues' board decided that they didn't want a repeat of the 'near thing' against Celtic and asked for a cancellation of their match with Cowdenbeath (or did they feel that the Blue Brazil represented a greater threat than the Hoops?) due to six players being named in the Scottish League squad, and having Meik, Buchanan, Bob Hamilton and Nicholson all carrying injuries.

Cowden chairman Andrew Dick termed the request a disgrace and warned that he had backers. The game was duly called off. Rangers increased their lead at the top of the league, despite being idle, as Kilmarnock beat Aberdeen 4-2.

Once again a story appeared in the paper about the death of Alan Morton. This time the tricky little winger was reported to have been electrocuted. The allegations couldn't have been further from the truth and Morton played a starring role in a 5-2 win at Hamilton, a match which also heralded the comeback of Meik from injury.

Rangers were in no mood to go easy on opponents and hit Ayr United for nine at Ibrox in mid-November. Fleming scored four times and in the papers the following day, it was noted, 'Rangers don't usually hammer teams.' An explanation was offered, though.

Apparently Morton was hurtling down the wing when he was cynically halted in his tracks. That, intimated the reporter, was the catalyst for all-out attack and, as the Wee Blue Devil was bruised from head to toe in the incident, 'no leniency' was the cry from the Light Blues.

Darvel lad Bob Ireland left the club in the wake of the game, citing the unfortunate circumstance of playing in the same position as Davie Meiklejohn. 'I have no chance of getting a game,' he said as he clinched a move to Liverpool.

With just four weeks to Christmas, Meik signed for a new team – although there was no reason for Gers fans to panic. He was teaming up with Jacky Robertson and the staff at the *Glasgow Evening News*, who had started coaching classes for youngsters.

That same day, Rangers signed young goalkeeper James Dawson from Camelon Juniors. He made his debut for the Alliance team in a match against Falkirk at Ibrox and, naturally, recorded a shut-out in a 5-0 win. He would go on to make a name for himself as 'Jerry' Dawson, after the big goalkeeper of the same name who had kept goal for Rangers in the early 20th century.

December proved a sensational month for Rangers with four successive wins and a trip to Troon to play badminton. By the end of 1929, the Light Blues were top of the league by a point from Aberdeen, and had two games in hand. A Happy New Year indeed.

In the traditional New Year's Day game, Rangers pulled off an important 2-1 victory over Celtic despite the match at Parkhead being played in atrocious conditions. It had been 28 years since the Gers had last won on the ground of their great rivals, and newspaper columnist Jacky Robertson knew exactly who he was crediting for the win. 'Meiklejohn played the finest centre half-back game I have seen in years. This game should go down in the annals of history as "Meiklejohn's Match". With anyone less competent in this position, I doubt if Celtic could have been prevented from winning.'

Napier had given Celtic the lead but on the stroke of half-time McPhail was brought down by Geatons, and Morton dispatched the penalty to tie the scores. He shocked watching spectators by taking no run-up and simply slamming the ball into the net. Meik was described as the 'master of the skidding ball, while heading well'. George Brown scored the winner for Rangers but still Aberdeen refused to be shaken off.

The following day, Meik missed a penalty against Partick Thistle, but Rangers still won 2-1. From the gate receipts, Rangers sent a cheque for £100 to a fund which had been set up in the wake of the tragic Glen Cinema disaster in Paisley, in which almost 100 youngsters had lost their lives. Smoke from an old reel of film filtered through from the viewing room to the cinema itself as children watched a matinee film. Someone cried 'fire', and in the panic to escape the building, many children were crushed to death in the stampede.

After the match with the Jags, Tommy Muirhead spoke of his intention to hang up his boots at the end of the season and become a journalist, while Andy Cunningham was announced as player-manager of Newcastle.

A blizzard put paid to Rangers' next match, at Brockville Park, Falkirk, although 8,000 people had already been admitted to the ground but the players hadn't even bothered to travel, with Meiklejohn and Muirhead electing to head for Firhill to see Partick Thistle play Morton. Despite the call-off it had been a successful festive period for the Gers, although the same could hardly be said for Celtic who lost all four of their matches during this period.

Next up for the Light Blues was a Scottish Cup first-round tie at Hampden, with the game against Queen's Park attracting an astonishing crowd in excess of 95,000. Meiklejohn received a blow to the head from the heavy, wet football and was forced off for lengthy treatment. Despite this obvious handicap he returned and was named man of the match.

Saturday 25 January was D-Day as Rangers hosted Aberdeen in a match the press said was a title decider – at the end of the first month of the year. The Dons' dangerman Benny Yorkston was superbly shackled by Meiklejohn and Rangers won 3-1 to move two points clear with three games in hand.

Meik was back in the wars during Rangers' next match, a 4-0 romp over Kilmarnock. He fell awkwardly on his left arm and ended up playing out the game on the right wing. But he was determined he wasn't missing any more action and helped Rangers to a battling 5-2 Scottish Cup third-round win at Motherwell plus a 1-0 success at Tannadice.

The 1929/30 campaign was rapidly becoming arguably Meiklejohn's best in light blue, which was quite something considering the sterling service he had given since joining up at Ibrox ten years previously. His maturity was there for all to see and his influence over team-mates was at an all-time high.

However the master tactician was powerless to stop Rangers crashing to a 3-1 home defeat against Hearts – as he was at Celtic Park helping Scotland defeat Ireland along with four of his colleagues (three for Scotland and two in the colours of the Irish). Meik was up against 'Scoring Joe' Bambrick, Ireland's on-form Linfield striker, who had netted six against Wales in his previous international outing.

But he didn't get a sniff against Meik, who later said, rather diplomatically, 'I have nothing but praise for the Ireland defence, especially Bob Hamilton, my club mate, and wasn't Portsmouth Bob Irvine a grand raider? Despite difficult conditions, it was a grand game.'

Next up for Gers was a Scottish Cup tie against minnows Montrose. Rangers cruised to a 3-0 win but once again Meiklejohn was injured. He picked up a loose ball and strode forward before being clattered by Williamson, the Gable Endies' centre-forward. Meik was off for eight minutes being treated for a suspected broken collarbone but insisted on returning to the field and playing out the remainder of the match.

He missed the next match, a win at Queen's Park, in which he was joined on the absent list by George Brown, a schoolteacher, who was forced to work. Mind you, Queen's were also minus their very own teacher, R.G.C. Peden.

Rangers announced plans for a close-season tour of Canada, sanctioned by the Dominion Football Association. It was proposed that they would play 12 matches with an extra game against Arsenal in New York also a possibility. The team was set to travel through the Rocky Mountains and all over Canada to far-flung outposts not normally associated with soccer.

Meanwhile, the Gers were drawn against Hearts in the semi-finals of the Scottish Cup and the day before the Hampden tie, Jamie Marshall, who was studying medicine, was given permission by Struth to give a lecture called 'The Human Body and How to Keep Fit'. Elsewhere, the rest of the players enjoyed a game of golf at Troon – before promptly thumping the Tynecastle side 4-1 in front of

92,048. Victory came at a price though, as Meik, Morton, Archibald and McPhail were injured.

A few days later it was Meiklejohn's turn to get a day off training to take part in a charity match between the Southern Division Police and the 'Jingling Geordies' at Shawfield – as referee. All proceeds were earmarked for the Gorbals' Ward Old Folks Treatment Fund.

The following night, Rangers – minus their cup semi-final walking wounded – beat Ayr United 3-0 at Somerset, and Meik learned that he had been chosen to skipper Scotland against England at Wembley. Gray, Craig, Morton, Buchanan and Fleming were also called up. Rangers trainer James Kerr – who had recently nursed ex-Celt Patsy Gallacher back to full health – was asked to look after the fitness needs of the team.

Rangers were closing in on the league title with the win at Ayr putting them six points clear of Aberdeen, with two games in hand, and next up was Clyde at home. A goal from Muirhead and a Fleming brace were sufficient for a comfortable 3-0 win but it wasn't until later that they discovered second-bottom Dundee United had drawn 2-2 at Pittodrie, a result that ensured Rangers were crowned champions for the 18th time. The title win also allowed them to overtake Celtic. In the previous 11 seasons Rangers had won the championship nine times, and this was their fourth in a row.

With the league wrapped up, attention turned to the forthcoming Scottish Cup Final with Partick Thistle. Before a ball was kicked, the Jags won the first battle – to see who could wear their first-choice colours. At that time Thistle wore dark blue shirts, and it was the Maryhill men who won a toss of the coin to decide the issue. Rangers were torn between sporting white jerseys and black pants, and the blue and white striped jerseys from their early days.

Before the cup final, half-a-dozen Gers stars made the trip to London by train for the annual Auld Enemy clash. Meik, winning his 15th cap, helped the Scots edge the weight stakes in the half-back area with the visitors weighing in at 34st, as opposed to England's 33st 11lbs. It was the first time that one club had contributed more than half the team, apart from the first international in 1872, when Queen's Park players made up the entire 11. In the 1900 fixture at Celtic Park five Gers players had made the team, but the inclusion of

Meik, Gray, Buchanan, Craig, Fleming and Morton set a new record. The team stayed at the plush Bloomsbury Hotel, near Covent Garden, and everything seemed set for a Scottish success.

Forty special trains left Glasgow's Central Station and the army of Scottish foot soldiers numbered in excess of 30,000. Before the game, and ever the optimist, Meik said, 'Nothing can prevent us winning. I have every confidence in my men. The changes we have been forced to make will not weaken us in any way. We will undoubtedly miss Gallacher, but Buchanan and Fleming will add power to our side. You may depend for your life on Jock, and if Jamie Fleming has just a little bit of luck, he may indeed make history. He will let the Saxon defence know he is there.'

Meiklejohn got part of his prediction spot on for Fleming did just that, scoring twice, but three goals in four minutes set England on the way to a famous 5-2 victory. Meiklejohn played well but the Scotland fans in the 90,000 crowd were left reeling when England went four up in the first half hour.

There were dreadful scenes outside the ground before kick-off as thousands of supporters with tickets were refused entry because the terraces inside were full. They rushed the police and knocked down gates which saw thousands more get inside the ground.

The following Saturday, cup final fever gripped Glasgow and just shy of 105,000 were at Hampden for the Rangers–Partick Thistle clash. After a dour struggle in awful conditions the game ended 0-0, and it was reported that Meik had held the Rangers defence together in the face of constant Partick pressure. Five minutes before half-time, Thistle's Johnny Ballantyne 'laid out' Meik and two minutes later Gers enforcer Buchanan 'laid out' Ballantyne, after warning the Partick player that he was 'going to get him'.

For the replay, blue shirts were banned 'by mutual consent'. Rangers wore white shirts with blue shorts while the Jags opted for brown and gold hoops. Almost 104,000 spectators paid to see yet another enthralling encounter between these two Glasgow rivals and looked on as the influential Alan Morton was badly injured after just 15 minutes.

Despite their one-man disadvantage Fleming put Rangers ahead, but Torbet equalised on 71. Tully Craig was on hand, though, to clinch Rangers' sixth Scottish Cup in the 85th minute. The winner came about when Marshall was through on goal only to have his heels clipped. Meiklejohn's free kick was headed clear by Lambie but only as far as Craig, who lobbed Jackson in the Thistle goal from 25 yards.

Both teams were wined and dined in the F&F Restaurant in Buchanan Street, Glasgow, and reporter 'Waverley' said, 'It was difficult to get a word with Davie Meiklejohn, so busy was he receiving congratulations, a considerable number of which were from ladies!'

Meik said, 'Considering we finished with ten men, our victory was splendid. Proud I am to be captain of a winning team. Thistle put up a magnificent fight, they were worthy opponents.'

But rather than put their feet up on yet another successful campaign, Rangers' end-of-season schedule was among the most hectic around with seven games scheduled in just 11 days. Struth must have been glad that the major honours had already been secured.

Just three days after winning the cup Rangers lost 1-0 to Airdrie at Broomfield but on the same day, at Ibrox, 21,000 – the biggest crowd in Scotland – saw the reserves grab a narrow Scottish Alliance Cup first-leg lead over Kilmarnock. However it wasn't all good news as reports filed through that Carl Hansen, the Danish former Rangers player, was seriously ill in a Norwegian hospital.

Due to unforeseen circumstances, Rangers' Canadian tour was brought forward a week and they were set to sail on the same day as the Glasgow Charity Cup Final. Provisions were made to have the boat standing by at Greenock for departure immediately after the game.

Before then though, it was games galore, and Meiklejohn even managed to fit in a benefit match for ex-Hearts manager John McCartney where he scored as the West beat East 3-2.

The Light Blues duly disposed of Partick Thistle and Third Lanark en route to setting up a Charity Cup Final against Celtic. It was an exciting match, watched by just over 35,000, and they saw Rangers lead twice through Marshall and Fleming only to be pegged back twice. Tom Hamilton pulled off three great saves in extra time to deny Celtic the win.

The final was to be decided on corners but as both teams had managed four and a replay was out of the question due to Rangers' impending tour of Canada, it was down to the toss of a coin, the first time, it is believed, the destination of a trophy had been decided in this way.

Meiklejohn had already won the toss at the start of the game and again at the beginning of extra time. Then he made it a hat-trick to secure the silverware for his team. Afterwards, he said, 'I may not be a good captain, but I'm certainly a lucky one!'

As Rangers set sail for Canada, laden down with silverware, rumours were rife that the great Everton centre-forward Dixie Dean was set to sign for the Ibrox club.

15

Gers stars' brush with death

RANGERS' tour of the US and Canada in 1930 was hailed a great success. Played 14 won 14 was a record that both players and management could be proud of, and they maintained that fine Rangers tradition of never having lost a game on foreign soil.

However, while travelling through Canada and just after they had negotiated the vast Jasper Park, which took six hours to pass through from start to finish, the party almost met with tragedy on an unimaginable scale. As their train was shuttling along in the direction of the iconic Rocky Mountains, it left the rails for a split second – perhaps akin to an aeroplane rapidly losing 1,000 feet while in mid-flight – and the party was left with that horrid, sinking feeling.

At that particular moment, the players were looking down hundreds of feet into a valley which housed the shacks of British settlers, many of which were timber dwellings, and drinking in the sights and sounds of rural Canada. Their high vantage point allowed for views so breathtaking that an impromptu concert in the train compartment was halted for a few minutes. However that vantage point could quite literally have proved their downfall with the train track precariously following the outer line of the mountain, leaving nowhere to go but down.

Shaken, and stirred, it took quite a few moments for the players to regain their composure as the realism of what might have been fully sunk in. Most dealt with the scare by peering blankly out of the train window.

It was all a far cry from the fantastic send-off the players had received when they hopped aboard the train at St Enoch Station, destination Princes Pier, Greenock, and ultimately North America on board the sprawling Anchor-Donaldson Line ship, SS *Andania*.

Long before the hour of departure, crowds had arrived to secure the best vantage points and extra police and railway officials had been drafted in to prevent enthusiasts from rushing the platform. The moment the players left the adjacent hotel they were hoisted upon shoulders and carried to the platform by well-wishers, eager to show their appreciation of the victory over Celtic.

Hundreds of supporters, unable to gain access to the departure platform, made for adjoining platforms where, at the extreme ends, they were able to give their favourites a fitting send-off. As a train in the next platform steamed out of the station, many supporters jumped on to the lines and crossed over to the compartments being utilised by the players. It was mass hysteria on a scale not unlike that reserved for The Beatles a couple of decades later.

After an enjoyable voyage, the team arrived refreshed in Quebec, and Struth said, 'The time on board the SS *Andania* passed all too quickly, as the players enjoyed many a game of deck billiards and quoits, but the "championship" remains undecided until the journey home! All we need now is Jamie Marshall, who is following us on the SS *Aquitania*. We shall watch Kilmarnock play the Car Steel team in Montreal tomorrow evening.'

Rangers' first match, in Toronto, was delayed 24 hours, a void which the players filled by partaking in a round or two of golf. But when they arrived in Montreal they were given a rousing reception by townsfolk and dignitaries alike – and Archie Walker's Pipe Band made them feel right at home.

On the evening before the game, the tourists were guests of honour at a banquet thrown by the Old Timers Club, a group of expats from Govan, and the hospitality was on a lavish scale. Dr Givens, a member of the Old Boys Club, presented Struth with a beautiful Loving Cup in appreciation of the team's record-breaking season. The good doctor then thanked the players for making the trip across the Atlantic, and Meiklejohn replied on behalf of the Rangers. Before the opening match, against Ulster United, the players journeyed to the town centre to place a wreath on the Cenotaph.

The game itself was reckoned to be one of the best seen in Canada and, after a titanic struggle, Rangers emerged victorious by the odd goal in seven. Morton and Fleming, with a brace each, were the scorers.

From Montreal the party moved on to Hamilton, Ontario, where once again the crowds turned out in great numbers to greet the 'famous tourists' which prompted the following remark from Gers skipper Meiklejohn, 'We met some kent faces from the Old Country, and the hand shaking that took place was enough to spoil our golf!'

Rangers received the freedom of the city from the Hamilton mayor, and Ex-Bailie Duncan Graham was presented with a gold key. After lunch the players were taken to Niagara Falls, where they enjoyed an afternoon's sightseeing.

That night, Rangers took on and beat Hamilton Thistle 3-0. Ten thousand spectators watched a clever Canadian combination push Rangers all the way until the full-time training of the visitors made the difference. Bob McDonald's brother was playing for the opposition, but he couldn't prevent Fleming grabbing another brace and Willie Nicholson a single. Meik made his first start of the tour and helped keep out the Canadian forwards.

A 520-mile train journey to New York was next on the agenda for the party. There they met the New York Nationals, who had promised to lower the colours of a Rangers team on foreign soil for the first time. A crowd of 20,000 watched the Nationals almost stay true to their pre-match boasts but despite an exceptionally narrow pitch, which proved a real handicap for the Scots, Rangers emerged with a 5-4 victory.

Tom Hamilton conceded three goals before half-time and Rangers found themselves 3-1 down. But the tourists were made of stern stuff and managed to force their way back into the game before smashing home the winner. Young Jimmy Smith and Bob McPhail scored two each and Alan Morton the other. It was a brilliant recovery and the crowd gave Rangers a wonderful ovation at the close of play.

Another new experience awaited the players the following day when they 'did' Broadway. They were invited on to the stage at The Palace and introduced to a cosmopolitan audience by Chick York, of York and King, Vaudeville's top-line promoters. Chick dubbed the players 'the world's champion soccer team', which had men, women and children rising to their feet in admiration.

Next up for the Light Blues was the match they had vowed not to take on – a meeting with the infamous Fall River. The corresponding fixture from the 1928 tour had brought Rangers into contact with a team of roughneck, tough-tackling players who cared not a jot for reputations and set about their task, and the opposition players, with gusto. This time, though, Rangers were missing four players due to injury before the match, but still managed a highly creditable 3-2 success in front of a crowd of 10,000. Bob Hamilton, Fleming, McPhail and Morton were absent and it was left to Smith, Brown and Meiklejohn – who hit the winner – to keep the blue flag flying high.

There was little rest for the party before heading back to Canada for a match against Car Steel United in Montreal. The match turned into a pleasant Saturday afternoon's football and the Scottish champions were able to show everything that was good about our game. Smith scored a fine hat-trick and other goals were collected by Brown and McPhail.

It was then on to Winnipeg where Fort Rouge Rangers lay in wait. On arrival in the city the Rangers party was well looked after and had a fleet of luxury motor cars and guides put at their disposal. The day before the game they were feted by the Caledonian Society, and the only criticism was the almost tropical-like weather, which was far too hot for football. Regardless, a crowd of 10,000 was present as Rangers beat their namesakes 4-2. The players still managed to put on a dashing exhibition of fine play on a dry-as-a-bone surface and were able to play at a slower pace than previous games. Goals by Archibald, McPhail and Fleming, who scored twice, clinched Rangers' sixth win in a row.

Another civic reception awaited the players and management when they arrived in Edmonton. They were then shown round town before lunch with city fathers. There was of course a game to play and once again Smith was the star of the show, scoring a hat-trick before the interval and putting in a determined shift. The other goals in the 5-0 romp were scored by Marshall and Archibald.

Next stop Vancouver, with St Andrews providing the on-field opposition. After sitting out the previous match, Meik returned to the heart of the Rangers half-back line where he formed a formidable partnership with Jock Buchanan and Tully Craig. Rampant Rangers turned in a fine exhibition of football and ran out 7-1 winners. Fleming scored a hat-trick and the other goals were collected by Morton, Marshall, Archibald and Muirhead.

Following their visit to Vancouver the party moved on to Victoria in British Columbia, the westernmost point of the tour, and once again they were treated like kings, first of all touring the area in luxury transport before being guests of Premier Tolmie in the evening. It was game number nine on the itinerary and much of the football served up was in keeping with that age old phrase, 'saving the best until last'. Rangers ran out 8-1 winners and Smith collected his third hat-trick of the tour, while Marshall and McPhail notched two each. Nicholson was also on the scoresheet.

Smith was rested for the next game, against Calgary United, no doubt more to give the opposition a rest than the hungry youngster. This time, though, Marshall 'performed the hat-trick' as the tourists racked up a similar score to the previous game. Other goals were collected by Brown, with a double, Archibald, Craig and Fleming.

Before the action, Rangers manager Bill Struth had been presented with a buffalo head by leaders of the St Andrews Caledonia Society, and the players were entertained to a banquet and dance where they found no lack of partners. During the course of the evening Mr McGregor, of Edmonton, presented the Rangers management and players with a scarf pin made from gold found in the local river. After the game a large crowd turned out to cheer the party on their way to Chicago.

The Windy City had a surprise in store for the Light Blues as the travellers were greeted not by gale-force winds but by rainstorms. Sparta, made up of Chilean expats, provided the opposition but proved no match for the Gers, who ran out 4-1 winners. Goals by Morton, McPhail, Fleming and Marshall had Rangers on easy street despite being held 1-1 at the break. After the game, and yet another civic reception, Meiklejohn was presented with a Chilean banner to mark the occasion. Eleven games, eleven wins, and still three matches remaining. Could the Gers end the tour with their 100 per cent record still in place?

Rangers moved on from Chicago to Detroit, where they played a night match against a local select under artificial light. Dozens of high-powered arc lights had been positioned around the pitch and 8,000 fervent fans were in attendance. Against strong-going opposition the Scottish champions played brilliant football and ran out 3-1 winners thanks to goals from McPhail, Nicholson and Brown, although reports suggest the winning margin would have been even greater were it not for the referee striking off two perfectly good goals.

After the match it was all aboard the night train – destination Cleveland, Ohio, and a challenge match against Bruells. Kick-off was scheduled for 8.30pm but there was a delay, and when the action finally got under way, a double by Smith and one from Nicholson helped the Light Blues to a 3-1 win – the 13th of the tour, and unlucky for Bruells.

It was then on to New York where Rangers would play their final match before the seven-day return voyage to Southampton. Old foes Fall River provided the opposition and Rangers signed off in style with a thumping 6-1 victory. The match had aroused tremendous interest in the Big Apple and fully 20,000 were present. The visitors led by the only goal at the break but turned in a fine exhibition of football in the second half to win at a canter, despite temperatures of 88 degrees – in the shade. Smith grabbed all the headlines with another four goals and Fleming scored twice. At the final whistle the crowd stood as one to give the Light Blues a rousing cheer. Alan Morton, injured by a clumsy tackle early on, was replaced at the break by Nicholson – the first time, it is believed, that Rangers used a substitute in a match.

The Light Blues returned to Great Britain aboard the SS *Berengaria* having played eight matches in Canada and six in the United States, and covered 15,000 miles in the process – and Struth was delighted that his side had maintained their record of never having lost a match on foreign shores.

And, after 51 days away, there was just as big a crowd at Central Station to welcome home the players as there had been on their departure. Struth said, 'You must remember what the players had to do. The conditions of the tour called not only for playing ability, but required willpower, determination and a steady resolution to keep the touring record of the club right.

'The players were conscious – as captain Meiklejohn will tell you – that the prestige of Scottish football, as much as that of the Rangers club, was in their keeping, and their purpose was to maintain it from the moment they stepped off the *Andania* to the time they set foot on the *Berengaria*.

'We met some very capable sides. They were all fit and fresh – and waiting for us. We were giving away a handicap in the sense that in 35 days of actual land travelling, we played 14 matches, an average of a game every two-and-a-half days. We had to cover 8,000 land miles to play these games. By land and sea, we traversed around 15,000 miles.

'Our most severe test was to have been the return match with Fall River in New York – the last match of the tour. A condition of our meeting Fall River was that we wouldn't play them on their home ground. This was a sequel to our visit two years ago. We played them on the fourth match of our tour and won 3-2, which looked good for America, so when we met them again in New York we were told, plainly and pointedly, that we were in for it. We insisted on a playing surface of at least 105 yards by 60 yards.

'It is not easy to convey the feeling of tension felt by everyone when the teams came out. The atmosphere was electric. An England–Scotland international or a cup final gets you in its grip, but this was something different and more deadly. To show they meant it, Fall River had signed several good players and the crowd hummed with excitement. We had already played three matches that week and the boys had to summon all their courage and vitality for a final big effort.

'Within a minute of the start, McGill, the old Third Lanark back, came into violent collision with Alan Morton. Result, a dislocated finger and a badly damaged knee for Alan. I am not going to say anything about the accident except that it was of a kind that determined me on one thing – for once we were going to adopt the American system and bring out a substitute.

'I let Alan limp along until the interval and then sent on Willie Nicholson. Two nights before, we had played against 13 men, 11 and two substitutes, against Bruells at Cleveland. Still, it was not our intention to make use of substitutes. At the same time, we meant to have a square deal.

'Our boys played as if the cup depended on it, and when it was all over and they had won by six goals to one, they were as happy as if they were taking home the Statue of Liberty. The American Scots in the crowd were frantic with delight.

'It was a strenuous tour and, of course, our train almost met with a nasty accident when it came within a whisker of going over the edge into kingdom come, but the sail home did us the world of good. Alan Morton is about all right again, as is Jamie Fleming, who had three stitches put in round about the eye, while Sandy Archibald is recovering from a nasty leg injury. Tom Craig also had a knee knocked.

'It cheered us all up wonderfully to receive cables from the club members at the annual meeting – one to Ex-Bailie Graham, one to myself and another to captain Davie Meiklejohn.'

A lasting memory to those Americans who witnessed the Rangers party sightseeing between matches would forever recall Bob McPhail and Jock Buchanan's continuous clowning around and the mouth organ that was permanently attached to the face of Sandy Archibald.

But the players knew how to behave themselves, and when one Fall River player invited his Rangers counterparts for a drink after the match, and they politely declined, he was heard to mutter, 'Fancy living in Scotland and not drinking. What a waste!'

One remnant from the notorious Fall River match ended up in Scotland. The match ball was presented to junior club St Andrews United by Meiklejohn, a regular visitor to the historic Fife town. The ball was used in the club's opening league match against Dunnikier.

But the tour belonged to Jimmy Smith: 18 goals in just seven matches was a phenomenal record, but it was just the beginning of a special career in the light blue shirt of the Rangers. The goal machine had arrived and supporters back home were in for a real treat.

Rangers' complete tour record:

21 May: At Toronto – beat Ulster United 4-3
24 May: At Hamilton – beat Hamilton Thistle 3-0
25 May: At New York – beat New York Nationals 5-4
30 May: At New Bedford – beat Fall River 3-2

31 May: At Montreal – beat Car Steel 5-2

3 June: At Winnipeg – beat Fort Rouge 4-2

5 June: At Vancouver – beat Edmonton 5-0

7 June: At Vancouver – beat St Andrews 7-1

9 June: At Victoria – beat Victoria West 8-1

11 June: At Calgary – beat Calgary United 8-1

15 June: At Chicago – beat Sparta 4-1

18 June: At Detroit – beat Detroit Select 3-1

20 June: At Cleveland, Ohio – beat Bruells FC 3-1

22 June: At New York – beat Fall River 6-1

Goalscorers: Jimmy Smith 18 (7 games), Jamie Fleming 14 (9), Jamie Marshall 9 (8), Bob McPhail 7 (9), George Brown 5 (10), Alan Morton 5 (8), Sandy Archibald 4 (10), Willie Nicholson 3 (7), Tully Craig 1 (10), Davie Meiklejohn 1 (10), Tommy Muirhead 1 (5).

16

Meik wins a tenth league medal

A S CARTOON character Betty Boop was making her big screen debut – and the last inhabitants of Scottish island St Kilda were being evacuated to the mainland – Rangers were preparing for the new season and Meik was chasing a tenth league gong.

But the Light Blues received an eve-of-season blow when Jamie Fleming was injured during the Clyde Sports fives. Jimmy Smith, fresh from his scoring exploits in Canada and the US, was drafted in and responded magnificently with doubles in Rangers' opening league matches. He then fired the only goal of the game at Dundee as the Gers preserved their 100 per cent start.

However, Struth 'rested' Smith for the next game, at home to Motherwell, which finished all square. Hamilton Accies were the surprise early league leaders but were edged 1-0 in the next game at Ibrox. Meiklejohn missed a month's action through injury and while the team struggled in his absence, he was back in situ for Leith Athletic's first visit to Ibrox, helping the Light Blues thump the Portobello side 4-1. Rangers then journeyed to Belfast to officially open New Windsor Park and enjoyed a motor tour of surrounding countryside on the morning of the match.

Another short spell on the sidelines for Meik coincided with the launch of a new sports craze in Glasgow – mini golf. It was the brainchild of the *Daily Record* and punters were invited into their Hope Street offices to play the game. First up was Meik, a keen golfer, who played both courses, St Andrews and Prestwick. The fabled 19th hole was a café and the sport, a variation of indoor putting, was quick to catch on.

The Scotland international was back in his usual position for the Glasgow Cup Final against Celtic at Hampden. A crowd of 71,806 observed an impeccable minute's silence for the 48 victims of the R101 Airship disaster, before the Glasgow Police band played 'Abide With Me' – and then all hell broke loose. The game was one of the rowdiest Old Firm matches on record, and afterwards Celtic boss Willie Maley – always a controversial figure – complained to the SFA about the performance of the referee and the rough tactics employed by Rangers.

There was bad blood throughout the game, which Celtic won 2-1, and Meiklejohn was the victim of a particularly brutal tackle from behind which went totally unpunished by the referee. Maley's actions in complaining drew heavy criticism from readers of the *Daily Record* with one correspondent in particular pointing out that McGrory had tripped Meik three times, and three times the referee failed to take any action. Another letter suggested that Scarff, the Celtic forward, lashed out constantly at Rangers players, and when the crowd urged him to 'play the game' he put his finger to his nose in a gesture of defiance.

It was felt that Celtic had committed more fouls than Rangers, and Maley's complaint was merely a smokescreen to deflect criticism from his poorly-behaved players. Regardless, relations between both clubs plummeted to an all-time low.

Rangers were struggling in the league and sat sixth in the table, behind Motherwell, Dundee, Partick, Celtic and Cowdenbeath. Successive wins over Aberdeen, Falkirk and Queen's Park hauled them up to third, and when they thumped Morton 7-1 – to make it four wins in 21 days – their title challenge was back on track.

This pleasing run of form ensured a better atmosphere at their annual dance in the Grosvenor, where the players paid for the board of directors to enjoy a sumptuous meal. Meiklejohn made a speech on behalf of his team-mates and Tom Vallance, one of the club's earliest stars, presented medals to the players for their efforts the previous season.

Rangers ended November with a 5-1 win over Clyde at Ibrox, but reporters had to rely on a linesman relaying info up to the press box due to a thick blanket of fog which had engulfed the entire playing surface. The Light Blues were equally as relentless in the month of December, thumping Hibs, East Fife and Cowdenbeath – the latter 7-0 – before enjoying a brief Christmas break.

For Meik, though, the festive season meant a great deal as he became engaged to Annie Pearson on Boxing Day. His new fiancée might not have been too happy to read the following report in the *Daily Record*, 'Davie's engagement does not mean early wedding bells at Ibrox. The Rangers star won't be in a particular hurry to blossom into "the young guidman" stage. Davie is not quite yet tired of being single.' Prophetic words, as it would be seven years before the couple would walk down the aisle.

Rangers' barnstorming run came to an abrupt halt the day after Boxing Day when they lost 3-0 at Tynecastle. It left Celtic one point clear going into the Ne'erday game at Ibrox, the first match between the great rivals since their 'falling out' at Hampden in October.

A crowd of 83,500 braved sub-zero temperatures to see Alan Morton fire home the only goal of the game with a fantastic shot. The players' reward for such an important victory was a night at the Alhambra Theatre to see the musical comedy *Stand Up and Sing*, starring Scottish dance-hall legend Jack Buchanan.

The Scottish Cup campaign paired Rangers with Armadale Thistle, and the match took place at the latter's Volunteer Park. It was like a home from home for Morton who worked close by for the United Collieries Company. Rangers won 7-1, although Johnny Simpson grabbed the headlines with nine goals for Partick Thistle in their 16-0 hammering of Royal Albert.

Rangers could only draw their next match, 1-1 at home to St Mirren, which left them level on points with Celtic but with a game more played. Goalkeeper Tom Hamilton's unbroken run of 122 matches came to an end due to an injury received in the match at Armadale and young Jerry Dawson deputised.

It was a tough time for Rangers and they crashed out of the Scottish Cup to Dundee before losing at home to Airdrie in a league encounter. Jimmy Smith was recalled for the next match, a trip to Shawfield, and responded by scoring five in an 8-0 romp, but despite his goal in the following game at Ayr, Rangers squandered a 2-0 lead – after Meik limped off injured – and the only saving grace was that Celtic also lost, which allowed Motherwell to return to the top of the table.

But successive wins over Hamilton, Aberdeen and Leith Athletic allowed the Light Blues to leapfrog Motherwell and Celtic, and despite a three-point lead over the latter they had played two games more.

It had been something of a stop-start season for Meiklejohn but he received the perfect pick-me-up when he was chosen to skipper Scotland against the English at Hampden Park, and he would be partnered in the half-back line by former Maryhill team-mate John Miller, who was plying his trade in Paisley. Archibald, McPhail and Morton were also chosen for a game watched by Prime Minister Ramsay MacDonald.

Just a few spectators short of 130,000 crammed into the national stadium and saw the Scots deservedly win 2-0 thanks to goals by Stevenson and McGrory. The scores were tied at the break and England, with their main goal threat Dixie Dean nullified by the towering presence of Meiklejohn, failed to make an impact on the home goal.

For the opening counter, Archibald collected a Morton corner and shot for goal. The ball came back off the post and ran along the line. Stevenson and McPhail went for it, and while it was widely believed that the Rangers man got there slightly ahead of the Motherwell player, the goal was credited to Stevenson.

Meik said, 'At half-time I felt we could still win. We were even more confident than before. The wind, I would say, was as difficult to play with as against. Then that glorious 20 minutes of good Scottish football, two of which minutes we punctuated with a goal, and brought about our glorious victory. We worked harder than ever before. We had, apart from beating England, to make the public realise that we were not nearly such a poor side as we were said to be. We had to win, and that's why I'm now smiling over my first successful captaincy against England. I am so proud.'

Rangers entered a Monday night encounter at home to Ayr United level on points with Motherwell and three ahead of Celtic, but for over 50 minutes they failed to break down the Honest Men. The goal was coming though and from an Archibald corner, Meik bulleted home an unstoppable header. That was the signal for the floodgates to open and two from McPhail, and singles from Marshall and Morton saw Gers run out 5-1 winners.

Before the next match, the SFA requested the services of Meiklejohn for Scotland's international summer tour of Austria, Italy and Switzerland. Rangers refused permission owing to the fact that their skipper hadn't had a decent close-season break since 1927.

There were just three league matches to play and Rangers were in the driving seat. A 1-0 win over Hibs left the Gers on 57 points, three ahead of Celtic, who had a game in hand. Motherwell were out of the running, leaving the destination of the title a two-horse race involving the Old Firm.

More than 43,000 turned up at Ibrox for the penultimate league match, against Partick Thistle, and a McPhail strike put the Light Blues ahead at the break. In the opening moments of the second half, Meik fell and hit his head on the ground while trying to clear a low ball. He played on with concussion, but Thistle equalised late on to take a share of the spoils.

Celtic put the pressure on by winning at Leith, but victory over East Fife at Methil secured a 19th flag for the Ibrox side. Goals by McPhail, Smith, Marshall and Archibald – the pick of the bunch – ensured a ninth successive league win and a fifth title in a row. The stuff of champions. Before the game, though, Meik realised he had forgotten something, and sprinted back to the dressing room, but would go no further than the door. Someone shouted, 'come in', but he refused, saying, 'No fear, it's bad luck to go back in, once out!' It worked, and he collected his tenth league medal.

The following Saturday, Rangers once again trumped their old rivals. The pair met in a Glasgow Charity Cup tie at Parkhead and goals from Morton and Smith earned Rangers a draw after being two down. There were no further goals in extra time but the Light Blues progressed to the semi-finals on a count-back of corners, four to one.

Meiklejohn was outstanding in the last-four tie with Partick Thistle, when a goal by Smith took them through to a final meeting with Queen's Park. The Hampden encounter ended 2-1 to Rangers, thanks to Smith and Marshall, and it was a fitting end to yet another successful season.

17

Meik stunned by Thomson tragedy

MEIKLEJOHN lost another long-standing team-mate, Tommy Muirhead, to football management when Muirhead accepted the gaffer's job at St Johnstone. Muirhead had been stationed in Perth with the army and had grown close to the Muirton club.

Alan Morton was the only Ranger who hadn't put pen to paper and it's believed the hold-up was down to the fine details of a possible benefit match. Elsewhere, a young striker by the name of Sam English, who had been making great headway at Yoker Athletic, signed for Rangers. In return, the Light Blues arranged to play the junior club in a friendly match.

It is a wonder the deal was carried through at all, as manager Bill Struth was engaged in playing golf at St Andrews, partnered, of course, by his skipper Meiklejohn. The duo were taking on all comers during a week-long golfing holiday in the Fife town.

English made his debut in the opening league game of the season when Dundee visited Ibrox. The Light Blues showed no signs of rustiness and the Northern Irish striker scored twice in a 4-1 win. Three days later, Jimmy Smith notched a double as Airdrie were brushed aside. This Rangers team looked like scoring a couple every time they took to the park but they suffered a setback next time out, losing five goals – and both points – at Motherwell. Like a wounded animal, though, the Gers came out fighting at home to Morton and English was in stunning form, hitting five in a 7-3 rout. It was a fantastic start to his senior career by the rookie striker.

St Mirren were next up and Meiklejohn's performance was described as 'majestic' as he opened up the Saints' defence time and again with a superb range of passing, and capped a great display by thundering home the second goal direct from a free kick.

By the end of August, Rangers were in their usual berth at the top of the league and had scored twice as many goals as their rivals. Next up was a visit from Celtic, a game that would never be forgotten – but for all the wrong reasons.

On the morning of the match, a *Glasgow Herald* scribe speculated as to which of the Glasgow super powers would emerge triumphant. He said, 'The game of the day is undoubtedly at Ibrox and will draw the first true big crowd of the season. It should also provide us with an opportunity to judge the qualities of both sides, and to learn which member of the Old Firm is to be the dominant partner this year.

'If consistency counts for anything, Celtic will start favourites. In my opinion they are stronger on the right than their rivals – Wilson and the two Thomsons are a strong trio, whereas Fleming and Meiklejohn, at outside right and right half back, will be out of their usual positions.

'Both teams have been experimenting of late, probably with this game in mind, but Celtic seem to have found nothing better than they had last season, and will revert to type.'

But the big team news for Rangers fans, something sure to cause disappointment within their ranks, was that English was a major doubt and not expected to take his usual place at centre-forward. He wasn't even listed in the *Herald*'s 'probable teams' section. It was reported that Smith was being drafted in as a replacement, and that the veteran winger Alan Morton had been preferred to the youthful Nicholson. If only.

Almost 80,000 spectators filed into Ibrox and the majority were hoping for a home win, but what started out as just another Old Firm match would go down in history as the day a Celtic goalkeeper tragically lost his life.

When the teams emerged from the tunnel, Gers fans were surprised to see English sporting the number nine jersey. Whether or not it had been a managerial ruse on the part of Struth we shall never know, but at the start of the game nervousness was obvious in every movement. Was it more important not to give away possession than to retain it? Mistakes were made and an unnecessary number of fouls conceded. It was an exhibition unworthy of the league champions against the Scottish Cup holders.

The teams resembled boxers trying to size up one another, and when they attempted to land blows, they struck fresh air. Chances were at a premium in the opening 30 minutes and only Celtic's Napier had an effort of note. Then just on the interval the Celts almost came a cropper. McPhail carried a ball upfield and played it through to English, but the pass was long and the opportunity lost.

With the wind behind them after the break, Rangers opened strongly, but the football world stopped just five minutes in. John Thomson threw himself at the feet of English in a brave attempt to prevent a goalscoring opportunity and paid the ultimate price. From still shots of the incident it looks as though English has his leg planted on the ground, and it is Thomson's momentum that carries his head on to the Rangers player's knee.

At that moment, though, it is said that the haunting shriek of Thomson's fiancée could be heard above the noise of the crowd. However, one man more than most, Davie Meiklejohn, realised the severity of the incident almost immediately and ran behind the goal to the terracing populated with Rangers supporters. Being unaware of the extent of the goalkeeper's injuries, they were jeering and shouting for Thomson to get up. Meik instructed the fans to quieten down, and within a matter of moments silence had blanketed the terracing.

The popular Fife-born keeper had suffered a depressed fracture of the skull and after receiving lengthy treatment on the park he was stretchered off and taken to the Victoria Infirmary, where he died later that night.

The game restarted with Chic Geatons in the Celtic goal, but play was dull and unentertaining and the game ended in a goalless draw.

News of Thomson's death was made public at around 10pm on the Saturday and cast a giant shadow over the city and throughout

Scottish football. A post-mortem was carried out and a fatal accident enquiry ordered. In the course of this enquiry, Glasgow's procurator fiscal interrogated several Rangers and Celtic players.

The coffin containing the remains of the young goalkeeper was conveyed from the Victoria Infirmary to his home at Cardenden, in Fife, and remarkable scenes were witnessed at Trinity Congregational Church, Glasgow, when a memorial service for the player, who had represented Scotland several times, attracted thousands of people.

So dense was the crowd that there were genuine fears for the safety of those seeking admission to the church, and police reinforcements were summoned to regulate the struggling throng. The church, which quickly filled to capacity, could only accommodate half the number who came to pay their last respects, and a second service was held.

The size and personnel of the crowd that gathered in the vicinity of the church prior to the service was due to the widespread popularity which Thomson enjoyed, not only in the football community but with the public generally.

At 2.30pm, when the doors opened, 2,000 men and women tried to gain admission. In their haste to get inside they rushed the doors and some even scaled exterior railings. Many became wedged in the doorway and women shrieked with alarm, but eventually two policemen managed to force a passage up the middle and succeeded in stemming the oncoming rush.

The service was conducted by the Rev H.C. McClelland, minister of the church, but a number of Thomson's football colleagues were unable to gain admission. Among them was Peter Wilson, Celtic's right-half, who was scheduled to read one of the lessons. Meiklejohn stepped in to cover for his rival and looked visibly shaken by the whole affair. The congregation fell silent while the 'Death March' was played by the organist at the conclusion of proceedings. Sam English sat head bowed throughout the majority of the service, looking a pale shadow of his former self.

In the course of a tribute to Thomson, Rev McClelland described his last act on the football field as one of superb courage and of supreme and unfaltering loyalty. He added, 'John Thomson did not give his life for a goal – he gave his life for an ideal.'

A striking tribute to the Celtic goalkeeper was commissioned by the Rangers Supporters' Club in Bridgeton. It took the form of a crown of white coronations surmounted by an emblematic white dove, and with the word 'Remembrance' upon it in silver letters. Showing in a shop window at Bridgeton Cross, it attracted the attention of thousands of people from early in the forenoon until late at night. The constant stream of pedestrians who passed before the window was regulated in the evening by members of the Bridgeton club, and their efforts prevented a cessation of trade at that part of the street.

There was another large gathering a few hundred yards along the Old Dalmarnock Road where people filed in a dense crowd past a number of wreaths from Celtic supporters on show in the windows of a funeral parlour. The tribute of the Sacred Heart supporters was a harp of white carnations, with the words in gilt lettering, 'Never forgotten – to our beloved goalkeeper'.

The funeral at Bowhill Cemetery, in Fife, was witnessed by a crowd of almost 40,000, many of whom had walked from Glasgow to Fife. Two special trains from Glasgow carried nearly 1,400 people and thousands more travelled by rail and road from all parts of Scotland. Industry halted and schools were closed as the village of Cardenden stopped for the service.

Every player who had taken part in the game was present with Struth and Meiklejohn spearheading the Rangers representation. Members of various supporters' clubs, both Rangers and Celtic, carried tributes.

The totally blameless English cut an increasingly forlorn figure as the months and years passed, and a week after the funeral he visited Thomson's parents at their home in Fife. They assured him they attached no blame to him for the tragic accident and wished him well.

Just five days after the awful tragedy, Rangers hosted Third Lanark, and English was on target in a 4-1 win. Struth had decided to rest the Irishman, with Smith down to play, but he contracted flu on the morning of the game and English was a last-minute replacement.

Just 48 hours later, Rangers picked up a valuable 3-1 win at Firhill in a game which saw Meiklejohn struggle through the final half-hour with a 'dicky leg'. It was felt that the injury would cost him another cap when Scotland faced Ireland the following Saturday. One correspondent remarked, 'I did hear that certain selectors had "gone off him", which is a funny way of remembering his match-winning exhibition against England.'

As it transpired, the injury failed to keep Meik out of the Ireland game but, as a precaution, Struth rested him for the 4-1 win over Aberdeen the midweek prior to the international. Gers defender Bob McAulay won his first cap for Ireland and was also in opposition to team-mates McPhail and Brown.

A crowd of 40,000 turned out at Ibrox for the match and saw McPhail grab the third in a 3-1 win. With the scores tied at 1-1 McGrory was fouled in the box and, as there were no other takers, up stepped skipper Meiklejohn to take the kick. However his precision shooting deserted him and he fired wide of the post. Goals by Stevenson and McGrory ensured a Scots win though.

Afterwards, Meik said, 'I am honoured to be skipper of such a clever team. A hearty congratulations to all of the lads, but especially the younger players, who more than held their own against a good Irish side.'

Rangers and Celtic were then involved in a titanic struggle in a Glasgow Cup semi-final. The teams played out a thrilling 1-1 draw at Celtic Park before replaying the tie – at Ibrox – the following midweek. Again it finished all square, 2-2, but it took a dramatic injury-time goal from Marshall, with more than a helping hand from Meik, to set up a second replay. The ever-dangerous McGrory had scored twice for Celtic, and Archibald for the Light Blues.

Ibrox was the venue for the third and final match between the Glasgow giants and all that separated the teams at the end was a brilliant Jimmy Smith goal. It was a deserved win though, as just before Rangers scored Alan Morton found himself through one-on-one with Celtic keeper Falconer when a whistle sounded. Morton stopped and kicked the ball away, only to discover that the whistle hadn't come from referee Mungo Hutton but from a member of the crowd. The three very entertaining games attracted a total crowd of 122,160 spectators.

Sandwiched somewhere in between the thrice-fought Old Firm semi was a league match against Cowdenbeath at Ibrox. English took his place in the starting line-up, despite having been on the end of some awful challenges in the first tie at Parkhead, but scored twice as Rangers romped to a 6-1 victory. Meiklejohn and Dr James Marshall also managed to find the net twice each. Meik opened the scoring on 18 minutes with a powerful free kick but his second was described as 'a thing of beauty'. He dribbled past a few defenders before rifling home a shot from the tightest of angles.

Next up was the Glasgow Cup Final against Queen's Park at Hampden, and Rangers ran out worthy 3-0 winners. Some 50,000 spectators saw Meik 'hold Queen's dangerman J.B. McAlpine in the hollow of his hand'.

The following Saturday, though, it was payback time and Queen's raided Ibrox to pull off a smash and grab 1-0 win thanks to a goal by McAlpine.

But Rangers had more pressing problems when it was discovered that the club's 'domestic' cat had wandered off from Ibrox. An article in the *Daily Record* stated, 'Lost, stolen or strayed. The domestic cat has strayed from the Rangers pavilion and the finder will be rewarded by Mr Struth on delivering the goods.' A black, full-grown feline of the Isle of Man species, 'Puss' was a big favourite with players and officials.

The club showed the true meaning of the term 'strength in depth' when five Gers players – including Meik as skipper – were named in the Scotland side to face Wales in Wrexham. The manager was obviously confident in the remainder of the squad to dispose of Dundee United at Ibrox, and how right he was as a hat-trick by English and a double from second-team striker Murray contributed to a 5-0 success.

Meanwhile, Scotland won in Wrexham for the first time since 1899, when they had roared to a 6-0 victory. This time the winning margin was far closer, 3-2, but the performance was equally pleasing. From Liverpool, the night before the match, captain Meik said, 'I like our team. They are all fit as fiddles, so watch us lay that 30-year never-win-at-Wrexham bogey!' Meiklejohn led from the front and inspired the Scots to their historic success.

In the match programme, the editor stated, 'The Rangers are the greatest side in the football world – and we are meeting nearly half of them this afternoon!'

After the game it transpired that there had been initial doubts over whether Meiklejohn and Brown would be able to play against Wales.

One of the earliest pics of Meik as a Ranger, taken in the early 1920s

William Wilton signed Meiklejohn for the Light Blues

Lining up for Scotland (second right, back row) in Wrexham before a drawn match with Wales in 1927. Picture courtesy of the Scottish Football Museum

Another early shot of the fledgling star

Rangers' cup final hero of 1928

Part of Rangers' all-conquering side of 1929/30. Meik is on the left-hand side of the back row. Picture courtesy of the Scottish Football Museum

Some kids try to climb the Hampden wall before the sold-out 1928 final

RANGERS CAPTAIN'S MESSAGE.

I am proud and happy to be captain of the Rangers team that won the Scottish Cup after 25 years striving. In our hour of victory we think of our old team mates, Arthur Dixon, Tommy Cairns and Bert Manderson who helped to keep the colours of the old club flying and who with the welfare of their former chums at heart, sent us a message of good cheer just before the great tussle began.

D. Meiklejohn.

Meik's Scottish Cup winning message

With goalscorers Tully Craig and Jamie Marshall after Rangers's Scottish Cup replay win over Partick Thistle in 1930

Legendary Rangers manager Bill Struth had a great relationship with Meiklejohn

Meiklejohn in action

Tragedy on an unimaginable scale as Johnny Thomson is carried into an ambulance at Hampden Park

Scottish Cup heroes against Kilmarnock, from left, Bob McPhail, Sam English, Davie Meiklejohn and Jamie Fleming

Skipper Meiklejohn and his Scotland team-mates line up alongside their English counterparts

Joking with some German players – and team-mates Jerry Dawson and Jimmy Smith – at Ibrox ahead of a friendly match in 1936

DAVID MEIKLEJOHN RETIRES

Dear "Waverley,"—After a long spell of activity in the grand old game, I feel that many friends might be interested to know that I have decided to retire at the close of the present season.

I have had many expressions of goodwill both from followers of my own club and others, and these I appreciate deeply. I should like you, through your popular page, to convey my thanks to all these friends, known and unknown.

Yours sincerely,

David D. Meiklejohn

Announcing his retirement from the game

Working as a reporter with the Daily Record

Meiklejohn won silverware as manager of Partick Thistle in 1951

Meik's Thistle players training at Firhill in 1957

The late, great Sandy Jardine represented Meiklejohn as he was posthumously inducted into the Scottish Football Hall of Fame in 2009. Courtesy of SNS Pics

Meik marries his sweetheart Annie Pearson

Meik and Celtic captain Jimmy McStay were big rivals

International captains Meiklejohn and T.P. Griffiths, of Wales

Wearing the latest fashion – Jazzy Jumpers – are Rangers stars, from left, Meiklejohn, Tommy Muirhead, Tommy Cairns, Arthur Dixon and Alan Morton

Former Scotland star Jacky Robertson said in his Sunday Mail *column that anyone missing a penalty should go to jail. Meik missed one against Celtic!*

And just a fortnight later, Meiklejohn was awarded the bouquet of roses by the same paper for another man-of-the-match performance

Meik wasn't a dirty player, but took no nonsense from opponents

To this day, Meiklejohn remains one of Rangers' most decorated players

"MEIK" MURMURING SADLY THAT "HE WIS FAUR OWRE AULD FOR THIS STUFF" SCORED THE ONLY GOAL.

But all good things have to come to an end…

The type of boots and ball used in Meiklejohn's day

Meik shakes hand with an opposition captain during a tour of North America

Third Lanark press but Meik, third left, and Gers keeper Jerry Dawson stand strong

Meiklejohn captains Scotland against Ireland at his beloved Ibrox in 1931. Picture courtesy of the Scottish Football Museum

Brown, a schoolteacher, travelled on a later train and therefore didn't have to ask permission to leave work early.

Meiklejohn, on the other hand, had received a reassuring message from home to tell him that his sick father was on the mend. Alexander had been dangerously ill in the previous week but was progressing favourably. This news obviously had a positive effect on Meik as he played one of his best games in an international jersey.

The following Saturday, yet more representative honours were bestowed upon Meik as he and six of his team-mates were called up for the annual Scottish League v English League match at Celtic Park. McPhail notched the winner as the Scots won 4-3 and afterwards skipper Jamie McStay, of Celtic, said, 'Didn't Davie Meiklejohn play grandly in defence and attack.'

It was then off to the pictures for the Rangers players to see the new movie in town, *Up for the Cup*. It was showing at the New Savoy, in Glasgow, and the Light Blues were given seats at the front of the house. A British comedy by Sidney Howard, *Up for the Cup* told the story of a Yorkshireman who goes to London for 't'coop final'.

With the winter months coming in, and conditions underfoot difficult to say the least, English came into his own. Successive trebles against Leith Athletic and Falkirk kept Rangers on the shirt-tails of league leaders Motherwell, who were two points ahead but had played a game more.

There was a change of sport before the next league match, at Pittodrie, when a Rangers side comprised of Meiklejohn, Morton, McAulay, Fleming, Marshall and McPhail journeyed to Dalmuir Billiards Hall to take on a local team. The hall was owned by Gers keeper Tom Hamilton and the visit brought the Ranger heaps of publicity. W.D. Greenlees, the Scottish amateur champion, agreed to face Alan Morton in a challenge match.

Mid-December proved a stumbling block for the Light Blues with just a point to show for a draw at Aberdeen and defeat at Dens Park, Dundee, where all five other Glasgow teams had bitten the dust.

Turkey and stuffing was off the menu for the Gers squad with their Boxing Day clash against Motherwell at Ibrox falling into the 'must win' category. The Steelmen were five points clear at the top of the table but hadn't reckoned on a Meiklejohn masterclass and English scored the only goal of a hard-fought encounter. The following day's match report stated, 'The star turn of the afternoon was undoubtedly Meiklejohn. He stands alone as Scotland's best half back. Perhaps a shade slower and less powerful, but his craft and sense of position continues to increase.'

The battle for the title was on and if Rangers were to make it six in a row, they had to weave their way through January without losing a single game. First up was Celtic on New Year's Day and the first-half display from the blue corner of the Old Firm was described by former Scotland international Jacky Robertson as 'the best football witnessed from any team this season'. He added, 'Their fast, accurate, on-ground passing was a joy to behold. Meiklejohn was in a class of his own – I've never seen him play better.'

The game was watched by the new Chief Constable of Glasgow, Percy Sillitoe, and one wonders if he was of the mind to take action five minutes after the restart when Meik suffered a nasty punch to the kidneys. He was forced off the field for ten minutes but returned to play his part in a 2-1 victory, courtesy of goals by Archibald and Marshall.

The following day, Partick Thistle were the visitors to Ibrox but Meik failed to make the team after his injury the previous afternoon. 'Whitey' McDonald deputised and helped Rangers register a 4-0 win. Meik also missed out on taking part in Patsy Gallacher's testimonial match at Celtic Park. A Scottish League Select were beaten 10-7 by Patsy's Falkirk/Celtic Alliance, and one wonders if Meik's presence may just have kept the score down.

The inspirational skipper returned in time to face St Mirren at rain-lashed Love Street where Jamie Fleming's double ensured Rangers kept up their title challenge. Following an 8-2 win over Brechin City in the first round of the Scottish Cup, after which Struth ruled out talks of a planned close-season tour of Argentina, Rangers thrashed Ayr United 6-1 but remained three points adrift of Motherwell, albeit with a game less played.

On Saturday 30 January, rampant Rangers thumped Raith Rovers 5-0 in Kirkcaldy with English notching his third hat-trick in as many games. However, the crowd of 18,000 was surpassed by a 20,000 attendance at Ibrox – for a reserve match.

Back-to-back wins over Hearts – in the league and Scottish Cup – set up an interesting run-in to the season, and when English scored twice in a 6-1 win over Third Lanark everyone was looking out for the Motherwell score – but they had clocked up a similar result at Tannadice against Dundee United.

The following week, Rangers won 6-1 against Queen's Park at Hampden, with English scoring four to take his season's tally to 38, but Well won a tousy encounter at Tynecastle to remain five points clear with two games more played.

The scene was set perfectly for the Scottish Cup quarter-final tie at Ibrox between the top two teams in the country. Some 88,000 spectators looked on as rain lashed the playing surface and players struggled to keep their feet. However they fell silent when Meiklejohn was struck on the head by the ball – and was knocked unconscious. Later he would say that it felt like a 'galvanic shock running down my arm' but the moment he came round, he was straight back on to the field. Goals by Murray and McPhail saw Rangers emerge victorious and book their place in the last four.

But there was no time to rest on their laurels and Dundee United lay in wait. The Rangers squad limbered up by shooting some golf at Troon on the Lochgreen Course, where Meik had to be content with second place behind Bob McAulay, a 'smashing golfer'. The Rangers skipper took his disappointment out on United and English scored twice in a 5-0 romp. Motherwell carved out a fine win at Celtic Park to maintain their advantage with just five games left to play.

Bob McPhail scored Rangers' 100th league goal of the season during a 3-0 win over Kilmarnock but a last-minute goal at Fir Park gave Motherwell a 1-0 victory over Partick. Nerves were becoming frayed but the title race would have to wait as the Scottish Cup semi-final against Hamilton took precedence. Rangers swept into the final with a 5-2 win as Well thumped Dundee 4-0 to edge ever closer to winning the championship.

And the Steelmen's cause was boosted seven days later when Third Lanark left Ibrox with both points after a thrilling 4-3 win. Meik played well but missed his half-back partner Jimmy Simpson, who was rushed to the Western Infirmary after receiving a blow to the face.

Rangers were invited to tour Denmark in the close-season but were forbidden by the SFA after it emerged that a match against a select side was part of the itinerary. The Danes insisted it was necessary because their club sides simply weren't strong enough to play against the likes of Rangers, but the stubborn football authorities refused to back down.

The Light Blues visited Central Park and thumped Cowdenbeath 7-1, but even though Motherwell drew 0-0 with Partick Thistle the destiny of the title was still in their hands. Rangers were six points behind with two games in hand. Realistically Well needed three points from their two remaining games to prevent the Light Blues landing a sixth successive crown.

And there was further bad news just around the corner when the Scotland selectors decided Meik and McPhail weren't fit enough to be considered for a team place against England, despite both playing the full 90 minutes against Cowdenbeath – and McPhail bagging a hat-trick. And it transpired that the Scots could have done with both players as they crashed to a 3-0 defeat at Wembley. Gers keeper Tom Hamilton suffered an injury to his sciatic nerve in London and was considered a major doubt for the Scottish Cup Final.

On Scottish Cup Final day, Motherwell thumped Cowdenbeath 3-0 to move within touching distance of the title and Rangers fought out a 1-1 draw at Hampden against Kilmarnock. Just seven days after being snubbed by Scotland, Meik and McPhail were named joint men of the match, with 'Barrhead Bob' scoring the equaliser before having a perfectly good goal ruled out.

The replay took place four days later at the national stadium in front of 105,000. This time there would be no controversy over disallowed goals as Rangers ran out 3-0 winners thanks to goals from Fleming, Archibald and English. For the third goal, Rangers were awarded a free kick and, as Marshall shaped up to take it, he was overruled by Meik, who looked set to attempt one of his famous rocket shots. Instead he cleverly lofted the ball over the Killie wall and English headed home to seal Rangers' third Scottish Cup in five years.

Rangers suffered a hangover when they dropped a vital point at Shawfield and Clyde became the only team that the Light Blues hadn't beaten that season. The title race was over and Motherwell, who had scored 119 league goals, just one more than Rangers, were worthy champions. They eventually won the league by five points despite English contributing 44 goals in his debut season, a remarkable feat considering the Irishman had been playing junior football just the campaign before.

Rangers vowed to wrestle back the title the following season but it seemed they would have to do so by paying lower wages. The game was struggling financially and one club chairman said, 'Wages have to be reduced next season. We will have no £5-a-week men at our club!'

Rangers ended the campaign by winning their fifth successive Glasgow Merchant's Charity Cup. They beat Queen's Park 3-1 in the semi-finals before thumping Third Lanark 6-1, with McPhail notching a hat-trick and English a brace.

Meik was one of 20 players who re-signed for the new campaign but Bob McAulay joined Chelsea in a 'mega-bucks' £6,000 deal, while Jock Buchanan was given a free transfer. Former players Tommy Muirhead and Andy Cunningham proved a success elsewhere, with the former winning promotion with St Johnstone and Cunningham guiding Newcastle United to FA Cup glory.

At the beginning of July, English and his wife were guests of honour at the unveiling of a statue in memory of the late John Thomson. Manager Bill Struth was among the invited guests.

It was then on to the course for Meiklejohn and co with Muirhead and Cunningham joining him at St Andrews for a week's golf.

Back at Ibrox, there was a changing of the guard in the backroom team with former Ger Arthur Dixon, who played over 400 games for the club, replacing Jamie Kerr – who moved to Hearts – as trainer. Dixon had been manager of the Dublin Dolphins.

18

Mr Popular!

A GROUP of Rangers players opened the new season by partaking in a cricket match against the West of Scotland CC. They didn't win but covered themselves in glory by pushing the pros all the way, thus ensuring a round of applause as they made their way into the pavilion after the match.

Then it was on to the Rangers Sports Day, watched by 25,000. They saw the cream of world athletics strut their stuff and where the prize money on offer rivalled any other UK meeting. Rangers won the fives after wins over Partick Thistle, St Mirren and Third Lanark.

The season proper opened with a shock defeat at Love Street and after the first month of the campaign, St Mirren, Hamilton and Cowdenbeath occupied the top three league places. Meiklejohn had been asked to fill in at left-back for the first few matches but he was described as 'a fish out of water' and more often than not had been 'posted missing'.

Struth moved to solve the problem position by snapping up Mason from Camelon Juniors. The youngster made his debut against Third Lanark, and Meik switched back to right-half. Smith and Archibald scored two each as rampant Rangers won 5-0 and just one week later, Smith lived up to his 'Mr Consistency' tag by helping himself to a hat-trick as Rangers thumped East Stirling 4-0 to return to their rightful place at the top of the league.

With the first Old Firm game of the season looming, the Light Blues were dealt a blow when Meiklejohn was injured in a 6-2 Glasgow

Cup rout of Queen's Park, but the tough-as-teak skipper was in his usual place for the Parkhead clash in which a Bob McPhail goal earned a 1-1 draw. Director Joseph Buchanan wasn't able to attend the match as he was in London, lifting the prestigious Diamond Jubilee Cup, the Blue Riband of the Scottish section of the Bakers' and Confectioners' Association – for his bread, which was said to be the tastiest around.

In a battle of the Scottish and English cup winners, Rangers proved far too good for Newcastle United when the sides met in a midweek clash at Ibrox. English scored twice, and Archibald and McPhail were also on target as the Light Blues won 4-1. The Geordies had led 1-0 at half-time but Meiklejohn took over and there was only one team in it after the break. That night, the Magpies were guests of Rangers at the St Enoch Hotel, where boss Andy Cunningham said, 'I didn't realise Rangers were so good!'

But revenge must have been foremost on Cunningham's mind when the sides concluded their two-part 'Best of British' contest at St James' Park a week later. A crowd of 22,000 looked on as McPhail missed an open goal with the scores tied at 0-0. English then had a header saved by Magpies keeper McInroy, which prompted the following comment in the press the next morning, 'Had it been a league or cup game, McPhail would doubtless have charged the goalkeeper over the line, but he refrained because it was a friendly!'

And how Rangers would rue his decision as Newcastle scored five times after the break without reply. It was a dejected Rangers party that headed straight back up the road on the 10pm train.

The defeat south of the border spurred Rangers on to a Glasgow Cup Final win over Partick Thistle, in which the half-back partnership of Meiklejohn and Brown was outstanding. Simpson was injured in the first half and when Gray and Meik were involved in a bad collision, the former was forced to play the rest of the game with one eye completely closed.

In their next league match, Rangers found Morton a tough nut to crack at Ibrox and held a slender 2-1 advantage with ten minutes of the second half played. Then Meik gave the signal – McPhail switched to inside-right, Marshall stepped in one and Smith took over the outside-right berth. The Light Blues stepped up a gear and the skipper, who had led by example in firing home the first goal, steered his side to a well-earned 6-1 victory. Before the match there was a minute's silence for Bailie Buchanan, the former Rangers chairman, and the Govan Burgh Band played 'Abide With Me'.

Ibrox was again covered in a thick blanket of fog for the visit of Tommy Muirhead's St Johnstone. It was so difficult to see and on this occasion, George Brown had to shout up to the press box to tell journalists that it was McPhail who had opened the scoring. A 3-0 win, allied to a 4-1 victory at Falkirk the following week, put Rangers clear at the top of the league. They wanted their title back and would stop at nothing to achieve their ends.

The next day, 400 people turned up at a 'Sportsmen's Own' social evening in the Macgregor Memorial Church to hear Meiklejohn speak about comradeship. The evening, hosted by the Rev John T. Boag, from Govan, also heard the Rangers star read the lesson, as well as motivational speeches from other guests.

At the beginning of December, Aberdeen – Rangers' main title challengers – were at Ibrox for a clash of the titans, and proved a tough nut to crack until English broke the deadlock with the first of two smartly taken goals. Marshall grabbed the other in a 3-1 win. English was a wanted man and Ireland asked Rangers if they could play him against Wales. Rangers agreed but only if he was played in a specific position, a request which the Irish turned down. But when faced with a striker crisis they appealed to Rangers to release him, which they did. English scored but Wales won 4-1.

Meiklejohn recovered from a leg injury in time to play against Hamilton at Ibrox. Rangers cruised into a three-goal lead at half-time but needed a Marshall goal in the dying seconds to rescue a point in a 4-4 draw. John Allan, who scored Hamilton's fourth goal, was a cricketer first and foremost.

The good doctor Marshall was on target again as Rangers thumped St Mirren 4-0 on Christmas Eve to draw level on points with Celtic, but with three games in hand.

Once again, though, dissenting voices were the order of the day when Rangers invited Austrian cracks Rapid Vienna to Ibrox for a glamour friendly in January 1933. As a result of the hastily-arranged match, Rangers' Scottish Cup tie with Arbroath was brought forward, which prompted some folk to criticise the Light Blues for putting their own interests ahead of the Scottish game. Two of the most outspoken clubs, Clyde and Motherwell, asked the SFA to postpone the match, but they refused. Fans were urged to 'reserve their seat at Lumley's in Sauchiehall Street – Centre Stand 5/- and East and West Stands 3/6'.

A controversial match at Ibrox on Hogmanay resulted in the referee, Watson, being struck on the head with a stone – and knocked unconscious – after he allowed a Jamie Fleming goal to stand. Ayr United players protested vehemently that the ball hadn't crossed the line but the referee said otherwise, and Rangers salvaged a 3-3 draw.

Meiklejohn was injured in the match and was out of the Old Firm game three days later. In that first fixture of 1933, Rangers missed a host of gilt-edged chances in a 0-0 draw. The rain lashed mercilessly down on to the pitch and gale-force winds made any clever play almost impossible. However, one match report read, 'I feel that Davie Meiklejohn's old head would have won the game for the Gers.'

Tom Vallance was a guest of the club, as was Herr Weiss, secretary of Rapid Vienna. When told that Rangers had never been beaten by a continental side, he remarked, 'Well, we will do our best to alter that. From what I have seen today, they are a team worth beating.'

Later that night, Meik, who was an active Christian, joined the Rev A.C. Craig at the Glasgow South Nelson Street Congregational Church for a 'Sportsmen's Own' men's evening. The Rangers star read the lesson in the absence of his Ibrox colleague Jamie Marshall, while Charles Ledington sang the solos.

The *Daily Record* then instigated a month-long competition to find Scotland's most popular footballer of 1933. Reporter 'Waverley' listed 12 players and asked supporters to forecast the top three. Up for grabs was a first prize of £200. An envelope, with the writer's final selections, was lodged at a city centre bank and would remain sealed until the closing date. To be in with a chance of winning, fans had to name the same top three as 'Waverley', and those would then go into a hat, with the winner drawn by the bank manager.

The competition proved incredibly popular and thousands of entries poured in from all over the country. And no one could argue with the scribe's choices which, in reverse order, were: Neil Dewar (Third Lanark); George Stevenson (Motherwell), and the overall winner – Davie Meiklejohn. George Brown, Dougie Gray and Bob McPhail also made it into the top 12 but Meik was 'officially' the most popular player in the country.

With the latter stages of the flag race looming, Motherwell had emerged from the shadows as a genuine contender to retain their title and when East Stirling led Rangers 2-0 at half-time in a league match at Bainsford it looked as though the Steelmen would move clear at the top. However, goals by Campbell and Smith, who scored twice, ensured joint billing at the summit.

There were further howls of derision from dissenting clubs when the Scottish Cup tie between Rangers and Arbroath was postponed due to fog, and clubs insisted the Red Lichties had missed out on a big pay day due to Rangers' selfishness.

Regardless, the Light Blues pressed on with their contest against Rapid and 56,000 saw a 'match to remember'. J.T. Davis of Bury was appointed match referee and the Austrian cast of *White Horse Inn*, a hit play performing at the King's Theatre, in Glasgow, met the Rangers players a couple of days before the match.

The Rangers line-up for this historic first visit of a continental team to Ibrox was: Dawson, Gray and Bob Hamilton; Meiklejohn, McDonald and Brown; Archibald, Marshall, Smith, McPhail and English.

The year before, Austria had trounced Scotland 5-0 in an international challenge match and Rangers were keen to take revenge. The Light Blues were 2-0 down at the break but rallied to score three times in the second period to share the spoils in a 3-3 draw. Smith scored twice, once from the penalty spot, while McPhail got the other. Raftl, the Rapid keeper, was sensational in the second half and was carried shoulder-high from the field after the game.

Bill Struth's decision to switch Sam English to centre-forward and Smith to outside-left was hailed as a masterstroke. One scribe added, 'Meiklejohn's headwork was delightful and he was shooting in the second half like a Gatling Gun!'

Afterwards, both clubs retired to the St Enoch Station Hotel for dinner and Ex-Bailie Duncan Graham, the Rangers chairman, presented the Austrians with a silver Loving Cup. In return, Rangers were presented with an arbeiten, inscribed 'Until we meet again!'

The Austrians stayed on for Rangers' Scottish Cup tie against Arbroath 48 hours later and saw the Gers squeeze through 3-1. That night, Rangers hosted their annual dance at the Grosvenor and, once again, the Austrians were present.

There wasn't much love in the air when Rangers travelled to Fir Park 72 hours before Valentine's Day for a top-of-the-table clash against Motherwell. McPhail and Meiklejohn, who had a twisted knee, were missing but goals by Fleming, who scored twice, and Smith, gave Rangers a 3-1 victory in a bad-tempered affair.

Dougie Gray was injured in a rash challenge 30 minutes in and was forced to withdraw from play. A fortnight later, Rangers edged Dundee 6-4, and with Well losing 4-2 at Hampden, the Ibrox club streaked four points clear with eight matches remaining.

Once again the Rangers defence lost four goals, this time against Hearts, although a McPhail hat-trick helped them salvage a point. And it was McPhail who notched the Light Blues' 100th league goal of the season a week later in a 6-2 romp at Rugby Park. The win put the Gers seven points clear at the top, although Motherwell had two games in hand.

The following night, Meik again took part in a 'Sportsmen's Own' evening at his local church. Sharing the bill with the Rangers star was James Clarke of the British Boxing Board of Control, who talked about sport in other countries. Meik read the lesson at the popular event.

Early the following week Meiklejohn was named in the Scotland team to face England at Hampden Park, but the skipper-in-waiting said, 'I'm not 100 per cent fit. I'm fit, but not fighting fit and I would never put Scotland in danger.'

The inspirational half-back was given a fitness test on his troublesome knee the day before the match but failed to convince either himself or the trainer that he could do the team justice. He was immediately withdrawn, and said, 'I appreciate the compliment paid me by the selectors, and I should have liked to play, but feel I am placing the interests of my country first in standing down. It would be terrible if I went out and broke down. I only hope our boys win. No one could wish them better luck than I do.'

Meik dined with the team before the match and then joined the 134,000 crowd to watch Scotland win 2-1 thanks to a double by Jimmy McGrory. The team played well and Bob McPhail was voted star man.

The following Monday, Meik travelled with the Rangers party to Dublin for a friendly match against Dolphins. The players were welcomed to the Irish city by the mayor, and more than 20,000 watched Rangers win 3-1, but Morton was badly injured in the first half when he stepped in a hole. English scored twice and Simpson got the other.

Rangers required just three points for the league title following an eventful trip to Pittodrie in the middle of April. Smith grabbed the Light Blues' goal in a 1-1 draw that saw the scorer take a bad knock on the knee which made it swell to twice its normal size. Gray received a cut above the eye and the referee took ill during the match.

The following Saturday, Rangers clinched their 20th league flag with a single-goal win over Queen's Park at Ibrox. McPhail was the man who prompted jubilation on the vast terraces, although Meik was described in the press as 'outstanding' and hit the bar with a free kick.

Afterwards, English was again at the centre of speculation regarding a transfer to Liverpool, and ten players – including Meiklejohn – signed on the dotted line for another season at Ibrox. Morton – Bill Struth's first Rangers signing – was invited to take a seat on the Ibrox board.

The following Monday, a staggering 38,000 watched Rangers win the Second XI Cup with a 2-1 win over Celtic, but two nights later Meik twisted his knee in a charity match at Newcastle. He was still fit enough, though, to visit Lockie Memorial Mission Hall, in Kinning Park, for the annual display of the 80th Glasgow Lifeboys, with English as his aide-de-camp.

The knee injury kept Meik out of the Glasgow Merchant's Charity Cup, which was won for the sixth successive time with a 1-0 win over Queen's Park in the final. It was the end of yet another successful campaign for the most popular player in the country.

19

Little continental action for Meik

RANGERS set off on their European adventure in the middle of May 1933 with Berlin the first stop on their itinerary, just as Adolf Hitler was 'assuring' the western world, 'Germany does not want war.'

Simultaneously, the German Chancellor was making many demands on the League of Nations, the international organisation whose principal mission was to maintain world peace. Britain's plans for a Disarmament Convention were accepted by Germany, although they were secretly beavering away in the background with plans of their own, and they didn't involve peace.

Rangers had agreed to play five games in Germany before heading over the border into Austria for a return match with Rapid Vienna. There was also the provision for a fixture in Paris on their way home.

Seventeen players – Dawson, Gray, Russell, McDonald, Meiklejohn, Kennedy, Simpson, Brown, Craig, Archibald, Main, Marshall, Smith, English, McAulay, McPhail and Fleming – made the trip. They arrived in Berlin after a marathon train journey from Glasgow, in which they were entertained by George Brown and his ukulele. They were welcomed to the German capital by representatives of the German FA as well as hundreds of enthusiastic local football supporters.

Their first match, against Post Club Berlin, was easily negotiated and Smith, with a hat-trick, was the star turn. His first goal, from an almost impossible angle, was wildly appreciated in the stands. McPhail and Fleming were also on target. The weather was awful but 30,000 spectators attended and were treated to a first-class display of football by Rangers, who maintained their record of never having lost a match outside the UK.

One unfortunate incident, towards the end of the match, saw Lemberger 'knocked senseless', after a 50-50 challenge. Meiklejohn's troublesome knee kept him out of the action.

A three-hour train journey from Berlin to Hamburg was next on the agenda and a 20,000 crowd saw the Light Blues continue their tour in style with a 3-1 win over Hamburg Victoria. This time, overhead conditions were far kinder, and the game was played in tropical-style weather. Smith was again to the fore and scored twice, with Marshall grabbing the other. The crowd appreciated Rangers' play, especially their head work, and all three goals were celebrated by the home fans in enthusiastic style.

Once again Meik was missing, but assisted manager Struth at the side of the park. One interesting footnote concerned the award of a somewhat dubious penalty kick to the Germans shortly after Smith had opened the scoring. So soft was the award that even the German supporters aimed a barrage of protests in the direction of the referee.

It was back to thunderstorms when Rangers played their next match, in the north-western city of Bochum. A rain-affected attendance of 4,000 saw a Rangers side prove just too strong for their favourites. Doubles from English and McPhail, and a single by Fleming, completed the scoring and 5-0 didn't flatter the tourists.

Next up though was a tough encounter in Dresden, and 30,000 saw a match played on a hard, bumpy pitch, although the biggest obstacle seemed to be the ball, which was incredibly light and difficult to judge and control. Smith opened the scoring in the sixth minute when a clearance rebounded off the referee's head and landed at his feet, which left him a tap-in. Of Dresden, Struth said, 'It's a fine city. There's lots of sightseeing – the difficulty is deciding where to go. Everybody is well and enjoying themselves.'

On the last day of May, however, Rangers' proud unbeaten record came to an abrupt halt when they were defeated by a Bavarian Select team. It was the fifth and final match of the German tour and the Light Blues seemed jaded from their previous matches. The Germans took the lead but McPhail equalised just before the break. Smith hobbled off injured and with Rangers down to ten men, Rohr scored his second of the match midway through the second half. Try as they might, Rangers just couldn't find a leveller, although late on McPhail was robbed of a second when a German stopped the ball on the line with his hand, an act which went unpunished by the referee. The team received a standing ovation from the 30,000 crowd after the match.

Rangers left Germany for Austria where they were afforded a wonderful reception in Vienna, and presented to the mayor. Struth said, 'A programme of entertainment on a lavish scale has been drawn up. It looks as if we are about to have the time of our lives.'

Sadly the team suffered a second successive defeat on foreign soil, although the clash against Vienna fell into the 'titanic' category. Some 40,000 fans turned out in sweltering heat to see a ding-dong tussle eventually won 4-3 by Rapid. Before the start, the Rangers players and officials were presented to the president of the republic, and the crowd showed their appreciation.

Brown, Marshall and Simpson scored for the visitors but just when it looked like they might be wearing down the Vienna defence for a fourth time, the hosts broke free and scored the decisive goal. Afterwards, McPhail conceded that the Austrians had deserved their victory. The secretary of the Austrian FA then told Struth that the Rangers were the best foreign side to visit his country in the last ten years. From the ground, the tourists were driven to the Grand Hotel to be entertained to dinner.

From Vienna it was on to Paris for a few days' break before travelling home to Glasgow via London. From the capital, Meiklejohn said, 'The teams we played against are exceptionally keen, and they play the game in the best sporting spirit. The crowds were equally sporting. They gave us a splendid reception – win or lose – and it was a pleasure to play before them. Football on the continent is of a very high standard.'

He added, 'It was unfortunate that we met the best two teams so late in the tour, otherwise the results might have been different. We played six matches in 19 days, which surely is a sufficiently strenuous programme for anybody.'

Asked whether there was any possibility of an early formation of an international league of association football, Meik said that so long as the continental teams remained amateur he didn't see how such a thing was possible. Nevertheless, he said, they would always be welcome opponents.

As a postscript to the successful tour, reports spread like wildfire that two of the players, Craig and McAulay, had been detained by police in the French port of Calais, and that the manager had remained with them. 'Not a vestige of truth in it,' said Struth. 'We simply walked from the train on to the boat at Calais. Then we arrived in Dover. Craig and McAulay each had a bottle of scent which the Customs officials inspected. They were invited to open their bags, which they did, and they were told to proceed. McAulay had to pay a shilling or two duty on the scent.

'The other players had gone through Customs and got the first train to London. Craig, McAulay and I travelled on the relief train. There weren't many minutes left but the first train left without a second's delay, and those few minutes made all the difference. That's all there was to it.'

It was a surprise that Struth didn't have to pay excess duty on the haul of mementoes brought back from their successful tour. From the German FA, Rangers received a bronze plaque, with silver plate inscription; from the Austrian FA a silver salver; from the Sportklub Rapid a cup; and from the Austrian Propaganda Association, another beautiful cup. Each Rangers official was presented with a gold badge by their opposite number at Rapid.

At a dinner in Munich, the German Commissioner of Sport presented Rangers with an illuminated address, which was to be framed and hung in the Ibrox pavilion. In fact, a number of opera singers had been present at the closing banquet in Munich. Due to injury, Meiklejohn, McAulay and Craig failed to take part in any of the games.

20

Clean sweep for the Light Blues

AFTER missing out on game time in Germany and Austria, Meiklejohn was back in the groove with an appearance in the Rangers five-a-side team at the Glasgow Tramways Sports Day at the beginning of June – then, as was 'par' for the course, it was on to the fairways of St Andrews for a round or two. There he teamed up with old pals Tommy Muirhead and Billy McCandless, just as the latter had been appointed manager of Dundee.

One report from St Andrews stated, 'Davie Meiklejohn has been playing some real good stuff on the Old Course, mostly par, and a bit too hot for the opposition, although he and partner George Brown – not the Rangers George – had to give best to a pair from Grangemouth in a teethy foursome. But the Ibrox captain and his partner lost little time in taking their revenge – with interest.'

With the new season rapidly approaching it was time to get back to training. His final round at the Old Course was a thing of beauty and he recorded a par figure from his scratch handicap. He had also managed to eliminate a difficulty with his chip shot, which had been troubling him until his partner put him right.

The league flag was unfurled at the annual Rangers Sports Day and to put the icing on the cake, Meik and co won the fives for which they received brand new Kodak cameras. New signing Torry Gillick, who had been drafted in from Petershill Juniors, made his debut in the trial match between the Blues and Whites at Ibrox. A crowd of 15,000 rolled up and gave donations to the Elder Park Cottage Hospital.

On the eve of the first league match, Rangers fans were disappointed to see Sam English move to Liverpool. The fee, £5,000, was a record for the Anfield club. English had been struggling to keep Jimmy Smith out of the team and made the move to reinvigorate his career – a decision which was vindicated when Smith scored an astonishing ten goals in the first two league matches. First up he hit four against Airdrie to get Rangers off to a flying start, and just 72 hours later he contributed a double hat-trick in a 9-1 romp over Ayr United.

Hibs and Rangers drew a blank in the next match at Easter Road, and the report read, 'Hibs's Walls–Wallace front partnership looked like doing the business, and would have done so, but for the uncanny watchfulness of Davie Meiklejohn. The Ibrox master – who was injured just before half-time – has been more mobile before, but put an almost absolute stranglehold on Flucker, who was seeing a lot of the ball. Cheer up boy, you won't have Scotland's best centre-half against you every week!'

Normal service was resumed in front of goal the following Saturday when Rangers hit Clyde for six with, almost inevitably, Smith bagging a double. Meik missed the game due to a rib injury suffered in the match against Hibs and was absent again when the Light Blues lost 2-1 at Fir Park. But he was fit enough to play a part in a charity match between the Ministers and the Press at Cathkin Park, where he ran the line for top referee Willie Bell. The Unemployment Matinee Guild Fund benefitted from the gate money, which totalled almost £15. Meik then refereed a Boys' Brigade match before signing autographs for youngsters at a BB rally.

Meiklejohn still wasn't 100 per cent fit and when Scotland's selectors met to name their team for the match against Ireland, he said, 'I may be fitter than I was a year ago, but it's one thing playing for Scotland and quite another playing for the Rangers.' The following day, though, the inspirational player took his place in the starting line-up against Celtic at Ibrox, and placed a free kick neatly on to the head of McPhail for the opening goal. The match finished all square at 2-2.

In mid-September the famous Arsenal headed north for a challenge match at Ibrox, but before a ball was kicked the clubs had another score to settle – on the fairways of Turnberry. When the Rangers party arrived at the Ayrshire course the Londoners were waiting for them, clubs in hand and ready to do battle. The great Alec James – the Highbury Wizard – was also present, but with no more than a camera in hand he was tasked with being 'official snapper'.

The first tie out on the course was Meik and Archibald against Frank Hill and David Jack, and the golf on offer for those who had chosen to watch was first class. The Rangers pair went round in 75 but were beaten by the better-ball score of 73. Tom Hamilton and Bob McPhail squared the match with a solid win over Pilson and Carruthers. The remainder of the ties were all square, and thus the match ended in a similar vein. One Arsenal player commented, 'The team that comes here to keep fit ought to be the best in the world.'

To the match itself and a crowd of 37,000 watched the English league champions take the game to their hosts in the early stages, but goals from Smith and McPhail settled the issue. Meiklejohn, who was said to have a grip on James, was forced off injured when both James and Cliff Bastin fell on top of him and left him with a hip injury, but he was back on after treatment.

After a thoroughly competitive game, played in a great spirit, the players adjourned to the St Enoch Station Hotel for dinner and speeches. Each Arsenal player received a silver cigarette case and Sir Samuel Hill Wood, the Arsenal chairman, said, 'We have seen football which we are not in the habit of witnessing in England. In fact, we have been taught a mouthful.'

Meik's hip injury kept him out for a couple of weeks but he was fit enough to travel to London for the return match against Arsenal. An eight-hour train journey was spent playing rummage and bird-spotting from the windows of the carriage. At another table, Meik, Arthur Dixon and Rangers secretary Rogers Simpson played bridge.

Rangers were met at Euston Station by Sir Samuel while a 'well kent' face was also waiting on the platform – ex-Gers goalkeeper Willie Robb, who was working in London. After the party had checked in and freshened up at the Hotel Russell, they made for His Majesty's Theatre to take in a show.

Some 40,000 fans were present at Highbury the following night and witnessed one of the greatest displays of football ever seen. Rangers, it was said, rose to the occasion and played some quite brilliant stuff. Fleming scored twice and Dr Marshall got the other in a 3-1 win, and the players were roared off the field at the end of a pulsating 90 minutes.

Arsenal director George Allison said, 'The Rangers are good enough to meet England. I have seen nothing better.' Meiklejohn and Brown were the pick of the bunch and played the entire game 'with their sleeves rolled up'. Captain Meiklejohn said, 'I think we have done a spot of good for Scottish football. It was hard work, but it was worth it.'

At the after-dinner event in the Café Royal, the Rangers players were presented with a pair of field glasses as a memento of the occasion.

It was then back to the daily grind of the nine-to-five and with youngster Torry Gillick making his debut Rangers edged Partick Thistle 4-3 in a thriller at Firhill, but still they trailed league leaders Motherwell by three points.

Rangers and the SFA were on collision course just days later when the Light Blues accepted an invitation to play Racing Club de Paris in the French capital on the same day Scotland were due to face Austria. The Scotland selectors wanted Meiklejohn, McPhail, Marshall and Brown, but the French side had stipulated that Rangers must field their full league team. The game may have been seven weeks away but it was a matter that was set to rumble on.

Midway through October, Rangers faced Clyde in the Glasgow Cup Final at Hampden. Meiklejohn was supreme and led his side to an easy 2-0 win. It was generally accepted that the Rangers skipper had slowed up just a little, but that his tactical awareness more than made up for any deficiencies in his speed. In fact, after Rangers had beaten Kilmarnock 3-1 at Rugby Park a couple of weeks later, the *Daily Record*'s 'Waverley' said, 'Physically, Master Meiklejohn seems to be a better specimen of footballing humanity than a year ago when for the Scottish League he played one of the greatest games of his international life. Again at Kilmarnock he was immense. Davie's positional play was a positive education, a joy, and he has the perfect understanding with George Brown, a willing pupil.'

By the middle of November, Smith had scored 24 league goals, including successive hat-tricks against Clyde and Queen of the South, yet the Light Blues were still four points adrift of Motherwell. And that deficit widened even further when they lost 3-1 at St Johnstone, who were involved in a bitter tug-of-war with Sheffield Wednesday for their manager, Tommy Muirhead.

That night, Meiklejohn handed over a cheque for £666 to a Mr Lamont at the Picture House in Sauchiehall Street, after he had come up trumps in a football picture puzzle competition in the *Empire News*. All parties stayed to watch *Prince of Arcadia*, starring Carl Brisson.

The much-hyped Scotland v Austria game was on the horizon and Rangers, backing down in their tussle with the SFA, cancelled their match in Paris. Meik was chosen to skipper the Scots but picked up an ankle injury against Falkirk four days before the big match. On the morning of the game, the Austrians toured Ibrox before going to the Commodore Picture House in Scotstoun where they saw the German film *Morgenrot*. Meanwhile, Meik was receiving intense treatment at Ibrox, and was said to be making good progress.

The physiotherapy did the trick and he lined up alongside club-mate Brown in a Scotland team desperate to avenge an earlier 5-0 defeat to the Austrians. A crowd of 62,000 witnessed an intriguing tussle that ended in an honours-even 2-2 draw. Meik opened the scoring with a stunning free kick but the visitors fought back to secure a draw.

At the after-match dinner in Glasgow's Grosvenor Restaurant, the Austrians were fascinated by haggis while some old acquaintances – forged when Rangers played Rapid Vienna – were renewed.

The following weekend, Rangers clawed back a point on leaders Motherwell when they secured a 2-1 victory at Aberdeen but once again Meiklejohn was injured when he received a knock on the head – from a wet ball. He was unconscious for fully five minutes but when he came round he was straight back into the heat of the battle. Brown wasn't so fortunate, though, and was forced off after picking up a leg injury. The Light Blues soldiered on and got the points, while Motherwell drew 2-2 with Third Lanark.

Meik celebrated his 33rd birthday by playing his part in a 7-2 win over Airdrie at Broomfield. Flu victim Jerry Dawson was replaced by

Canadian keeper George Jenkins. With Motherwell losing at home to Clyde, Rangers cut the gap to five points and had two games in hand.

Young Alec Venters, signed from Cowdenbeath, made his Old Firm debut in the Ne'erday game and scored the opening goal in a 2-2 draw. Meik started the move which led to Celtic keeper Joe Kennaway dropping a Bobby Main cross and Venters was in the right place at the right time to knock it home.

A fortnight later, Rangers hosted Motherwell at Ibrox and more than 80,000 paid to see the action. Rangers were best in every department and doubles by McPhail and Fleming secured both points in a 4-2 win. Meiklejohn's experience shone through and he was described as 'cool and accurate'. The Light Blues were now three points behind but with two games in hand.

Rangers were in record-breaking mood on Saturday 20 January – and tiny Blairgowrie were on the receiving end. The Scottish Cup first-round tie attracted just 5,000 spectators to Ibrox but they witnessed a display of shooting that stands as a record to this day. Rangers won 14-2 and Jamie Fleming scored nine. In fact, such was the performance of Malcolm, the visiting keeper, that some pundits named him their man of the match.

Fleming scored four in the first half – his first after just 30 seconds – and added a handful after the break. It was 12-0 when Fechlie scored Blairgowrie's first, and Lynch scored the final goal of the afternoon with just 30 seconds remaining.

As a postscript to the match, letters arrived at local newspapers accusing Rangers of being unsportsmanlike in hammering the minnows although, rather significantly, none of them came from the Blairgowrie area. Everyone connected with the club insisted they had enjoyed a great day out and had been treated with the utmost respect by those at Ibrox. 'Waverley' said, 'Teams like Blairgowrie take their chance of almost humiliating defeat each time they enter the Scottish Cup – that's just the way of it.'

Fleming was at it again the following Saturday when he scored five in a 6-0 win over Dundee at Dens Park. After 14 goals in just eight days he was predictably hailed as the best centre-forward in the country. However the striker drew a blank in Rangers' next game, against Third Lanark at Cathkin. Smith scored all three goals in a match that saw Thirds' Carabine ordered off despite Meiklejohn pleading with the referee to show clemency. A reporter described Meik's actions thus, 'It's just what you would expect of a player with the sense and judgement of the Ibrox captain.'

Rangers were box-office sensations wherever they went. At Ibrox, for a Scottish Cup third-round tie against Hearts, almost 70,000 watched the sides battle to a 0-0 draw. The following midweek, more than 47,000 crammed into Tynecastle – a midweek record at the Gorgie Road ground – for the replay, and just before kick-off hundreds more jumped the barricades and got in free.

Such was the crowd inside the stadium, though, that an ugly downward sway ensued and many supporters swarmed on to the track and playing field to avoid being crushed. Others screamed for the attention of the ambulance men. The scenes were in stark contrast to the beginning of the day when Rangers players such as Meiklejohn, McPhail and Brown had spent a quiet morning taking advantage of Ibrox Stadium's brand new billiards room.

Once order had been restored on the Tynecastle terraces, goals from McPhail and Fleming helped Rangers pull off a 2-1 victory to earn a quarter-final tie with Aberdeen at Ibrox, in which Smith scored the only goal of the game.

Saturday 10 March was a pivotal afternoon in the race for the championship as Rangers returned to Tynecastle and beat Hearts 2-1 in a hard-fought match, while Celtic thumped Motherwell 3-0 at Parkhead. The Steelmen were a single point ahead – but had played two games more.

Rangers played the first of their matches in hand at Douglas Park, Hamilton, and a late Archie McAuley winner – the Light Blues' 100th league goal of the campaign – was sufficient to take them back to the top of the pile. It was also the afternoon that Meik was linked with the vacant manager's job at Arsenal – even though he denied applying for the north London post. But the league was far from all over and Motherwell were given renewed hope when Kilmarnock took a point from Ibrox – although Well then lost their next game at home to Partick Thistle.

The sides played football leapfrog as, first of all, Motherwell beat St Mirren 3-1 to regain their advantage, before Gers beat Third

Lanark 1-0 at Cathkin 24 hours later to claim top spot. Venters scored the only goal against Thirds but Meik played a real captain's part by clearing a shot from Hassan off the line with Dawson lying on the ground.

Next up, Rangers beat St Johnstone 3-0, and Motherwell pounded Airdrie 6-3 at Broomfield, but while these two rivals indulged in a Scottish League shoot-out the once-mighty Celtic were an incredible 25 points behind Rangers in 11th spot.

But the last day in March proved significant on two fronts. A Dr Jamie Marshall goal was enough to beat St Johnstone in the semi-finals of the Scottish Cup while, just a few miles up the road in Paisley, a Jimmy Knox hat-trick gave St Mirren a 3-1 win over Motherwell which all but ended their title hopes.

A 2-1 win over Aberdeen at Ibrox, coupled with another Motherwell dropped point, put the Light Blues on the verge of another championship success. Meiklejohn was inspirational against the Dons and turned it on in front of the Scotland selectors, who had one eye on the forthcoming Wembley international. But there was to be no fairytale return for the veteran half-back and the berth went to Alec Massie. Scotland lost 3-0 but Meik was there to support the team.

The following weekend, Meiklejohn was back in light blue as Rangers took on St Mirren in the Scottish Cup Final at Hampden. The popular captain got the first big call right – the toss of the coin – and elected to shoot with the wind in his favour. St Mirren's hopes were gone in a flash as Nicholson, with a double, Main, McPhail and Smith put the Buddies to the sword.

On the Monday morning, Scotland's top football correspondent, 'Waverley', said, 'Rangers proved themselves one of the best combinations in Scottish football this century. Meiklejohn had Scotland cap Johnny Miller on toast. He played the veteran's part skilfully – his value is inestimable!' At the close of play, Meiklejohn was handed the match ball by the referee, Mungo Hutton, but sportingly gave it straight to Saints striker Jimmy Knox.

The same afternoon, Motherwell completed their fixtures with a win at Ayr which put them on 62 points – one ahead of Rangers, who had three games to play – and the Light Blues duly clinched their 21st league title with a 3-1 win at Falkirk. It was their 12th in 15 seasons and the three occasions on which they had failed to win it, they had finished second.

To win their latest crown they had remained unbeaten since November, and had won 16 of their last 19 games – a phenomenal display of consistency that was rightly rewarded with the country's premier prize. Congratulatory telegrams arrived from Vienna, Berlin, Finland, Canada and more, and Rangers were invited to play in a tournament in Amsterdam the following week – although they politely declined.

In their final game of the season, a 1-1 draw at Hampden against Queen's Park, Smith notched his 41st league goal of the campaign – and Rangers' 118th in total. Twenty-six players – including Meik – were immediately retained for the following season.

There was speculation over manager Bill Struth's future, though, with Arsenal desperate for the Rangers gaffer to succeed the late Herbert Chapman. Struth insisted he was staying put and duly led Rangers to glory in the Glasgow Merchant's Charity Cup. Bobby Main scored the only goal of the final against Celtic, which meant Rangers had lifted all four senior cups in the same season – a remarkable achievement. After the Old Firm match a report suggested, 'Davie's calculations are never more than a few inches out.'

It had been another remarkable season in the history of a truly remarkable club. Forty-eight official games played and just two had been lost, with 151 goals scored against just 47 conceded.

A couple of days later the Rangers players were much in demand – as referees. Meik took charge of the Glasgow Schoolboys Charity Cup semi-final at Tinto Park, Govan, between Glasgow South and Glasgow West. The same night, Dr Marshall had the whistle for a charity match at Cappielow between doctors and teachers.

Rangers ended their season's work by playing in a couple of five-a-side tournaments. First up was a trip to Belfast to compete in the annual Constabulary Sports Day and it was a strong five – Meiklejohn, Craig, Kennedy, Main and Smith – who carried away first prize by beating Linfield in the final, with Main scoring the only goal in the dying minutes.

Following their Irish adventure, five Rangers players headed for the Parkhead area of the city for the Glasgow Tramways Sports Day.

Some 20,000 spectators packed into Helenvale Park and the gates had to be locked well before start time. Meik, McDonald, Venters, Smith and Main clinched the fives crown with a clinical 3-0 defeat of Clyde in the final, after they had edged out Celtic in the semis by virtue of having earned one more corner. A report said, 'Meiklejohn was Rangers' general, and made the ball do the work.'

But that final football engagement didn't signal a mass departure on holiday for Rangers still had the small matter of a challenge 'cricket' match to help them unwind after a long but successful season. Twelve players, including Meiklejohn, Kennedy and Smith, as well as a couple of guests, took part in the match at Whitehaugh, in Paisley, against a Buddies select. A good crowd witnessed the match and over £20 was taken for the Kelburne Pavilion Fund.

The footballers put up a sound display although, quite clearly, one or two of them would have been more at home hitting the bigger ball. The match ended in a draw with Meiklejohn managing just three runs after being bowled out by Smallwood. Smith fared little better, scoring seven, while easily the best for the Rangers Select was Tommy Crosskey, from Albion Rovers, who hit 68 before being bowled out. Of course it helped that he was a semi-professional with Carlton Cricket Club.

Just a few days later, a *Daily Record* correspondent took a number of youngsters on a tour of Ibrox and their official guide was none other than the club captain himself. The report read, 'Genial Davie Meiklejohn, one of the most popular players in Scotland, was the first man we met when we arrived at Ibrox Park to take a peek behind the scenes. Davie is one of the most obliging footballers I know. He is the essence of politeness and always willing to impart his fund of football knowledge, gained from many years of experience, to young people.

'When we asked him if he would give us a few words of advice, he said, "Always remember that you are playing for a team, not for yourself. Good combination is good football. Don't be individualistic. When you are in possession and you see a man better placed to get a goal, give the ball to him, don't carry on and try to score yourself. Nine times out of ten, if you carry on, you will be dispossessed, and the chance will be lost.

"'And another thing, when you are heading a ball, never shut your eyes. I know a number of players who do that and it makes it very difficult for them to place the ball. I used to do it myself, but I've got rid of that bad habit. Keep your eyes wide open and before the ball touches your head have your mind made up what you are going to do.'"

And so to the summer holidays.

21

Lucky 13 for skipper

AT THE beginning of July 1934, Meik and his fiancée set sail on a week-long Mediterranean cruise, lapping up the sunshine and soft drinks before returning to shore and going their separate ways. While Annie Pearson slotted back into Glasgow life, the Rangers captain joined Bob McDonald for five days of non-stop golf at St Andrews where, it was said, he was as well known in the old university town as the British Open champion himself, Bobby Locke.

By this time Meiklejohn had moved home, just a mile or so up the road to Cardonald and a comfortable terraced house in Arbroath Avenue, which was still only a five-minute car ride from Ibrox. But football was still the furthest thing from his mind after his stint on the Old Course for he headed straight from Fife to the Ayrshire town of Girvan – and even more golf. He was taking part in a special matchplay tie where he partnered Bill Struth against Bob McDonald and George Brown. The links course was also a favourite for Gers players, and looked out on to the famous old rock at Ailsa Craig as well as distant Kintyre. Meik and Struth gave away five shots and still won by a single.

On his return from the coast, Meiklejohn discovered that teammate Dr Jamie Marshall had been transferred to Arsenal, then the world's richest football club. He had quit his job in the Research Department at the Royal Infirmary to move lock, stock and barrel to London.

With pre-season training in full swing, Rangers entered a five-a-side team for the Clyde Sports, although Meik's place had to be taken by goalkeeper Jerry Dawson when he turned up late. He said, apologetically, 'I didn't think the fives started until later in the day.' Once again, though, the crowd were furious with Celtic's time-wasting antics, and let them know.

To the cricket field went six Rangers players, including Meiklejohn, Morton and Gillick, to take their place in a Footballers XI against the 'serious' players of Golfhill CC, a club from Dennistoun. The Footballers pulled off a stunning victory, running out winners by 31 runs. Rangers trainer Arthur Dixon, a semi-pro cricketer in his native Oldham, was first in but was bowled out for a duck – and the Footballers thought they were in for a long night, but fought valiantly and eventually came through. Jimmy Simpson scored a dozen, Meiklejohn contributed 14, Gray 15 and Gillick 12, while Dixon atoned for his earlier embarrassment by taking a couple of wickets.

Rangers began the new season with real vigour and thumped Dunfermline 7-1 at East End Park in a bad-tempered encounter. Former Celtic player Johnny McFarlane left the boot in a couple of times on Meik and the Ibrox captain eventually went toe-to-toe with the Pars hardman. Both players were booked but Meik had the last laugh as Smith picked up where he had left off by scoring six goals to get Rangers off to a flyer.

During a display of total dominance against Dunfermline, Meik was in a class of his own and the scene was set for him to once again exert his influence over a Rangers side bristling with talent and confidence.

Next up was a challenge match against Rapid Vienna. The Austrians fielded nine players who had made the trip to Ibrox the previous year, but not even a visit to the Empire Theatre the night before could inspire them and Rangers ran out 3-1 winners. Some 50,000 watched the Austrian keeper play the game of his life to keep the score down.

The lead-up to the Rangers–Motherwell league match was dominated by talk of the emergence of a new 'super power' in the Scottish game. The general consensus was that the fixture had overtaken the Old Firm game in terms of importance. Motherwell were now considered Rangers' greatest Scottish rivals. However, Scott Duncan, the manager of Manchester United and one-time Gers forward, said, 'Rangers would struggle to finish in the top half of the English Second Division.' He then insisted it had been a private conversation with a reporter, and not for publication.

Motherwell arrived at Ibrox and, in modern day terms, 'parked the bus'. Meik scored the only goal of the game with a beautifully taken shot that beat the keeper all ends up – especially after taking a slight deflection. Rangers deserved the points, it was said, 'because of Meiklejohn's masterly performance'. Another reporter said, 'On his form of the three games seen so far this season, Meiklejohn is surely Great Britain's best half-back. If you want to see the perfect football brain work in tandem with delightful execution, go to Ibrox and keep your eye on the Rangers captain all day!'

At the beginning of September 1934 the *Daily Record* ran a football clinic for youngsters, and one part was called 'How to Become a Demon in Defence'. Naturally it featured Meik, and he said, 'My general method of play is to keep a particularly close watch on the wing support, without forgetting that there is a "foe" near the touchline, and another in the centre.

'On the full-back in my rear I depend for intercepting the outside man, and on my centre-half I depend for an attack which goes past my other flank. We of the defence are all dependent more or less one upon the other, and the greater the feeling of dependence, the greater the team spirit, the sounder and stronger the understanding among us, the better equipped is the side to attack as well as defend. From goal to front rank there should be a sympathetic tie which makes for unity. And isn't unity strength?'

The Light Blues were scheduled to visit Kilmarnock on a Wednesday evening but the game was re-scheduled at the behest of the Kilmarnock Shopkeepers' Association, who asked that it be brought forward 24 hours as Wednesday was their half-day. 'When teams like Rangers visit town, we want to be open,' said a spokesman. Meik missed out due to injury but Rangers proved too powerful and won 3-1.

The first Old Firm match of the season was looming and Arthur Dixon had his hands full trying to get Meik and Archie McAuley ready for the Parkhead encounter. He had no luck with the skipper but a Smith goal – his ninth of the season – gave Rangers a 1-1 draw.

However Meiklejohn was with the Rangers party when they headed south for London to face Arsenal. The players looked resplendent in their new club ties, which were light blue in colour with a gold diagonal stripe. There were small circles on a blue background with RFC entwined. Like everything else associated with the club, they were first-class.

Jerry Dawson proved the star man at Highbury and 53,000 spectators saw the teams fight out a 1-1 draw. Cliff Bastin scored for Arsenal and Bob McPhail returned the favour. Dr Marshall played a grand game for the Londoners, and afterwards, chairman Sir Samuel Hill Wood said, 'To realise what London thought of Rangers, you had only to look at the crowd. Both Arsenal and Rangers represent what is best about football in both countries.' Each player was presented with a commemorative weather glass.

Just seven days after the Arsenal match, Manchester City arrived in Glasgow for a challenge fixture between the holders of the Scottish and English cups – an unofficial 'Battle of Britain'. Quick-thinking McAuley scored the only goal of the game after the City keeper had failed to hold a fierce Meiklejohn free kick. Afterwards the players dined at the St Enoch Station Hotel and the Rangers directors presented City players with a case of Sheffield cutlery, while the Rangers players were given chromium-plated reading lamps. The following day, both sets of players spent the day at Ayr races.

At the after-match bash, Meik said to City's Scottish player Matt Busby, 'Hard luck, losing in the final minute, I think the play deserved a draw.' Meik was being the perfect host but Busby, who would go on to manage Manchester United, replied, 'Wait until you come to Manchester, we'll knock the stuffing out of you!'

With the miserable month of October looming, Meik discovered a pastime that would keep him occupied during the dark winter nights – contact bridge. He signed for a team based in the Ibrox area and played in their opening fixture against the Rothley club, at their HQ in India Street, Glasgow. Rothley won by 540 points although Ibrox were to be encouraged by an excellent showing against a group of such experience.

But the Ibrox skipper wasn't about to swap football for the tabletop game and he led by example as Rangers beat Hibs 4-2 to extend their advantage at the top of the league. The talented half-back, who simply didn't score ordinary goals, opened the scoring with a real corker of a strike. Waiting on the penalty spot at a corner kick, he met the goalkeeper's fisted clearance perfectly and smashed the ball into the back of the net.

A couple of days later, a party of Rangers players and officials left Central Station bound for Manchester and the second part of their 'Battle of Britain' clash. The journey south was a merry one with players indulging in a card game and singing. Happiest of all, though, was goalkeeper George Jenkins, who was to meet his sweetheart in Manchester. She had travelled over from Canada just to see him.

However, Meik started to show signs of the flu, and was packed off to bed the moment the party arrived at the Midland Hotel. The skipper failed a fitness test on the morning of the match but was present, along with 25,000 others, to see Manchester City win 4-2 and become the first team to beat the Light Blues on English soil.

For their troubles the players were presented with gold watches, and Sam Cowan, the City captain, showed a touch more class than his team-mate Busby when he stood up and made a speech. The first thing he did was apologise for fouling Bob McPhail during the match. Cowan said, 'Bob beat me fair and square and I tripped him. I knew I had done wrong when my team-mates gave me a row. I apologise fully to Bob.' And McPhail accepted with trademark smile.

The Rangers players arrived back at Ibrox to discover they had a new team-mate, Mohamed Latif, an Egyptian international who was studying physical training at Jordanhill College. He had been sent to Scotland by the Egyptian government on a three-year course so that he could go back to North Africa and teach the subject in schools. The man the fans nicknamed 'Hammy' made his debut alongside Meiklejohn in the Rangers Alliance side against Hibs at Ibrox.

Rangers hit something of a little form dip and after losing the Glasgow Cup Final to Partick Thistle they were beaten 2-1 by Clyde in a top-of-the-table clash. Manager Struth, it was said, regretted not asking for a cancellation despite being without McPhail, Dawson, Smith and Simpson.

The following week the Light Blues, desperate to get back on track, travelled to Dumfries and edged Queen of the South 3-2 in a fiery encounter.

Meiklejohn was fuming with referee Willie Bell when he awarded the hosts an equalising goal midway through the first half, despite the ball being nowhere near over the line. Meik protested vehemently and was booked for his troubles. Bell produced his little black notebook and asked the Ibrox skipper his name. 'You know my name fine well,' Meik was reported to have said. 'Give me your name,' insisted Bell, and back it went to and fro until Meiklejohn relented and told the referee his name.

St Johnstone topped the table at the beginning of November, three points ahead of the Light Blues – with the sides due to clash at Ibrox. The match was played amid a thick blanket of fog but Gillick had no problems finding the route to goal and scored twice. Fellow young gun Venters chipped in with another and Rangers won 3-1.

At one point in the match Meik lost possession and a team-mate cried out 'Hoi, Meik, get it over here,' which prompted a reporter to say, 'What a brave lad, not many players would dare to "coach" the Rangers captain!'

Fourteen years after leaving Raith Rovers to join Rangers in a £250 deal, Sandy Archibald decided to depart Ibrox and return to his native Kirkcaldy. He sold his house in Mosspark and moved to the Kingdom – and 24 hours after joining as a player, he was appointed manager at Stark's Park.

So how do you replace such a stalwart as Sandy? With an ice hockey player, of course. That was the unlikely scenario when Struth confirmed his interest in Scottish international goaltender 'Scotty' Milne.

The Glasgow-born Canadian travelled from North America to Scotland in a bid to win a contract – at either ice hockey or soccer. The former Prince Albert Mintos footballer was predominantly an ice hockey player, but had recently earned something of a reputation in Canada as a first-rate goalkeeper. He was training at Ibrox and Rangers gave him a run-out in their Alliance team. In the end, Milne was signed by Glasgow University's ice hockey team and was capped for the Scots against England.

Just a week after the departure of Archibald, Rangers striker Jamie Fleming left for Ayr United. He had signed nine years previous from St Johnstone and in 291 games had scored a staggering 228 goals. Two stalwarts departing in the space of seven days in some ways heralded the end of an era. Meiklejohn was now the longest-serving player at the club.

But he led them back to the top of the league with a sterling performance against Albion Rovers in which Smith notched a hat-trick in a 5-1 win.

Later that week, though, the victory was overshadowed by the sad news that Rangers chairman Ex-Bailie Duncan Graham had passed away. The club postponed their annual dance as a mark of respect to the man who had joined the board in 1917. Deadly Jimmy Smith made it eight goals in three games when he paid his own tribute to Graham by firing a hat-trick against Queen's Park at Hampden.

Russell Moreland quit as manager of Third Lanark and Meiklejohn was immediately linked with the post but distanced himself from the job, insisting that he wasn't interested. When Rangers lost 4-1 to Hearts at Tynecastle, at the beginning of December, Princes Street newsvendors were screaming, 'Read all about the title collapse of the Rangers!' But the Light Blues were still one point ahead of Hamilton with a game in hand.

Meik wasn't feeling the pressure, though, and was in good form when he presided at the Glasgow Inverness-shire Shinty Club's concert in the Highlander's Institute. He had tried to trace his ancestors but the furthest north he could get was Fife. He said, 'That's good enough for me. Most of the wise people in Glasgow come from Fife! Sport is bringing the nation together.' The concert was a great success.

Perhaps there was something in the Edinburgh newsvendors' headlines as Rangers suffered an almost-unheard-of second defeat in a row. Kilmarnock came to Ibrox and inflicted the first loss on the Light Blues at their home ground for more than three years, but Rangers responded in the best possible manner by thrashing Dunfermline 8-1. Goal machine Smith scored four times while Meik was also on target, but sadly he suffered an injury in the next home game, against Motherwell, and was out of the Ne'erday Old Firm fixture at Ibrox. Some 83,000 were present to see an incredible match in which Rangers eventually gained the upper hand. Venters and Gillick scored in a 2-1 win and after the game, former player James Bowie was named as the club's new chairman.

January proved a pivotal month in the race for the title as Rangers won four games in a row to send them four points clear of Celtic, and with a game to spare. Meiklejohn missed all four encounters through injury but after a 2-1 win at Easter Road, the *Daily Record*'s 'Waverley' said, 'I give the title to Rangers. The only way they can lose it is if every player at Ibrox falls and breaks their leg!'

Meiklejohn made his return on Wednesday 6 February in a Second XI Cup tie between Hearts and Hibs at Tynecastle – in a scouting capacity. He accompanied Struth and the new chairman in a watching brief for new players. But he was back doing what he did best when Rangers hosted Airdrie. Described as 'the best man on the park', he played his part in a fine 3-1 win. Sadly, though, four days later he was attending the funeral of club legend Tom Vallance.

Rangers were strolling to another title but received a wake-up call at Falkirk when the Bairns looked likely to upset the applecart – before Meik took control of a 'shaky defence' and led his team to a 3-0 win. His inch-perfect pass to Venters created the second goal. The Light Blues now required seven points from seven games to win the championship. At the start of the match, both teams had run out on to the pitch sporting identical strips, so the referee made Rangers change to a white kit.

The following Saturday, Rangers turned in a brilliant performance to beat Motherwell 4-1 at Fir Park in the Scottish Cup quarter-finals. You would have had to have felt for Smith because despite scoring all four goals, Meik was named man of the match. 'Waverley' said, 'Davie Meiklejohn? Don't tell me he is an old man. He's a sprightly youngster with the craft of the experienced, and the brains of a master. I've heard it rumoured that Meik is finished with representative football. If I were a selector I'd place a pistol at the back of his neck and drive him to Hampden!

'Rangers fans have been very pessimistic recently, saying Meiklejohn must be dropped, McPhail has hit the slide – not a moan at Ibrox now, however. Meik and McPhail were the best on the park – by a distance.'

Wins over Queen of the South and Clyde followed – as did golf at Turnberry – and even a 2-0 loss at St Johnstone couldn't dampen the spirits. There were calls for Rangers' 'veteran' skipper to be included in the team to face England and 'Waverley' stated his case, saying, 'Davie is an experienced tactician and the selectors may be inclined to choose him and make him captain. I'd love to see the Rangers man get this great honour again, because if ever a man earned the applause of the public for his service to his country, and his loyalty to his first and only senior club, it is Davie. But I know that he, although thoroughly loyal, will not be disappointed if another gets the position.'

Before the team was announced, almost 103,000 turned up at Hampden for a Scottish Cup semi-final against Hearts. Torry Gillick got the Rangers goal in a 1-1 draw. Forty-eight hours later the selectors announced their team and there was no place for the Rangers skipper, but he had something else to cheer when Hamilton defeated Hearts 2-0 – a result that meant Rangers were champions once more.

In the replayed tie against Hearts, Meiklejohn suffered a thigh injury while making a last-gasp tackle on Hearts dangerman Tommy Walker. He was off the park for seven minutes and when he returned, with his leg heavily bandaged, he was moved out to the right wing. There he was again in the wars, and took another knock that forced him off on 73 minutes. Goals from McPhail and Main gave Rangers a 2-0 win and Meik was first on the park at the end of the game to shake the hands of every Hearts player.

After the match, Meiklejohn said of his injury, 'It was a strained muscle on my left leg above and behind the knee. I had to make a desperate tackle on Tommy Walker, and got the ball, but Tommy seemed to pull my leg with him. It was no fault of his – just a pure accident. I know Tommy would not hurt a fly.

'It was awful having to leave the boys to fight it out, but when I came back on I was just in time to see the second goal being scored, and it was one of the most beautiful bits of play in the match.

'Before kick-off I was also struggling with injury and Mr Struth said to me, "Shouldn't you stand down?" I told him I was playing in this match if I never played in another.'

Just ten days after Meik was left out of the Scotland team to face England, the selectors named their 17-man squad to take part in a close-season tour of Canada and the US and the Ranger was asked to be captain. He was unable to confirm his attendance, though, as it was felt that the double injury suffered in the match against Hearts could mean surgery after the season.

The week before the cup final, Meiklejohn was absent from the side that won 3-1 at Pittodrie – and his Hampden spot was anything but a certainty. Jamie Kennedy was standing by to fill his place. The manager gave his captain every chance to make the final but the duo were forced to admit defeat 24 hours before the big day and, as it transpired, Kennedy played the game of his life as Rangers beat Hamilton 2-1 to lift the famous old trophy in front of 87,000 spectators. Once again, Smith was the hero with both goals. Meiklejohn also missed the last three league games as Rangers won the title by three points.

He was present though at a night to honour his international team-mate Tommy Walker, who was handed a writing bureau and Westminster chiming clock for his services to football. The presentation was made at the Institute Hall of Livingston by Rector Thomas Cant of Tommy's old school, Bathgate High. George Brown of Rangers was also present.

But the Light Blues star proved his fitness ahead of Scotland's North American tour, and the players received a tumultuous welcome in New York before being driven to see the fabulous Madison Square Garden – but that's another story.

22

On tour with Scotland

A S SCOTLAND trainer Arthur Dixon was putting his players through their paces at the Yankee Stadium, home of the famous New York baseball team, a posse of journalists was waiting to talk to the famous Davie Meiklejohn. 'We know all about you, Davie,' said one reporter. In fact, one question on their lips concerned news back home that Meik was being linked with the vacant manager's position at Hearts. 'First I've heard of it,' was his polite reply.

The opening match of the tour took place in Philadelphia, against a German-American Select, and 9,000 were present. The pitch was far from perfect but the crowd were still entertained by an impressive display from the tourists. In fact, so excited did they become that they encroached far enough on to the park that they interfered with play.

But the experience for the players was by no means unpleasant and goals by Aberdeen's Willie Mills, who scored twice, and Hughie Gallacher, were enough to help register a 3-0 win. Meiklejohn, who was captain, 'directed operations' and 'hit the high spots', according to reports.

The party's impressions of Philadelphia had been favourable and on their arrival in the city, a police escort had been required to get them to their hotel as many hundreds of expat supporters turned out to greet them. Nothing stood in the way of police sirens and traffic ground to a halt. Once rested, a fleet of cars arrived at the hotel to take them to the First German Club where a reception and dance was held in their honour. A tartan-regaled band from the Philadelphia Transport Club piped the players into the exclusive club.

The party didn't have too long to spend in Philly as their next match took place the following night in New York against an American XI. On arrival in the Big Apple the players were again met by hundreds of passionate football supporters, waving an array of imaginative flags and banners. One conveyed a welcome from the Bronx football team while another party in a motor car followed the official Scotland charabanc and treated them to a stirring rendition of the Rangers anthem 'Follow Follow'.

On their first night in New York the players were guests of honour at one of the most important baseball matches of the season, between the New York Giants and St Louis, where two of the greatest pitchers in the history of the sport, the brothers Dizzy and Daffy Dean, were in action.

Scotland's game was played on the Polo Ground and 32,000 saw Dally Duncan score a hat-trick in a 5-1 victory. Although inclined to shoot wildly any time they got near the Scottish goal it was the Yanks who scored first in the 17th minute. Duncan and Mills soon had Scotland in front and when Tommy Walker was fouled inside the box on the stroke of half-time, the responsibility fell on the shoulders of Meiklejohn. He scored with a perfectly placed shot but the referee insisted he hadn't blown his whistle and made him take it again. The outcome was the same and the Scots led 3-1 at the break. Two second-half goals followed and Scotland could have scored at will, but decided to 'play the game'.

After the match, the players and officials were entertained to dinner at the Cornell Club by the Sportsman Brotherhood, a body that undertook the welcoming and entertaining of visiting organisations connected with sport of any type.

Tears were shed at the harbour in New York as the team prepared to set sail for Toronto. Hundreds of exiled Scots turned out to give the team a wonderful send-off. Meik was shaken warmly by the hand of an old Govan man who asked all about the old place. He said, 'We felt lumps in our throats as well. What it will be like in Toronto, goodness only knows. "Where's Tommy Walker?" has been a universally asked question. He is popular with the girls and if he gets home without taking a wife he will be lucky!'

With that the players boarded the vessel and set sail for Canada, and a trip to Niagara Falls, before the serious business of the football. After a bout of sightseeing they were given a civic reception at City Hall by mayor James Simpson. It was an incredible scene with the players seated in a semi-circle in the front row of the chamber, and after the speeches they filed past the mayor, who shook them all warmly by the hand.

Procession was then formed to the Cenotaph, which stands outside the City Chambers. Policemen had to clear a path through the huge crowd. After a short service the mayor accepted the wreath and asked James Fleming, president of the SFA, to lay it at the Cenotaph.

Meiklejohn sat out the match at Soldiers' Field as Scotland laboured slightly in the first half. Rangers winger Bobby Main, who had been a star turn in the first two matches, picked up an injury and thus the service into the box was somewhat limited. Willie Miller, of Partick Thistle, grabbed a double, and with Gallacher scoring the other Scotland still ran out worthy winners in front of 10,000.

A trip to Kitchener was next on the agenda and the Scots were seen at their very best as they hammered a rather bewildered Western Ontario 9-1. Mills and Davie Wilson, of Hamilton, notched hat-tricks as the side made it four out of four. The tourists returned to the United States for a match in Chicago against Illinois. Meik was again missing but goals from Mills (two) and Duncan secured a 3-0 win.

It was then back to Canada to face a Calgary FA XI and the Scots – especially Hughie Gallacher – were in dazzling form. The locals were mauled 9-1 with Gallacher helping himself to five, and the 5,000 spectators who paid their admission money were left purring at the skills on show. Skipper Meiklejohn occupied the rather unusual left half-back berth but was praised for his 'prompting' which unleashed myriad opportunities for the front players. Six games, six wins and 32 goals scored – the locals sure were getting value for money.

The next stop on the Canadian map was a trek that took the team farthest west, to Vancouver, where once again the tourists were treated like kings. The Premier of British Columbia greeted the Scots and two functions were arranged in their honour – a luncheon given by the city, and an evening banquet hosted by the governor of the province.

The match was played at Victoria, on Vancouver Island, which was reached by steam boat. Sailing down the Strait of Georgia and Hope Strait between numerous small islands certainly beat travelling from Glasgow to Edinburgh for a match at Tynecastle or Easter Road, and the day was complete when Meik was told he would be occupying his usual right-half position. The impressive Scots hit four first-half goals and while just one followed after the break, the contest was by then over. The spectators cheered the visitors at the end of the game, no doubt in appreciation of their 'thorough soccer education'.

The team remained in Vancouver for their next match, the toughest of the tour so far, against a team from a city known as 'the home of Canadian soccer'. Regardless of reputation the Scots dominated and missed a host of first-half opportunities thanks, mainly, to the brilliance of the Vancouver goalkeeper.

After the break, Meik almost snapped the post with a rocket shot but the breakthrough came five minutes before the end when Main whipped in a terrific cross and Gallacher pounced to nod home. After the game the Scots declared the Vancouver team – all Canadian-born – the pick of the bunch so far.

The next match was a somewhat strange affair. Winnipeg provided the opposition and scored twice but the Scots scored almost at will, deciding, however, that they would stop at seven. Part of the game was played under floodlighting which provided the referee and his linesmen with a real problem. The lighting was sub-standard and the match official had issues with 'shadows' and several times blew for infringements when none had taken place.

The Prime Minister of Manitoba kicked the game off in front of 5,000 and the tourists were soon into 'Wembley Wizards' mode. Mills, Miller and Gallacher posted doubles with Walker scoring a single. The finest move of the game was a Gallacher run from virtually his own penalty area when he tricked several players before slotting home for a quite sensational strike.

The next match, in Toronto against Eastern Canada, was another one-sided affair and the 6-0 scoreline hardly reflected the Scots' superiority. Tommy Walker was lauded as the game's outstanding turn and was the subject of a banner proclaiming him 'the world's greatest player', which raised a smile from the Hearts star.

It was back to the United States for the final game of what had been a rather satisfying tour. The School Stadium, in Newark, New Jersey, was the scene for a lively game in which the hosts were desperate to end the winning run of the Scots. Two penalty kicks were awarded and several of the home side were cautioned as the All Star Americans played a rough match, largely encouraged by the majority of the 8,000 crowd.

The hosts took the lead but when Gallacher was rather crudely brought down in the box, centre-half Meiklejohn rammed home the penalty kick. Scotland then produced some of their best football of the tour and goals by Duncan, Gallacher and Mills confirmed their superiority. Meanwhile, the Americans continued to resort to tough challenges – when they could get near their opponents.

By and large the American leg of the tour had been a great success, and the Scots had given their exiled patriots something to cheer. In truth, however, the football shown by the locals had been of a generally poor standard and it's doubtful if there was a real standout opposition player who could have held his own in the Scottish League.

The hospitality shown by both the Canadians and Americans had been first-class and, for that, the weary tourists were eternally grateful – but they weren't finished yet.

Journalist Dan Parker, of the *New York Mirror*, was rather sceptical about the tour's success. He wrote, 'I announce on behalf of the United States that the Scots can have their style of football, and we'll stick to ours. Soccer football at its best was played on the Polo Grounds by the all-star team from Scotland. It panicked 25,000 Scotsmen who turned out for the game, but its effect on the American spectators was that of a glass of water on New Year's morning – it left them cold.

'Soccer is ideally suited to the Scottish temperament. It calls for highly developed teamwork and individual skill of a high order. But it does not appeal to American taste because it isn't spectacular, and doesn't furnish enough opportunity for individual initiative.

'Nor is there enough variety in the game to appeal to American fancy.'

The plump lady may have hummed her tunes in the US, but the team trekked back to Canada to play the final matches of the tour. First up was yet another one-sided match, this time in Hamilton, Ontario, where the Scots thumped a representative side 10-1. After being criticised for 'letting up in front of goal' in previous games the Scots let rip, although they did take their collective foot off the gas before reaching total humiliation.

The crowd wanted goals, not necessarily by the Scots though, and they got them. Meiklejohn scored twice, one of them a contender for goal of the tour, a real 'zoomer' from all of 30 yards, which the home keeper first saw when he was stooping to pick the ball out the net. Walker hit a delightful hat-trick and the others were shared around.

The following night, the players took part in the final game of the tour before heading home to Scotland on board the *Duchess of Richmond*. But before the action came an SOS from the family of Meiklejohn who asked why they hadn't received any correspondence from the skipper, a man normally with a penchant for writing home. They had written plenty of letters, but none had been received by Meik. It was a mystery, but he would soon be home to regale the family with tales of soccer on the other side of the Atlantic.

Before playing their final game, in Winnipeg, the party motored some 40 miles north to Banff where it was discovered that lunch hadn't been picked up at the hotel before leaving. Never mind, the players called in at a little shop on the way and cleared the shelves of sandwiches and pop before stopping at the roadside for an impromptu picnic.

Then they went on to their destination where they met a group of monks who were only too happy to have their photographs taken, although not with Bobby Main, who was smoking. The team charabanc then stopped to allow the players to engage in a sulphur bath, apparently the thing to do in these parts.

A great reception awaited the players in Winnipeg, surely the most 'Scottish' town in all of Canada. They were waited on hand and foot and treated like royalty. The players were given the freedom of the city before playing at Carruthers Park in front of 5,000 spectators, which meant the Scots had attracted 100,000 people to watch them play football throughout Canada and the USA.

Floodlights were switched on near the end of the game but still left both goal areas in total darkness. It seemed that the Canadians had yet to master the art of how to properly use these modern contraptions. Regardless, Quebec Province were beaten 3-0 thanks mainly to a Walker double, which meant the team had played 13 matches and won the lot.

The squad then took to the high seas for the week-long journey home. Amid a deluge of cheers and tears they admitted to looking forward to the rest while at sea, due to the high volume of matches and travelling undertaken during their four weeks in North America. For one match alone they had travelled more than 1,000 miles, which prompted Grangemouth-based Partick Thistle star Willie Miller to say, 'From now on, I think I'll just walk to work in the morning!'

As the good ship *Duchess of Richmond* began its homeward journey, a telegram from the Premier of Canada, Mr Bennett, was winging its way to the SFA headquarters at Carlton Place in Glasgow. It stated, 'May I offer my congratulations to all upon the good sportsmanship and fine display of teamwork which characterised your stay in Canada. So many permanent friendships were created in the Dominion and I hope the visit can be repeated.'

23

Old Firm battle for supremacy

AS USUAL the Rangers players were spread far and wide during the close-season. Meik had just returned from a successful tour of the US and Canada with the Scotland team and was keen for a game of golf so off he went to St Andrews, where he passed on tales of his North American exploits to friends.

Jimmy Smith, on the other hand, headed for North Berwick and a caravan holiday. There, he watched an entertainment show at The Pavilion. He saw Tom Cable and Dot Carr indulge in a juggling act and when the former dropped a plate, Smith caught it quick as a flash. Cable quipped, 'I see you aren't just content with cups – you want the plates too!' The gag brought the house down and was a measure of how widespread fame was for the Ibrox players.

Early-season plans to introduce two referees at Scottish League matches was knocked on the head, which bothered Meiklejohn not a jot as he teamed up with old colleague George Henderson for a round on the Old Course. The pair had been in scintillating form but ran up against a duo just too hot to handle. A challenge had been arranged against professional golfing brothers John and Watson Gemmell, of West Kilbride, and the siblings were so much on top that even taking it to the 15th green was a real coup for the footballers. Watson finished with a round of 73 – which was championship form.

And Meik was still searching for success on the Fife fairways the following week when he teamed up with Old Course starter Jamie Alexander to play Tommy Muirhead and Alec MacBeaty, of Raith Rovers. The latter won a close game 2&1 with the winning combination posting a best ball of 72.

When the players turned up for training at the end of July – with Meik given an extra day due to his American exploits – one look at the car park by *Daily Record* correspondent 'Waverley' left him aghast. He said, 'The very thought of the players owning their own cars a few years ago would have caused howls of derision, but that's the way of it at the Rangers now!'

In those days players received what were termed 'close-season wages', which was a percentage of their actual salary but still sufficient to allow them a comfy life. Oh, and the car of choice, the Hillman Minx, was available for a cool £159 – or £175 for the deluxe model.

The normal curtain-raiser to the season, the Ibrox Sports, produced another Rangers success in the five-a-sides. Meik was joined by Brown, Venters, Smith and Gillick. Two goals by Smith in an Old Firm final was enough to see off the threat from Celtic but the fall-out from the match prompted calls for an official enquiry.

A crowd of 50,000 looked on as ugly scenes erupted – on the pitch. During a struggle for possession two players, one from each side, resorted to the sort of behaviour normally reserved for street corners. The players had to be separated but seconds later two others started to use brawn rather than brain and began kicking each other. Referee Mungo Hutton did all he could to keep them apart but required the assistance of those not involved in the brawling to help maintain order.

The referee – Scotland's number one at the time – submitted a written report on the matter and bosses at the SFA immediately promised an internal inquiry. Meanwhile, the victorious Rangers players were presented with silver tea sets for winning the competition. Storm in a tea cup?

Rather astonishingly, this very situation was all but repeated a few days later when Celtic held their sports day. Significantly, Rangers were represented by five completely different players – Jenkins, Winning, Fiddes, McAuley and Kinnear, effectively a reserve side – but they reached the final where they once again met Celtic. The hosts won the match but a ludicrous display of shoulder charging between McDonald, of Celtic, and Archie McAuley ensued when McGonagle, the home keeper, was hurt making a save. The players went at it hammer and tongs and only intervention by others prevented a full-blown 'rammy' taking place.

The following day in the *Daily Record*, 'Waverley' called for referees to stop shirking their responsibilities and to start sending players off. The scenes at both sports days had instigated a flood of letters to the paper calling for action to be taken against those who perpetrated the trouble.

Meiklejohn missed the first few games of the season proper due to injury but took his bow in a reserve league match against Galston at Ibrox. The Light Blues second string won 8-0 with four of the goals coming from trialist David Wallace, who played for Ayrshire junior side Kilwinning Rangers.

Meiklejohn's return to the first team was not without incident. After 20 hectic minutes of the match against Dundee at Ibrox the Light Blues found themselves 3-0 down. On the half-hour mark, Meik fired home a penalty and three further goals secured the win.

Ten goals for and just one against in their next two games, against St Johnstone and Partick Thistle, got the Gers back on track for their trip to Sheffield to face English FA Cup holders Sheffield Wednesday at Hillsborough. The game ended in a hard-fought 1-1 draw but there were handshakes all round at the end, before both sets of players enjoyed a post-match meal at a swanky hotel.

A Sheffield reporter said, 'Our centre-backs should study the technique of David Meiklejohn when he is heading the ball. Some of them just let the ball hit off their brow, but David is the best in the country at doing it properly.'

On the same afternoon, 250 miles north of Sheffield, the SFA met to discuss the shameful scenes during the five-a-side final between the Old Firm at the Rangers Sports Day but decided no further action need be taken. It was a real let-off for both clubs, who must have feared the worst, although others described it as a 'whitewash'.

Rangers' Egyptian star Mohamed Latif made his top-team debut in a league match at Easter Road against bottom side Hibs but failed to make any impression, being described in the papers as 'industrious but aimless'. The following midweek, Rangers beat Wednesday 2-0 in their return challenge match.

Next up was an Old Firm clash at Ibrox, the first time the sides had met since their infamous double-barrelled fives debacle. This time, though, the players were on their best behaviour – well, most of them – and 72,000 saw Celtic win 2-1.

With Rangers one up, Celtic keeper Joe Kennaway fouled Meiklejohn in the box. But Kennaway protested so long and loud that when the kick was eventually taken the Ibrox skipper saw his effort saved by the big keeper, who was booked for his behaviour. Five minutes later at a Rangers corner Kennaway tried to punch Meik, who somehow managed to dodge his right hook. The incident was witnessed by referee Hutton who, quite incredibly, failed to take any action against the Canadian.

The following midweek, Meik added to his collection of clocks when Rangers hosted Arsenal in a glamour challenge match at Ibrox. A crowd of 25,000 watched an excellent match, which ended 2-2, and afterwards the clubs retired to the St Enoch Hotel for dinner, where Rangers spoke highly of the English club. Rangers presented the Arsenal players with cutlery and in return they received large timepieces.

Despite being hampered by a lengthy injury list, the friendly match kick-started an unbeaten run that was to last two months. Rangers won 2-0 at Motherwell and Meik was described as 'tired' by the press. The report added, 'Meiklejohn can't handle too many games these days, but more than gets past by using his brain rather than his legs.'

The veteran half-back was rapidly approaching his 35th birthday and Struth tried to use his talents as sparingly as possible, although with the squad down to the bare bones he was needed more than ever, and never let the side down. Just 48 hours after the Fir Park encounter, Meik scored in a Glasgow Cup semi-final win over Clyde. He set the Light Blues on the road to victory and Gillick added a second.

There was no let-up as the games arrived thick and fast. Dunfermline were next up and it would have been an ideal opportunity to let Meiklejohn rest his weary legs, but with Jimmy Simpson and George Brown on international duty Meik's services were required. He had to rally his troops as Rangers were two down after just 15 minutes.

Once the captain had sounded the bugle, though, there was only going to be one winner, and Rangers scored six times without further reply.

Meik added to his incredible medal haul when the injury-hit Ibrox side beat Celtic 2-0 at Hampden in the final of the Glasgow Cup, in front of 48,000. The following Saturday, though, Rangers dropped a point at home to Hearts. George Brown scored for the Gers and they looked like cruising to victory, but key men Gillick and Smith were injured and Rangers were forced to see out the game with just nine players.

Clyde were then put to the sword despite the Light Blues' injury list reaching epidemic proportions. Venters and Drysdale scored two each as the club continued to pick up points against all the odds. At the start of November, Rangers had somehow managed to remain in the top three and were four points behind leaders Aberdeen but with a game in hand.

Meik took time out from his hectic schedule to appear on a radio programme to give advice to budding young players. He told boys how important it was to learn how to kick with both feet, as well as the value of being able to head a ball accurately. 'Heading a ball looks easy,' he said, 'but it isn't. Let me tell you, though, that practice makes perfect!'

A record league attendance of 33,578 converged on Pittodrie for the big first versus third clash and it was the Dons who came out on top by a single goal. Rangers suffered more injury heartbreak as Dawson and McPhail – who had just returned after a spell on the sidelines – were both badly injured after just 20 minutes. There was a hue and cry made after the match for the introduction of substitutes but the Scottish League were having none of it. It was said that the loss of injured players during a match was spoiling the entertainment for spectators.

Meiklejohn recharged the batteries by taking to the fairways of Dundonald with manager Struth before rushing back to Glasgow for the club's annual dance at the Grosvenor, where one can imagine there was more hobbling than dancing going on.

But the Light Blues battled on regardless and ground out wins over Kilmarnock and St Johnstone – they weren't giving up their title without a fight. The day after the St Johnstone match, Meik attended a 'Sportsmen's Own' with a difference – ladies were allowed to attend, and they would hear the Rangers captain read the lesson before referee W.G. Holborn sang the solo.

There was some bad news for Gers fans just a fortnight before Christmas when Torry Gillick signed for Everton. After travelling to Merseyside to sign his contract, he headed back up the road but was involved in a nasty car crash near his home town of Coatbridge. He hit a patch of ice and lost control of his vehicle. The car was written off and Gillick cut his hands on the broken glass but was otherwise unhurt. He was due to be married on Christmas Day but cancelled the wedding due to the transfer. The 19-year-old had spent just two years at Ibrox.

Rangers moved to plug the gap by snapping up Reid from Glenafton Athletic. A joiner from Mauchline, he was allowed to stay with the Glens while they were still in the Scottish Junior Cup. Of his transfer, he said, 'I would give my right arm to play for the Rangers!'

The Ibrox side were eight points behind Aberdeen in the race for the league championship and knew that a winning run over the Christmas and New Year period was imperative. It was the only way they would be assured of remaining in the hunt until the spring.

A 5-1 win over Albion Rovers was a decent starting point and winger Bobby Main grabbed his first hat-trick for the club. For his second goal, Main charged the goalkeeper over the line, which the press described as 'cheeky'. A 0-0 draw at Arbroath the following week was a blow, especially as Struth had pushed Meiklejohn forward in desperation. There was no shortage of goals in their next game, though, as Smith hit five in a 6-1 thumping of Ayr United.

A stormy Old Firm encounter on New Year's Day saw the Light Blues roar back from a 3-1 deficit to win 4-3. Was this D-Day? Sadly, violence erupted on the terracing when Smith clashed with Celtic goalkeeper Foley, after both had gone for a loose ball. McGonagle decided Smith's challenge was unfair and challenged the Rangers centre. Fighting broke out all over the ground and bottles were hurled through the air. Several spectators, including a young boy, were badly hurt in the melee. Others were crushed when they tried to escape the trouble. Fans spilled over on to the track and seven people were taken to hospital when a barricade near the covered enclosure gave way. Dozens more were treated on the spot for the effects of shock and fainting.

On the pitch, Meiklejohn was outstanding but was rested for the match with Partick Thistle on 2 January. Two from Smith and a McPhail goal moved Rangers into second spot, two points behind Aberdeen but with a game in hand. Rangers completed the busy holiday period with a 3-0 win at Dundee before heading for Troon, and a well-deserved game of golf.

A trip to Airdrie followed and a double from Venters put another two points on the board but a morning newspaper report stated, 'Meiklejohn's craft was visible in every move and his forceful play in the latter stages was largely responsible for the victory.'

When King George died in the middle of January a debate raged as to whether or not the Scottish Cup card should go ahead. It was decided to play the fixtures but that each ground would fly their flags at half-mast and players would wear black armbands. The Govan Burgh Band were primed to play 'appropriate' music during the tie with East Fife at Ibrox and, when the players had taken to the field, the crowd would be invited to sing 'Abide With Me' and 'God Save the King'. As it happened, the game was cancelled due to severe frost.

Celtic had been due to face Berwick Rangers away from home but Parkhead boss Willie Maley travelled to the Borders town for talks with club bosses and, immediately afterwards, Berwick withdrew from the competition. It transpired that Maley had offered Berwick £100 and a challenge match at Celtic Park later in the season – all expenses paid.

The day after Rangers beat East Fife 3-1 in their re-arranged tie, Meik was at Kelso Park in Yoker to give the young players of Victoria Park Amateurs some tips on the game and a talk aimed at improving their skills. The visit was scheduled to last for 30 minutes but two hours later, the Rangers and Scotland star was still there. He said, 'I enjoyed myself as much as the youngsters. They were about the finest bunch of boys I have ever had the pleasure of addressing.'

On the eve of Rangers' next Scottish Cup tie, Struth was installed as a Justice of the Peace and his players added to the celebrations by beating Albion Rovers 3-1 at Cliftonhill. However, the match was played on a 'skating rink' and the Light Blues emerged anything but unscathed from a dangerous encounter. Centre-back Jimmy Simpson was the first casualty of the afternoon when, with just 60 seconds on the clock, he was the meat in a Rovers sandwich and fell heavily on his face, splitting the bridge of his nose on the rock-hard surface. Meiklejohn, who had run towards him to accept the header, slipped and fell on his back, and he too crashed the back of his head off the surface. A fractured skull could so easily have been the outcome but, instead, Meik went on to turn in an excellent display at centre-half.

James Fiddes slotted in beside the skipper and, it was said, came on a ton through playing next to the old master. 'What a wonderful general is Davie Meiklejohn,' said 'Waverley', 'and one who shows the troops how to go about the job by personal example. His almost every movement, his changing of tactics, is right up to the minute, and fits in perfectly with the changing fortunes of the game.'

Rangers were on the verge of a fantastic run and Fiddes bagged a hat-trick as Dunfermline were mauled 6-2. Next up were St Mirren in the third round of the Scottish Cup and goals by McPhail and Smith were enough to take Rangers through. Those who couldn't make the game could see the highlights that night in a string of Glasgow picture halls.

Fiddes scored another couple as Third Lanark were brushed aside and the Light Blues moved menacingly close to Celtic at the top of the league. Two points behind but with a game in hand was the state of play. A Scottish Cup quarter-final trip north was next on the fixture list as Aberdeen stood in the way of Rangers and yet another semi-final appearance. The Rangers players walked from the train station in Aberdeen to the ground to stretch their legs.

The Pittodrie gates were closed fully 20 minutes before kick-off as more than 41,000 crammed into the stadium. The majority of the crowd were sporting blue and white and they belted out the national anthem with gusto as the teams took to the field. With the game goalless, Rangers were awarded a penalty kick. Up stepped a confident Meik but the keeper saved his effort and it took a Turnbull goal to put Rangers through.

As soon as the full-time whistle blew the Light Blue fans invaded the field and carried their favourites shoulder high to the dressing rooms, but the local police overreacted and mounted officers charged the supporters. Thankfully, though, no one was hurt.

Friday 13 March was anything but unlucky for a 16-year-old kid from Winchburgh as Rangers announced they were keeping tabs on young Willie Thornton. He had played two trial matches and scored twice.

Rangers made it 15 games unbeaten when they beat Clyde, Hibs and Queen's Park within the space of eight days. Struth used Meiklejohn sparingly, handing him a couple of 'half-holidays' for the games in which he believed he could get by without his skipper. But Celtic kept on winning too, and by the end of March the Gers still trailed by two points – albeit with a game in hand – while Aberdeen were struggling to stay in contention.

Next up was a Scottish Cup semi-final with Clyde at Hampden, and a stunning lob from Meik just two minutes into the game put Rangers ahead, although the captain was injured a mere 120 seconds later. He soldiered on, though, as did Main, Turnbull and Simpson, who also picked up knocks, and the Light Blues ran out 3-0 victors.

Meik was rested for the visit of Queen of the South and the team narrowly scraped by but the next match, at Hamilton, proved a tactical disaster for the manager, who decided to play centre-forward Jimmy Smith on the left wing and wideman James Drysdale through the middle. Rangers lost 1-0, their first defeat in 21 games, and by the time Struth changed it round it was too late. Celtic won 2-0 at Arbroath to move four points clear of Rangers – with just three games left to play. Rangers still had a game in hand but Celtic needed only two wins to secure the title.

Forty-eight hours after the debacle of Hamilton, the Light Blues travelled to Cathkin Park to face Third Lanark and it turned out to be a real battle both on and off the pitch. Two players were ordered off and three booked – a highly unusual stat for the 1930s – and the bad blood spilled over on to the terraces, where many arrests were made as fans fought for almost the entire second half.

After the game, Howe of Thirds lodged a protest with the referee about the colour of the language used towards him by one of the Rangers players. The Scottish League promised to look into the matter.

Five days after the 'Battle of Cathkin', the teams met again just around the corner at Hampden. The occasion was the Scottish Cup Final and 88,859 spectators filed into the national stadium where thankfully the bad blood from the previous Monday was conspicuous by its absence. The only goal of the game arrived when Meik played a great ball to McPhail, who outmuscled a Thirds defender and shot home. Meiklejohn almost scored direct from a corner but placed just a wee bit too much spin on the ball and it missed the target by inches.

With just six minutes remaining, Rangers keeper Jerry Dawson pulled off one of the best saves ever seen at Hampden when he dived full length to tip a Kennedy shot round the post. But the plaudits went, once again, to Meiklejohn, who, in the words of 'Waverley', 'was instrumental in everything Rangers did'.

But it would ultimately prove to be a bittersweet afternoon for the Light Blues as Celtic beat Ayr 6-0 to clinch their first championship in ten years.

With the season over, Meiklejohn and Struth were in action in the Fife village of Milnathort where they acted as linesmen in a charity game. The manager had grown up in the little village and was still as well known there as he was at Ibrox. Just days later, Meik signed on the dotted line for an 18th term at Ibrox – only three short of the longest-serving Ranger, Aleck Smith, a Light Blue for 21 years.

It was well known around the club that the skipper was keen to better Smith's record but the following season would prove an anti-climax for a Rangers great.

24

National pride

T HROUGHOUT a sparkling 17-year career at Ibrox, Meiklejohn won the princely sum of 15 full international caps. Contrast that to Mohamed Al-Deayea, the Saudi Arabian international who collected 178 between 1993 and 2006. And even Al-Deayea is lagging behind in the appearance stakes to Ahmed Hassan, the Egyptian attacking defender who had amassed 184 international appearances between 1995 and 2012.

Nowadays, though, there are regular international breaks built into the domestic season as well as a whole raft of World Cup qualifying games taking place constantly around the globe.

The first World Cup took place in 1930 – at the height of Meik's national popularity – but despite FIFA inviting every member country to participate at the finals in Uruguay, just 13 accepted. The home nations weren't members of the world governing body at that time although an invitation was sent out to England, who refused to participate.

The South American hosts were furious that no European teams had bothered to enter and it was only after FIFA stepped in that France, Belgium, Romania and Yugoslavia made the trip across the Atlantic.

By way of a protest, Uruguay refused to take part in Italy four years later. The four Home International sides were also absent, which was a great pity as it represented Meiklejohn's final shot at world glory. So British players of Meik's era were confined to the Home Internationals and the occasional friendly match but he maintained an excellent record against England, winning three and losing just one of his four clashes with the Auld Enemy.

In the twilight of his career, the close-season of 1935 to be exact, Meik was invited to captain a squad of Scottish footballers on a tour of Canada and the US. There was speculation, however, that following an injury-ravaged season he would have to go under the surgeon's knife for a small operation, but he was passed fit around a week before the trip and set sail along with the players for his third and final tour of North America.

David Meiklejohn's international record:

Home Internationals
4 February 1922 – Wales 2 Scotland 1
16 February 1924 – Wales 2 Scotland 0
14 February 1925 – *Scotland 3 Wales 1
28 February 1925 – *Northern Ireland 0 Scotland 3
4 April 1925 – Scotland 2 England 0
29 October 1927 – Wales 2 Scotland 2
25 February 1928 – Scotland 0 Northern Ireland 1
23 February 1929 – Northern Ireland 3 Scotland 7
13 April 1929 – Scotland 1 England 0
22 February 1930 – Scotland 3 Northern Ireland 1
5 April 1930 – England 5 Scotland 2
28 March 1931 – Scotland 2 England 0
19 September 1931 – Scotland 3 Northern Ireland 1
31 October 1931 – Wales 2 Scotland 3

International Challenge Match
29 November 1933 – *Scotland 2 Austria 2
*denotes scored in match

Scottish League caps:
26 October 1921 – Scottish League 3 Irish League 0
17 February 1923 – English League 2 Scottish League 1
15 March 1924 – Scottish League 1 English League 1
14 March 1925 – English League 4 Scottish League 3

7 November 1931 – Scottish League 4 English League 3
9 November 1932 – English League 0 Scottish League 3

Aside from taking his place on the 1935 tour of North America, Meiklejohn's penultimate appearance for his country came when he was named as reserve for the Scottish League team bound for Manchester to play their English counterparts. It was the first time the Rangers stalwart had been named as reserve and he admitted he was finally looking forward to travelling with the party with no pressure on, joking that he was set to make some 'easy money'.

The best laid plans, though…a few days later, Meik was called up to replace injured Hearts star Alec Massie and joined club-mates Sandy Archibald and Jamie Marshall on the right-hand side of the team. It was clear from the moment he replaced Massie that he was ready to write the headlines.

After the game, *Daily Record* reporter 'Waverley' said, 'Davie Meiklejohn is perhaps not quite the stalwart he was, but if he lacks anything in this department it is made up for in craft. Davie was our master man. He shepherded his fellow half backs through the game and his positioning was everything. He anticipated Johnston of Everton's every move and never put a foot wrong. The influence he has on his colleagues is immeasurable. It isn't too much to say that we won because we had a Meiklejohn, and England lost because they didn't.'

Meiklejohn and Archibald combined to set up Charley Napier of Celtic for the first goal and the Scots ran out 3-0 winners, their first success on English soil since victory at Burnley in 1914.

It was performances like the aforementioned that led to the talented right-half posthumously being one of the nominations when the sixth annual Scottish Football Hall of Fame dinner took place in Glasgow on Saturday 15 November 2009. Eight new inductees were unveiled, including four former Celtic players and the Glasgow club's first manager. But from a Light Blue perspective, it was the inclusion of Meik which finally set the record straight.

Nominees for the national Hall of Fame are put forward by football fans around the world, based on their contribution to the Scottish game, with the final list selected by a panel of experts from the world of football and the media. Thus, Meik joined Willie Maley, Jimmy

Delaney, Alan Gilzean, Bertie Auld, Maurice Johnston, Paul Lambert and Steve Archibald in the batch of inductees.

Sure, when you compare cap hauls and look at Meik's combined total of 21, it falls behind others who have 50 and 60 caps for their country. Times are different but the half-back's collection stands proudly alongside those from his own era. Others may have won more but Meiklejohn's career was blighted by injury, and while more often than not it didn't prevent him from turning out for his club he was always adamant that he would never risk playing for his country while less than 100 per cent fit. He was picked to play for Scotland on many other occasions but subsequently stepped down due to injury, often just the day before the match.

There is no question that representing his country was an honour Meiklejohn placed high up in his list of priorities and it was always with a heavy heart that he would withdraw from an international match. In fact, on one occasion he travelled to Wales for a game in Wrexham, saddled with the knowledge that his father was dangerously ill. He certainly wore the dark blue of Scotland with immense pride.

His cap haul, though, was a classic case of quality over quantity.

25

Meik's big anti-climax

THE 1936/37 season, Meiklejohn's 18th at Ibrox, should have been one in which the veteran campaigner could assert his influence over a rapidly changing Rangers team. Many of his former team-mates were in managerial hotseats up and down the country.

The likes of Billy McCandless, Tully Craig, Andy Cunningham and Tommy Muirhead, who had moved from the hotseat at St Johnstone to Preston North End, had made the step up from player to boss, but there was still a real desire on the part of Meiklejohn to continue playing as long as he could.

During his time in charge of Rangers, Bill Struth hadn't exactly been known for bringing through young players, instead relying on the tried and tested – and the youth – of other clubs. But that all changed as the end of the 1930s approached and players such as Tom McKillop, who played in a winning Rangers team against Celtic at the age of 18, pointed the way forward.

Struth had trained his eye on another young talent, Willie Thornton, a teenage centre-forward who received the perfect birthday present on his 17th birthday – a contract with Glasgow Rangers. The youngster, a product of Winchburgh Albion, had turned out several times for Rangers' Alliance team on an amateur contract.

But while there may have been a changing of the guard in the offing, Meiklejohn still had his part to play in reclaiming the league title from Celtic, who had won their first championship for a decade in the previous season. In those days players didn't sign two- and three-year deals, with their time at any particular club taking on the form of season-by-season contracts and, as usual, Meiklejohn had penned his present deal on the final day of the previous season.

Regrettably, Meik's first action of the close-season was to cancel a long-standing diary engagement. He had been invited to open the Glasgow Flower Show and been warned to take an extra pen or two as autograph hunters would be out in force. But the international half-back had a date with a surgeon at a Glasgow nursing home. It was believed, however, that he would be fighting fit for the start of the new season.

The day after the op, Meik received a visit from Struth who spoke with the surgeon and reported that the procedure had gone well and that his skipper should soon be up and about. The operation was a nasal one, the result of a broken nose sustained an incredible ten years previously following an accidental collision with team-mate Willie Robb.

'Waverley' said, 'It strikes me that if Davie has a recurrence of all the injuries he has sustained during his 17-year career, he'd better book a nursing-home berth for a long time to come.'

Meiklejohn's recuperation was indeed coming along nicely and after attending the Poloc v West of Scotland cricket match at Shawholm, he headed off on a Mediterranean cruise. He was back in time, just about, for the 50th anniversary of the Rangers Sports, and the annual five-a-side competition – or was he? He was billed to play alongside Brown, Venters, Smith and Turnbull but his place was taken by Simpson when he failed to show.

Rangers won the competition without the loss of a goal but many supporters were unhappy at Meik's no-show. It transpired, though, that the player had arrived home from the Med just hours before kick-off and it was thought unwise to rush him straight on to the football field. As the days and weeks passed, one began to wonder if there was more to his absence that day than met the eye.

It was decided that the player would sit out the first couple of games as he wasn't 100 per cent fit. He had missed part of training because of his nasal op, so it was decided to 'bed him in' gently. But the best laid plans...

While Rangers were drawing 0-0 at Dundee on the opening day, Meik played for the reserves at Ibrox in a 4-1 win over the Dens Park side. And he was enjoying a satisfactory game until the closing minutes when he picked up a niggling ankle injury. It looked a simple thing to mend but that initial prognosis would be well wide of the mark.

The players of FC Austria arrived in town at the beginning of the following week and after training at Ibrox, they expressed their hope that Meiklejohn would be fit to play against them in their challenge match. 'Waverley' said, 'It struck me during the course of our conversation that in Austria Meiklejohn is as popular as Herr Hitler would like to be!'

Dr Scharz, coach of FC Austria, said, 'I do hope this master footballer is able to play in our game,' and with that he turned to Struth, but he was giving nothing away with regards to team selection.

Just hours before kick-off, Struth informed the press corps that Meik had failed to make the team. 'He isn't quite ready yet,' was a cry he would repeat regularly as the season wore on. The Austrians were a tough nut, having reached the equivalent of the European Cup Final in 1936, but the Light Blues were too good on the night and won the match 4-1 with Bob McPhail scoring a hat-trick. The Austrians were criticised after the match for the use of their elbows and fists – and Jimmy Smith had the bruises to back up those allegations.

Rangers racked up five successive league victories as their skipper and guiding light looked on dejectedly from the stands. By the beginning of September, Meik was joined in trainer Arthur Dixon's room by the likes of McPhail, Main and Simpson as Rangers were once again struck down by a succession of injuries. Goalless draws against Arbroath and Third Lanark preceded a slender 3-2 win over Motherwell – thanks to a Venters treble – but Meik was nowhere to be seen at Ibrox that afternoon. Instead, he was in Methil, watching East Fife draw with Morton. He was there in a scouting capacity, and George Scott was the focus of his attention.

However, the skipper was at Ibrox on Saturday 26 September for an Old Firm Glasgow Cup encounter. He watched an enthralling encounter end 2-1 in Rangers' favour but knew nothing about the near disaster unfolding as the 64,000 spectators made their way out of the stadium. A woman had fallen on a stairway, which had led to hundreds more collapsing. More than 30 people were injured in the crush – with a further 11 hospitalised – and only the quick thinking of the emergency services averted a potentially fatal disaster.

In mid-October, Meik accompanied his manager at a meet and greet ceremony for the German party at the Central Station Hotel. The Germans were in town for a challenge match against Scotland at Ibrox. A massive demonstration outside Ibrox threatened to become violent and two men were arrested for their part in the protest. A banner read 'Who murdered Jewish footballers?' and the German players infuriated a large section of the 60,000 crowd when they gave Nazi salutes to the stands just before kick-off. Scotland won 2-0 thanks to goals by Jimmy Delaney.

Two days after the game, 'Waverley' said in his *Daily Record* column, 'I have been asked repeatedly of when Davie Meiklejohn is likely to be seen in a Light Blue jersey again. Sorry, I can't give the answer, and neither can anyone else. I saw him out with the boys the other day, and there was a strap of bandage around his right ankle.'

Despite being unable to contribute on the field, Meiklejohn was proving more than expedient off it as Struth put his expertise in assessing young talent to good use. The skipper was asked to run the rule over a 16-year-old Lanark schoolboy by the name of William Waddell. Along with director and former team-mate Alan Morton, he watched the youngster play on the wing for Forth Rangers. Representatives from Portsmouth and Albion Rovers were also at the game. The Rangers duo made enquiries about the boy but his parents intimated their desire for young William to continue his studies at Lanark High School.

A fortnight after watching Waddell, Meik made a rare appearance on the football field for the reserves in a home match against Kilmarnock. He was keen to play and while Struth was against the idea, the boss relented. The skipper played at right-half and performed well in a 2-2 draw but broke down after the game, just as 19-year-old Waddell was penning his first Rangers contract.

The following Monday it was reported that Meik tripped the light fantastic at the Rangers dance in the Grosvenor and 'danced in a manner that suggested his ankle injury is a thing of the past'! A youngster called Robert Ross, a teenage Govan right-half, was signed from Benburb. A replacement for the great man, perhaps?

Meik had managed just two second-XI games in the first three months of the campaign, a sad statistic that had supporters asking the inevitable – was he finished or would he rally and make a successful comeback?

In mid-December 1936, Meik said, 'The trouble is an ankle injury. It's the most irritating I've had in my entire career. Looks nothing at all but plays the merry dickens with my leg power. It is certainly getting better, but confoundedly slow. If it's anything to do with me, I won't let it finish me off. In fact, I'm hoping to be out on the field again around the New Year.'

The interviewer, 'Rex', of the *Sunday Mail*, said, 'Davie Meiklejohn, the greatest footballer of my generation, is fighting a stiffer battle off the field than any he fought on it,' and Meik ended, 'I would be heartbroken if I had to peter out in this way. I want to finish as I started – in a Light Blue jersey and on the field – not on a massage table. And, believe me, I'll do it!'

It was the sort of coverage that Meiklejohn would rather not have had, although some of the limelight was shifted off him in the coming days as a royal scandal involving Edward and Mrs Simpson rocked the country and plunged Great Britain into a constitutional crisis.

But while the injury list at Ibrox continued to grow, there was no doubt that the influence of Meiklejohn was missed more than most. His leadership, many said, was worth a goal of a start and never was it more evident than at Brockville, where the veteran played a starring role in a 5-1 win over Falkirk reserves.

Bairns director Bob Kirkwood, a member of the SFA Select Committee, said, 'I stayed at home to watch our Alliance team take on the Rangers, and Meiklejohn, despite his troubles, was head and shoulders above everyone else on the field. He gave the impression of having years of football left in him.'

This appraisal of the skipper led to many calling for Meiklejohn to be included in the Rangers team for the Ne'erday game against Celtic. It was a non-starter. There was a world of difference between playing against a Falkirk second string and a Celtic team on top of their game.

Instead, Meik continued his rehabilitation on Boxing Day against Hibs reserves at Ibrox in an Alliance League match, but he was in the Ibrox stand to see an Alec Venters goal secure a 1-0 victory over Celtic and no doubt harboured genuine pangs to get back out onto the first-team field where he belonged, especially as the Light Blues had been forced to play young McKillop – still a schoolboy – in the right-half position against Celtic.

It was a full month before Meik was fit to play again and he lined up for the reserves in a 'wee' Old Firm game against Celtic at Ibrox. The visitors won the match 1-0 and further bad news filtered through from Dumfries that Rangers had been knocked out of the Scottish Cup by Queen of the South. The stalwart defender salvaged a disastrous weekend by announcing he was set to marry his sweetheart Annie Pearson at the end of May.

Hearts found themselves minus a manager in the first week in February when David Pratt quit his post. It had become normal practice to link Meiklejohn with every vacant position under the sun and this job was no different. 'Waverley' informed his readers that on this occasion, though, were the Hearts board to make an approach, the Rangers star would express a readiness to discuss terms. He added, 'Even if Davie does not appear as Hearts manager, I think we have seen the last of him on the field. He is seriously considering retirement.'

The player continued to turn out for the Ibrox bridge team in the Western District League and when news came through that former Arsenal and England goalkeeper Frank Moss had been given the Hearts job, he decided it was time to try and salvage his playing career.

But there was a new 'crisis' looming at Ibrox as the club's cat had once again gone missing. Supporters, or other eagle-eyed residents of Govan, were asked to carefully decide whether or not they had seen Puss as the last time the *Daily Record* highlighted the moggie's disappearance, hundreds of cats had been taken to Ibrox.

Two wins on the trot, against St Johnstone and Hamilton Accies, clinched the First Division title for Rangers, the first time in 18 years that Meiklejohn hadn't featured in a single league match. He did play against St Johnstone reserves in an Alliance League match at Ibrox on Tuesday 20 April 1937 but that would be the last time he would pull on the famous light blue jersey. Fittingly, though, the game ended in a 4-0 win for Rangers.

Four days later, on the afternoon of the Scottish Cup Final between Aberdeen and Celtic, arguably the greatest ever Ranger announced his retirement in a letter to the *Daily Record*. It read, 'Dear Waverley, after a long spell of inactivity in the grand old game, I feel that many friends might be interested to know that I have decided to retire at the close of the present season.

'I have had many expressions of goodwill from both followers of my own club and others, and these I appreciate dearly. I should like you, through your popular page, to convey my thanks to all these friends, known and unknown. Yours sincerely, David Ditchburn Meiklejohn.'

Meik had barely time to draw breath before the season's end and his impending marriage to Annie Pearson, a 27-year-old from Angus Avenue, just a couple of streets away from his house in Arbroath Avenue, Cardonald. Annie had been born in Summerton Road, Govan, just a short free kick from the Rangers skipper's Sharp Street home.

The *Sunday Mail*'s 'Rex' reported on the wedding, 'So, Davie Meiklejohn is "way up a ky". He got a good send-off anyhow. After the wedding in the St Enoch Hotel, the Ranger and his party made for the Alhambra Theatre. Alas, he was discovered, and an announcement from the stage brought resounding cheers from the auditorium – and blushes from the man of the moment. I wish him well, for he was my youthful football idol – different from some in that he didn't possess feet of clay.'

Off the Rangers star went on his honeymoon and, on Monday 17 August, when normally he would have been relaxing after playing in the opening game of the new season, he was excitedly beginning another chapter in his life.

26

On the write track

WITHIN two months of penning his retirement letter, Meiklejohn had a new job – as a sports writer at the *Daily Record*. He joined 'Waverley', alias W.G. Gallagher, and his team at the paper's HQ: Kemsley House, in Hope Street, Glasgow.

The announcement was made on the front page of the paper under the banner headline of 'A Sports Scoop'. The message read, 'It is with pleasure that we announce that David Meiklejohn, Rangers and Scottish football star, has joined the sports staff of the *Daily Record*.

'David will conduct a special service bureau for footballers and followers, placing his great experience of the game at the disposal of our readers who have football problems to settle. He will also conduct special coaching classes for the young.

'With Waverley, Scotland's outstanding football journalist, and now with David Meiklejohn's special service, the *Daily Record* remains supreme for sport.'

Meik's opening message read, 'Good morning Boys, I am glad to tell you that I have joined the *Daily Record* and will help you all I can. If you have any little problems about which you would like me to advise you, write me, and I will try to put you on the proper lines.

'In a day or two, I will tell you all about the tuition classes we are going to carry on in Newspaper House. Boys' teams will be invited to apply for a date, and when that has been fixed, you will come here and have demonstrations of ball control and all the rest of it.

'We shall have goalposts, a net and a full-size ball, so that everything will be done in a practical way. I am hopeful of getting some noted players to co-operate with me in giving useful hints which may help improve your play, and lead to improved team work.'

Meik's daily column, 'Davie's Corner', soon achieved cult status and sackloads of mail arrived each week for the rookie reporter. His catchphrase was 'Ask me a question and I'll give you an answer', although his Monday column was more or less given over to summarising the weekend's events.

One of the first matches he reported on was Rangers v Motherwell at Ibrox. In his preview he said, 'This will be the first game between Rangers and Motherwell that I have ever watched, and I am looking forward to it immensely.

'I always derived great pleasure from playing against the Fir Park men, probably because the teams were so evenly matched that it resembled a game of chess. One match in particular instantly springs to mind. Ibrox, 1934, and the fine line between success and failure was never better illustrated.

'It was a ding-dong struggle and in the first half John McMenemy sent in a great shot. It looked a scorer all the way but the ball hit a post, rebounded on to Jerry Dawson's body, and was deflected past the post. Two minutes later, the ball came out to me from the Motherwell defence and I shot for goal instantly. The ball hit a post, rebounded on to Alan McClory's body and was deflected into the net.

'It was the only goal of the match. It was our lucky day and to the very last kick, we went at it tooth and nail, but that little turn of fortune pulled us through. In my earlier days, when I was playing right-half, I would lie in my bed the night before a game against Motherwell and think of all ways and means of grappling with the Stevenson-Ferrier wing. George Stevenson and Bob Ferrier were two grand players and I never had a cross word with either.'

On the Monday morning, after Rangers had defeated Motherwell 2-1, Meik reported, 'True to custom, I saw Rangers struggle to beat Motherwell. I enjoyed the game and it brought back happy memories of some great tussles with the Fir Park men.'

In a bid to prove Celtic's superiority over Rangers, one Parkhead supporter requested results from the last 20 years of Old Firm games.

This only served to highlight that Rangers had been the dominant force. The supporter didn't like it one bit and criticised Meik for showing a bias towards his old team. 'The facts don't lie,' Meik said. 'You asked for the last 20 years and you got them.'

Back came the reply, 'Well how about the 20 before them?' The former Ibrox skipper was always as fair with his pen as he was on the park and was praised for his ability to remain neutral in the white-hot atmosphere of an Old Firm game, despite his career-long allegiance to the Light Blues.

The first of Davie's tuition classes was held at Kemsley House and the recipients were the lads of Victoria Park Amateurs who listened to John Scott, vice-president of the Scottish Referees Association, explain the laws of the game and how to avoid the little pitfalls that trouble even the grown-ups.

On New Year's Day of 1938 Davie used his column to speak of his joy at finally being able to enjoy a wee dram at Ne'erday, and said, 'New Year – a happy time for all, but not the footballer. It's all right for me now, but I had a long spell when I envied the freedom of other people in being able to enjoy all the old Scottish customs.

'My programme on Hogmanay was the first house of a show and off to bed before The Bells had begun to ring. It was ever in our minds that tomorrow was the day of the big battle. No matter how Celtic might be going we knew we could expect the usual stern 90 minutes.

'My mind goes back to the many thrilling incidents that have occurred in these Ne'erday tussles. I suppose most supporters will never forget – and neither will I – that great battle in 1936. Both teams derived a great deal of credit from it. I can well recall how, in the first half, I wondered what had actually struck us. So mesmerising was the display of the Celts in that opening period that I and my mates worried about where it would all finish.

'Outplayed before such a gathering is not the sweetest pill for a player to swallow. And we were outplayed. Celtic led 3-1 when just before the interval we got a second. It came to us like a reviving tonic. In the pavilion, from feeling down and out we felt there was still a possible chance for us.

'Out we came with our tails up. Everything swung the right way for us, and we went on to gain one of the most hard-earned victories it has ever been my lot to share in. What a wonderful feeling to flop down on the massage table the moment I entered the dressing room. The smile of victory was ours, which was very pleasant, but who could withhold from Celtic the equal praise that was due them for their brilliant first half exposition of football as we all like to see it played.

'And now for today. I am still asked the same question as when I was a player: "Who do you think will win?" I can only give the same reply. When Rangers and Celtic meet, especially on New Year's Day, you can toss a penny if you have one left after Hogmanay.'

Readers loved Davie's Corner and the insight it gave them into the life of the professional player. Meik had a real flair for taking his reader on a journey into the inner sanctum of the dressing room, from which they could almost taste the acquired smell of liniment oil, or feel the crispness of the freshly laundered playing kit.

But it was the smell of baby oil that was all-pervading in the Meiklejohn household on the morning of Tuesday 13 September when they were blessed with the arrival of baby son Alexander Allan, and 'Waverley' instantly marked him down as a future Ranger.

But there was still life left in his daddy's boots as Meik came out of retirement for a great cause. He lined up for Patsy Gallacher's Old Internationalists in a fundraising match for Eastpark Children's Home which, by some quirk of fate, was positioned halfway between the grounds of Maryhill Juniors and Partick Thistle. The match took place at Largs Thistle's Barrfields ground and Meik's side beat Dave Bruce's Select 4-3. Meik was joined by former team-mates Tom Hamilton, Jamie Fleming and Willie Nicholson.

In 1939, with relations between Britain and Germany at an all-time low, Davie's Corner continued to provide much light-hearted relief for those about to suffer the harsh realities of war. He also took over the popular 'Spotlight' column usually written by 'Waverley' while the chief sports reporter was on tour with Scotland in the US. Meik told the tale of Tom McKillop, the young Ranger who was at loggerheads with the Ibrox club over the validity of his contract.

Meik wrote, 'He was a Ranger before heading abroad and on his return, Manager Struth wanted him back again. The problem was, he wanted to go elsewhere. He appealed to the league management committee to free him from the Rangers, but the committee ruled to vote in favour of my old club, citing that McKillop was a retained player and had re-signed for the Ibrox club. The irony is, I suppose, that young Tom was groomed to take over my place at Ibrox!'

Meiklejohn also wrote a rather interesting feature on the effect a new military training regime was having on football. The footballer-turned-journalist was emerging from the shadows of 'Waverley' and throughout 1939 he penned a long list of instantly readable features on topics such as evacuation during football matches, his old Parkhead adversary Jimmy McGrory and much more.

The following year, with the country struggling to come to terms with the news that the European conflict could be a lengthy one, Meiklejohn did his best to come up with a number of features – both serious and light-hearted – that could take readers' minds off the war for just a short period of time. He wrote extensively about the SFA's decision over whether or not to suspend competitive football during the war, the resultant east/west league split, and the rather interesting tale of Stanley Matthews agreeing to play for Rangers then turning out – with the Ibrox club's blessing – for Airdrie.

Wartime rationing affected almost every aspect of daily life and newspapers were no different, but while the government was keen for newspapers to keep people informed as to the goings-on in Europe the *Daily Record* was cut to just eight pages. That meant one page at best for sport, and sometimes just a column or two. Meik reported on the wartime league title going to Rangers, after a deciding match with Falkirk, and of the thousands of Gers fans who invaded the pitch just as the victorious players were receiving their prizes of War Savings Certificates from the Lord Provost.

In 1941 the former Ranger told readers that his old club were to play two games on the same day. On Saturday 16 August the Light Blues travelled to Firhill for a Southern League match against Partick Thistle, while Raith Rovers were the visitors to Ibrox for a North Eastern League match. Rangers pulled off a grand double by beating the Jags 3-2 thanks to a brace by Jimmy Smith and one from Alec Venters, while the others thumped Raith 8-1 with rebel player McKillop scoring three.

Rangers were still top dogs in Scotland and when the mighty Preston North End visited Ibrox for a challenge match, 35,000 watched the home side win 3-1, which prompted Meik to report, 'On this form, the Rangers would lick even a Panzer Division!'

But despite the sufferings of our troops abroad there was still a large number of football-going Glaswegians who couldn't leave the old rivalries behind, and when Rangers played Celtic at the beginning of September 1941 widespread hooliganism led to threats from the Chief Constable, the infamous Percy Sillitoe – slayer of the Glasgow razor gangs – and Lord Provost Sir Patrick Dollan, to halt the Old Firm fixture until the end of the war.

Meik reported that Sir Patrick said, 'Every latitude has been allowed the clubs and I am indebted to them for considerable support for war funds, but I would rather do without financial aid than obtain it at the price of good citizenship and the winning of the war.'

Meik said, 'Just before half-time, following the saving of a penalty kick by Jerry Dawson, who had fouled Delaney, the West End terracing became insanity fair. In a twinkling we were right back to the mad hooliganism of 12 and 15 years ago.

'Free fights, air thick with flying bottles, stretcher cases, policemen with drawn truncheons fighting their way through a surging mass to make arrests. A ghastly travesty of sport, a sickening spectacle for any decent-minded man. Order was only restored when Assistant Chief Constable Walter Doherty took command and led a strong body of officers from the pavilion to the storm centre.

'Personally I wished the referee had been invested with the power to stop the play and let me escape from it all. Years ago, when Old Firm games were frequently spoiled by similar happenings the authorities took drastic measures. They must do so again.

'When the rioting on the terracing stopped, some of the players began to introduce something of a similar nature on the field, and the second half was completely spoiled by indulgence in shady stuff. For 12 minutes, Celtic were without Delaney and Crum, who were both carried off on a stretcher to shrieks of delight from the hooligan element on the East terracing.'

Meik was also present at Easter Road on Saturday 27 September 1941, when Rangers – who had clocked up seven straight Southern League wins for the loss of just six goals – were routed 8-1 in one of the most astonishing games seen during the war. It was also one of the worst results in the club's history and Meiklejohn said, 'One of my colleagues in the press room was asked to repeat the score several times by his obviously bemused editor such was the surprise at the result.'

But even the events at Easter Road were overshadowed by developments on the day the SFA War Emergency Committee met to discuss the shameful scenes of hooliganism at the Old Firm game. Meiklejohn reported on the aftermath of the meeting and said, 'After a lengthy discussion on the matter, the committee decided to close Celtic Park for a month – and banned the Parkhead side from playing on any ground in Glasgow for the same period of time. On the re-opening of their ground, the club were ordered to post warning bills explaining to their supporters why this drastic action had been taken, in the hope that it might have a calming effect on the rowdy element.

'Celtic Football Club was also warned that their players must also behave more properly on the field, and accept the decisions of the referee more freely.

'There you have it, and it certainly is strong action which was totally unexpected by the football world at large. Clause number one means that the Glasgow Cup semi-final between the Old Firm, due to be played on the Glasgow Autumn holiday, is definitely postponed.'

Meik also penned a riveting feature on his old Ibrox colleague Dougie Gray, who became the longest-serving player in the country in 1942 when he embarked on his 18th campaign with Rangers, a haul that just eclipsed the author.

The following year, the enigmatic Peter 'ma ba' McKennan was the subject of Meik's pen. The Partick Thistle star had just been allowed home on leave from the army and made his way straight to his native Glasgow to see his family – after visiting his beloved Firhill, of course.

Meik spoke of Jags manager Donald Turner's good fortune at once again being able to utilise the incredible talents of the 'Maryhill Magyar', and the spin-off that would bring to supporters and team-mates alike. In McKennan's first match he scored twice to set up a Glasgow Cup Final with Rangers, who had defeated Celtic after extra time.

And Meiklejohn, who had fitted seamlessly into the role of roving reporter, told the footballing fraternity that Rangers had just won their third successive wartime championship – but weren't able to fly the flag in celebration of their success. He said, 'Rangers are already flying two flags, and it would've been three, had they been able to find someone to make it. Seems it's easier to win them than fly them!'

He was also on the spot to tell his army of readers to beware a change of kick-off time in the league match between Rangers and Aberdeen – 'it's so the Aberdeen players can make the last train home!'

And on the eve of the 1944/45 championship, Meik threw down the gauntlet to Scottish football sides when he begged the question, 'Who can stop the Rangers? They have won every championship since the war began.'

Rangers started off with a hard-fought 3-2 victory at Brockville, with Willie Waddell getting the winner, and a 4-0 success at Celtic Park the following week did little to suggest that anyone had paid heed to Meik's rallying call. Fast-forward to April 1945 and Rangers tied up the title with a bit to spare after a 4-1 win over Morton at Cappielow.

Rangers were then invited to Belgium to play a show game for the nation's troops. With the war all but won, chairman James Bowie was delighted to accept the invitation and Meik said, 'Rangers are old-time visitors to the Continent. They were never beaten there until a German Select XI, under the guise of a club side, beat them 2-1. So like the Nazis!'

Victory in Europe was achieved on the battlefields and not the football field on Tuesday 8 May and with the end of the war, the *Daily Record* once again upped its pagination. 'Monday Morning by Davie Meiklejohn' soon became a big hit with readers and in August 1946, the column read, 'As I sat (quite comfortable, thank you) in the guard's van on the long trek to Aberdeen, my thoughts turned back down memory lane, and to a time when the engine pulled in to Stonehaven. That very name was enough to recall an experience that at the time had Mr Struth all hot and bothered, and added some grey to his temples.

'Like Celtic, the Rangers club had been travelling on the Saturday morning train. Nothing untoward in that, but when it comes to the train having a breakdown it becomes quite a different story.

'The minutes ticked away all too quickly with the kick-off time getting uncomfortably near. We made it, however. Partially stripped in the train, we arrived Aberdeen 2.45, taxied to the ground and took to the field promptly at three o'clock – and were a goal up a minute later, thanks to yours truly! Maybe that is the real reason why this story is so vivid in my mind. Final verdict on that game of long ago – we were the luckiest team in the world to escape with a 1-0 win.'

Meiklejohn penned his final column for the *Record* in June 1947. He had accepted the manager's job at Partick Thistle and it was with a heavy heart that he bade farewell to his loyal army of readers, many of whom hadn't seen him on the football field but had merely become acquainted through print.

He said, 'I say farewell to readers of the *Daily Record* with many happy memories of my 10 years' association with this paper. In these years I have made many warm friendships, and I should like to take this opportunity of expressing my gratitude to the many people, both in journalism and in other spheres, who have helped me along the way. I owe them much.

'I have enjoyed every minute of my journalistic career, and it was not without a great deal of thought and consideration that I decided to take the dive into football management. But, as any ex-footballer will tell you, once the pavilion blood runs through your veins, the call to return rings often in your ears.

'When Partick Thistle directors kindly invited me to join them, the "homing instinct", which I believed had disappeared, came back to life. So there you have it, I have taken this step because I believe it is an opportunity to have an ambition realised.

'I shall always recall with deep satisfaction some of the highlights of my experiences as a football writer. One stands out vividly, and concerns the famous Moscow Dynamo. I was given the commission to go down to Stamford Bridge in the first game of the Dynamos' British tour, which was against Chelsea. I believe I was the only Scottish reporter on the job. It seemed at the time, very ordinary routine work, but how different was the ultimate outcome?

'When I returned, and tried to convey through these columns to *Daily Record* readers that something really big in football had arrived in this country, I found all around me unbelievers who were certain I had allowed my pen to run wild in estimating the Russians' ability.

'For the Dynamos' second game I went to Tottenham, where they played a reinforced Arsenal side. Through blankets of fog, from my position on the touchline where I had planked myself, I saw enough to convince, if I needed any further convincing, that our visitors were really good.

'The aftermath of this game is an experience I am not likely to forget. To anyone lost in a London fog miles from his objective – which in my case was our London office – the feeling is one of hopelessness. Here I was, not knowing which way to turn, and I had still to get my stuff over to Glasgow by a certain time.

'I was in a cold sweat as I tried to hail taxi after taxi only to be met with a negative shake of the head. I walked miles before a taxi driver took pity on me and took me to the nearest tube station. That was as far as he would go in the fog, but I will never forget him. He was my life saver.

'The Dynamos came to Ibrox, packed the ground as they did on every occasion in England, and those of you who were there will admit they had something.

'If I am looking for another highlight in my writing career, I like to think of the day when I signed up to join the *Daily Record* writing staff. It started in a small way, and some of you will remember the "Davie Meiklejohn Corner", which brought me into contact with hundreds of people whom I had never met, but between whom and myself there grew a feeling of intimacy which was as gratifying to me as I hope it was to them.

'From there I went on to bigger things. In my capacity as reporter I have always tried to be helpful. I know the truth has to be told, but as an old footballer I now realise that if a lad has a bad game, and is told so in a kindly way, he will accept and benefit from the advice which his elders have given him.

'So again it is goodbye readers. I wish you all the best, as I'm sure I have your good wishes to go along with me in my new venture. Thanks to all who have sent me congratulatory messages.'

So, after a ten-year absence, it was back to the cut and thrust of a game Meiklejohn had been forced to give up just a little prematurely.

27

In the hotseat

ONE afternoon, Meik was sitting at a window table in a café having a cup of tea with his *Daily Record* colleague 'Waverley'. He confessed that he had a problem. Partick Thistle wanted him to succeed manager Donald Turner, who had been 'moved upstairs', and he couldn't make up his mind. 'Waverley' admitted to feeling underqualified to advise him when, all of a sudden, the former Ranger stood up.

'I'll be back in a minute,' he said. He had spotted the Partick chairman James Leckie in the street and, after a five-minute conversation at the pavement's edge, he returned to the table. 'I've taken the job,' he said, with a nervous smile.

Meik was announced as the new manager of the Jags at the beginning of June 1947 after the Firhill board revealed that just one name had been put forward – that of the former Rangers and Scotland half-back. So it was back to Maryhill, the district in which his football career had kicked off some 28 years previously.

It was a timely appointment by the board as Turner's resignation had been tendered some weeks before. The reason for the delay had been simple – Meik was unsure of whether or not to accept the position. He had fallen in love with journalism and had been a decade at the typewriter. Leaving such a fulfilling profession was a massive gamble and one that he had refused to take when both Hearts and Clyde had previously come calling with lucrative offers and the promise of a free hand in team affairs. On both occasions, after mulling over the offers, he had opted to remain in journalism so it was a case of third time lucky for Partick Thistle.

Of course, gaining the services of such a well-respected and experienced campaigner was a major coup for a provincial club like Thistle and when the announcement was made, to say his appointment gave unbounded pleasure to the Jags faithful was an understatement. Another happy camper was Turner, who declared that he couldn't have wished for a more worthy successor.

On his retirement from the game, Meiklejohn's decision to enter journalism rather than remain involved in football shocked many. Here was a man with so much to give in terms of experience and knowledge and it was felt that one of the game's greatest ever tacticians would be lost to future generations of players. His appointment at Firhill thus allowed him the vehicle to impart that knowledge and mastery of tactics to a new group of willing pupils.

Partick had some fine exponents of the sport on the payroll, both young and experienced, and Meik's appointment gave real hope to Jags supporters who had been starved of success for some time as they hadn't won a major trophy for 26 years. Whether or not the new boss could deliver success in terms of silverware would be a question best kept for future seasons.

However, it was reported in the press, 'Davie Meiklejohn has all the attributes to become a first-class coach as well as a manager.' The new gaffer had been such a big success as a player that it seemed a foregone conclusion that success in the dugout would follow but the reality was that he had no experience in management, so the jury would remain out and in deliberation for the duration of his debut season at least.

Tragically, one of the first matters he had to deal with was unrelated to football. A few weeks after Meik took over at Firhill, Thistle trainer Jimmy Kennedy was struck down by illness while on holiday in Girvan. He travelled back from the Ayrshire resort by ambulance to the Western Infirmary where he underwent an emergency operation. The well-known football personality was allowed to return to his home at Leny Street, in Ruchill, after seemingly recovering, but he died shortly afterwards. Kennedy had succeeded Sandy Duncan as trainer in 1927 and his ability had been recognised at national level by the SFA and Scottish League.

He had played most of his football down south as a centre-half for Tottenham Hotspur, Leeds United and Watford, and at one time skippered Spurs. He was a tall, big-boned player, wiry and strong with a grand turn of speed. As a trainer many famous players passed through his hands, and his unobtrusive manner marked him down as a popular man in the game.

As one can imagine Kennedy's death, and the loss of such a big personality, cast a giant shadow over Firhill but with the dawn of a new season looming, Meik had to learn fast and prepare his players for the challenge ahead.

But the introduction of the new fixture list caused immediate consternation in the Maryhill boardroom. It had generally been agreed that the first Wednesday in August would host the lucrative Glasgow Cup ties but an edict from the Scottish Fuel Efficiency Committee, who were petitioning the Cabinet and calling for an absolute ban on all midweek sport during working hours until the fuel position improved, put paid to that.

The proposed Rangers v Partick Thistle first round tie at Ibrox was cancelled, and put back a fortnight. Desperately-needed cash might have been lost but it at least allowed Thistle stars old and new to attend a reunion organised by the supporters' club at the Ca'doro Restaurant, in Glasgow, which served as a welcome opportunity for the new manager to familiarise himself with those of a Partick Thistle persuasion.

The talented Peter McKennan made a timely return from injury while Meik received another pre-season boost when Alec McSpadyen – who had formed a lethal pre-war partnership with McKennan – announced that he was free of army duties and keen to resume his Jags career. Things were looking up. To this day, McKennan is still viewed by people of a certain vintage as the greatest player ever to pull on the red, yellow and black.

With the new season just days away, the feeling in the north-west of Glasgow was that Thistle were bang on course to have one of their best seasons for years but 'Waverley' urged caution, pointing out that his former colleague had not a magic wand, and reckoned Thistle supporters were getting a bit carried away.

For the club's official trial match, which was open to the public at 6d a head and the 'gate' earmarked for charity, Meiklejohn did indeed pair McKennan with McSpadyen. He was keen to find out if the duo could rekindle their almost telepathic understanding. Ten thousand spectators turned up at Firhill and left the stadium talking about one player in particular. Not McKennan or McSpadyen but young defender David Cummings, who was signed on the spot.

Fit-again McKennan, who had been sidelined for nine months due to injury, made a successful comeback while young goalkeeper Tommy Ledgerwood also caught the eye. Meiklejohn had one more important signing to unveil before the big kick-off, although this one would never don a Jags strip. It was former Rangers favourite Arthur Dixon and he had been brought on board to replace Jimmy Kennedy as trainer. He worked part-time as a masseur but assured his old team-mate that he would give no less than 100 per cent to his new post. Dixon would be assisted by former Celtic star Adam McLean.

And 'Lil Arthur' was busy on his first morning on the job, tending to McKennan, who had picked up a leg injury in the trial match. Thankfully it wasn't the same leg that had forced him to sit out a chunk of the previous campaign, although he did miss the first couple of matches.

But everything was geared towards Meiklejohn and co's first competitive game in charge, a sectional League Cup tie against Falkirk at Brockville. One of the most pressing issues requiring the manager's attention was who to start in goal. Ledgerwood was keen to play, although the recently de-mobbed Bobby Henderson was also available for selection.

On the morning of the game, Meiklejohn was asked if he thought the thrill of being a manager would be any different from that of the player. He deferred answering until 5.40pm – and after such a baptism of fire you can imagine his reply. There were 11 goals in the match and, thankfully for Meik, Partick grabbed six.

The Jags were 6-2 up with just 20 minutes to play and there were no doubt a few sweaty palms in the visiting dugout as they awaited the referee's full-time whistle. One can just picture Meiklejohn, Crombie coat and soft hat, churning up inside as his defence suffer an alarming fall from grace in the closing stages of the match, although the gaffer could not fail to have been impressed by the man operating in his old position, right-half Jackie Husband.

Wins over Queen's Park and Queen of the South followed before the Jags visited Ibrox. How strange it must have felt to be opposing his paymasters of almost 20 years. It was the long-awaited Glasgow Cup tie on Edmiston Drive and 50,000 saw a brilliant solo goal by Willie Waddell separate the sides.

With the nights drawing in Meik was rocked by a transfer bombshell from his star man. McKennan, at 29, decided that after 12 seasons at Firhill he wanted a fresh challenge. The move was criticised by certain members of the press who reckoned the player was being unreasonable given the manner in which the club had looked after him on his de-mob from the army. He had missed almost the entire previous season through injury but still the Jags paid his wages. The club decided to sit on it, but not for too long, and within a matter of weeks McKennan had agreed to sign for Bury in a £10,000 deal, a quite incredible sum in the days of post-war austerity.

At the 11th hour, though, McKennan changed tack and joined West Bromwich Albion. Within the space of 18 months the soccer nomad had moved to Leicester City, Middlesbrough and Oldham Athletic.

But Thistle were going great guns and led the league table – jointly with Motherwell – after eight matches, seven of which had been won. And when the teams met at the start of November in a crunch clash at Firhill, 23,000 watched the Jags win an action-packed match 2-1. Controversy dogged the ending to the game when a home player was alleged to have thumped Motherwell's Andy Paton after the final whistle.

The following week, football's great unpredictables – that's Thistle – lost five goals at home to Celtic to relinquish their lead at the top of the table. Mind you, they scored three corkers but their supporters in the 35,000 crowd still went home disappointed.

They bounced back quickly and regained their advantage with a narrow win at Third Lanark. Thistle remained in contention right up until Christmas when Meik made his first league trip back to Ibrox. And there was more than an element of luck in Rangers' 2-1 success as the Jags were denied a stonewall penalty in the final minutes. The result left the Maryhill men third in the table, five points behind the Light Blues, and having played two games more.

Thistle maintained the incredibly high standards set by the new manager until the end of the season and finished a very creditable third, behind just Hibs and Rangers. A 6-2 rout of fourth-placed Dundee on the final day of the season was the perfect way to draw the curtain on Meik's debut campaign.

Thistle were invited to spend part of their close-season on a controversial tour of Israel, which hadn't long been 'created' as a result of the Palestinian partition. Meiklejohn was keen to take his team to the Middle East but the dates available were unsuitable due to the inauguration of the Festival of Britain: St Mungo's Cup, which was scheduled to start in the middle of July.

As it transpired, Thistle lost in the first round to St Mirren and were left clicking their heels in frustration until the start of the campaign proper.

That season saw the Jags finish 11th in the table but they ended with a real flourish by winning the Glasgow Charity Cup. They disposed of Clyde in the first round before a Jimmy Walker goal was enough to KO Rangers in the semi-finals at Ibrox.

Hampden Park was the venue for the final against Celtic and both sides served up a cup final cracker. Bobby Howitt gave Thistle the lead on 17 minutes, following a great move, but Paton equalised midway through the first half. However, Walker was once again the last-action hero as he struck in extra time to ensure there were red and yellow ribbons on the cup. The Celtic defence simply couldn't cope with his 'catapult acceleration' and when he raced clear in the 97th minute to slot home, the Jags fans in the 51,000 crowd went crazy. Meiklejohn had just secured his first trophy as a manager.

The man of the match was Celtic's Pat McAuley but it was the all-round team performance of the Jags that won the day. Celtic's forward line was credited with creating more excitement while Thistle played all the football. The fiery forward punt and hell-for-leather follow-up of the Parkhead team failed to cut the mustard with Meik's young side, who possessed the greater collectiveness.

Many pundits reckoned the Jags were set to become a 'super-power' and battle their two main rivals for supremacy in Glasgow. Meiklejohn had developed a team packed full of young talent and, perhaps, now was their time to blossom.

But he hadn't lost his penchant for the golf course and as soon as the season was over he could be found on a variety of fairways, from Killermont Golf Club to his favoured second home of St Andrews.

Partick supporters were obviously happy with the brand of football the manager's young side was serving up and crowds fluctuated between 10,000 and 20,000 for home games. A mid-table placing the following season was supplemented by a run to the semi-finals of the Scottish Cup where they lost out to East Fife by the odd goal in three.

But Meik had shown that his team could compete with the best and in 1950/51 the Jags finished sixth in the league – one place above Celtic. They also reached the final of the Glasgow Charity Cup before losing 2-0 to Rangers at Hampden.

One other significant achievement that season was a home and away league success over Rangers, something they hadn't managed in 25 years. The second match, in January 1951, ended in a 3-1 win for the Jags thanks to goals by Crawford, Stott and McKenzie, but it was the manner of the victory which pleased the gaffer.

The game was described by one reporter as 'one of the most heart-pounding, incident-packed struggles I've seen in years'. It took place on a ground where players were ankle-deep in mud, but two men shone brighter than the rest – Willie Waddell of Rangers and Partick's hero Johnny McKenzie.

While Waddell equalised for Rangers on the stroke of half-time the second period belonged to the talented McKenzie, and he capped a masterly performance with a stunning 25-yard volley in the dying minutes. A crowd of 40,000 watched the Ibrox encounter and even the most diehard of Gers fans left the ground satisfied that they'd had their money's worth.

By February, though, Jags fans had little left to get them excited as they nestled in mid-table and had already exited the League Cup and Scottish Cup – then the letter arrived. It was from crack Austrian side FC Austria, the league team club who regularly supplied the bulk of the players for the national team. And the terms were decent – a 50/50 split on the gate. The board started getting excited. Thistle had never had a continental team at Firhill before. Then someone piped up, 'Isn't 19 May the date of the Scottish Junior Cup Final?'

And it was. But the showpiece junior game was scheduled for Hampden Park so what was the big deal? The deal was that the Firhill directors didn't want to 'steal' a few thousand people off the Hampden gate – it was the time of the season traditionally held over for a succession of junior finals, and the 'Scottish' was the cream of the crop. Here was a decision that had sporting integrity at its very core and fair play to Thistle for refusing to put their own needs – the match could have netted them in the region of £1,000 – before that of others.

One example of the positive atmosphere fostered at Firhill by the manager arose when goalkeeper Tommy Ledgerwood pulled off an incredible save against Rangers at Firhill. 'Oh, well done, great save,' was heard from the press box. On looking round, it was noted that the comment had been made by Bobby Henderson – the Jags' second-choice keeper who, but for the sensational form of Ledgerwood, would have been a first-team regular.

At the end of the season Meik granted Henderson a free transfer when the club could quite easily have commanded a healthy fee. It was another reminder of the manner in which business was conducted at Firhill.

The 1951/52 season was marred by the constant speculation over the future of McKenzie, the 'Darling of Firhill'. He had been linked with many a club but Meiklejohn finally broke his silence when reports appeared in several papers quoting him as saying, 'McKenzie may go to Manchester City.' It was also reported that City directors were to meet that night to decide whether or not to take him up on his 'offer'. Meik said, 'It's a lot of bunk. It's a complete waste of their time, and mine, for them to come up here because McKenzie is not for sale.'

One player Meik had signed, though, was his old Rangers team-mate Torry Gillick, who helped the club achieve a sixth-place finish – and once again it was higher than Celtic.

In 1952/53 Thistle made a rather inauspicious start to their league campaign and after four games they had managed just a solitary win – but they had their eyes on another prize. They had reached the semi-finals of the League Cup and Rangers stood between them and a place in the final.

Almost 50,000 watched the match at Hampden and while they saw Partick pull off a terrific 2-0 win, celebrations were muted at the end of the game. A goal by Wright on the half-hour put Thistle in front but this paled into insignificance when the players learned at half-time that trainer Arthur Dixon had suffered a heart attack.

Bobby Howitt fired home the clincher in the second period but as the players filed into the dressing room after the game, there was little celebration. They had just reached the League Cup Final for the first time in its 14-year existence but that mattered not a jot. Ironically, Dixon ended up in the same hospital ward as his one-time Ibrox boss Bill Struth. The popular trainer made rapid progress and was even expected to be fit and well for the final at Hampden between Thistle and East Fife.

At the national stadium Meiklejohn locked horns with another old team-mate – former Rangers goalkeeper Jerry Dawson, who was in charge of the Methil outfit. But it was Dawson who was wearing the broadest smile after just eight minutes when goals by Gardiner and Fleming had the Fifers two up. Both goals came as a result of some awful defending which must have made the manager grimace.

It could have been more but it remained at two until the break and one can only speculate as to the nature of Meiklejohn's half-time team talk, because within a couple of minutes Walker had pulled one back and the Jags were in the ascendancy. Suddenly they were passing like world champions and it was no surprise when McKenzie levelled matters with 17 minutes remaining. Off went the Jags in search of the winner, but with two minutes to go East Fife broke up the park and Christie swept home the decisive strike. It was a cruel blow to Meik's men but probably the fairest result on the day.

After shaking hands with his old team-mate, Meiklejohn said, 'I don't think we should have lost after coming back to level things, but that's football, you know, and the boys at least made a good show.'

The Jags had an early Christmas present in store for supporters – and it came in the shape of a 9-0 win over Airdrie at Firhill. Two goals to the good at the break, it was like the pantomime season in the second half as the rampant Jags scored seven times. And as far as the Diamonds were concerned McKenzie made the perfect panto villain, terrorising the visiting defence every time he got the ball.

Apart from McKenzie, the undoubted star of the show was Harvey, playing in Meik's old right-half position. He distinguished himself as the master craftsman – an apprentice Meiklejohn – and he managed a couple of goals.

The former Ranger had been involved in some real ding-dong tussles as a player, too many to mention, but when Thistle faced Second Division Cowdenbeath in the quarter-finals of the League Cup in September 1956 not even battle-hardened Meik could have predicted how hard his players would have to toil to get a result.

With the Jags leading 2-1 from the first leg at Central Park, pundits predicted a hefty home win. A fairly even first half ended 1-1 and it was felt that when the part-time Fifers tired in the latter stages, players like Tommy Ewing would run riot. Not so, and it wasn't until the 84th minute that George Smith's second of the game put the tie to bed.

The one-off semi-final against Dundee couldn't have been more different and a 'no-snore' draw was the end result after a boring encounter. At the end of the 90 minutes one supporter turned to his mate and said, 'Look, the fans are drifting away. Obviously they don't know there's an extra 30 minutes to play.' 'Really,' said the pal, 'My guess is that they DO know!' Yes, it was that bad.

In between that game and the replay, the Jags entertained Newcastle United in a glamour match under the auspices of the Anglo-Scottish Floodlit League and thumped the Magpies 4-1. Ten thousand spectators saw the fit-again Johnny McKenzie and Willie Sharp run the show. Three goals – two for the Jags – in a frantic two-minute spell had the crowd on their feet cheering even the great Jackie Milburn's counter for Newcastle. Ewing put the gloss on an encouraging scoreline for the Firhill men.

An unusual pre-match request saw Meiklejohn take a call from the Newcastle secretary Ted Hall, asking that no functions be organised on their behalf. 'We are coming north to do a job of work,' he said, as a matter of fact.

Next up for the Jags was a return trip to Ibrox for Meik and an opportunity for Thistle to qualify for the League Cup Final, although Dundee had exactly the same idea. It was a cracker of a match and by the end of the regulation 90 the Maryhill men did indeed have a final to look forward to. The game had everything, including five goals, lots of incident, and a screamer of a winning goal by Bobby Davidson.

Thistle had roared into an early two-goal lead but the Dens Parkers had managed to pull level before the break. Then came a moment of magic from Davidson, 20 yards out from a free kick, and the tie was won. Most people had expected him to thunder a shot in at goal but the crafty pivot deftly chipped the ball over the wall and into the back of the net. It was a blow to Dundee and one they failed to recover from.

Thistle limbered up for the cup final against Celtic with a home league match against Kilmarnock. Meiklejohn was hoping for a good performance and two points. In other words, a relatively quiet afternoon with no fresh injury concerns. What is it they say about not always getting what you want?

Tommy Ewing got Thistle off to a dream start with a goal midway through the opening period but Killie levelled on the stroke of half-time. And then it all started to go wrong. Joe Hogan, Andy Kerr and George Smith picked up injuries and Thistle were reduced to eight contributing players, but how they showed the old spirit of a Meiklejohn – and got their reward.

With just eight minutes left, Ewing – arguably the smallest man on the park – rose to head home a Jimmy Davidson free kick and both points, but more importantly the confidence such a defiant win would bring, remained in Maryhill. It was mad but true – and could only have happened at Firhill.

Quite incredibly, when the Jags met Celtic in the League Cup Final, they were left with just nine fit men when Smith and Davidson suffered game-altering injuries. But Thistle still looked the more likely team to emerge with the victory, even after extra time, and had two efforts brilliantly saved by Beattie in the Celtic goal.

In fact, one report suggested that when Celtic got close enough to Jags keeper Tommy Ledgerwood to read his thoughts, he read theirs first and pulled off a save or two. A crowd of 60,000 watched the teams fail to produce a goal between them in two hours of play – it was back to the drawing board.

Just hours before the replay, Meik received a massive blow when inspirational centre-half and captain Jimmy Davidson was told by medics that it would be too risky to have the stitches removed from a head wound sustained in the first game. He had played almost half the match with a bandage covering his forehead and was unable to head the ball – a particular strength of his.

Sadly, with 11 fit players but missing the influence of Davidson, Meik's Thistle were given a harsh lesson and lost three goals in the space of ten second-half minutes. The cup dream was over for another year.

Despite the defeat, Meiklejohn remained loyal to his twin ethos of bringing through youngsters and always trying to play the game in the proper manner. In 1958/59, tragically Meiklejohn's final season, the Jags started off well, beating Celtic 2-1 at Parkhead which placed them second in their League Cup section, and they followed that up with a midweek win over Arbroath in the Scottish League First Division.

But it was at Broomfield on Saturday 22 August 1959, that tragedy struck – Davie Meiklejohn had played a part in his last football match.

28

A tragic end

THE news came like a bolt from the blue. Davie Meiklejohn had collapsed in the directors' box at Airdrie immediately after his Partick Thistle side had lost a sectional League Cup tie 4-0. The Jags boss had been chatting to directors of both clubs when he suddenly fell to the ground.

The official doctor was in the players' room when he received the call but rushed straight upstairs to the stand, where he immediately tended to his casualty and summoned an ambulance.

It was initially reported that Meik had died 'somewhere between Broomfield and Glasgow's Royal Infirmary' as he was dead on arrival at the hospital. The cause of death was a coronary thrombosis, or heart attack, but a corrected entry in the death register shows that Meik was dead before the ambulance left the football ground and gave his place of death as Broomfield Park, Airdrie.

It was a tremendous blow to all who knew him and it wasn't long before tributes to one of Scotland's finest ever footballers started to pour in. Celtic legend Jimmy McGrory led the way by saying, 'It is a terrible shock. I knew him as an opponent of magnificent courage and skill – and as a colleague when he captained Scotland's international side.

'He was as true a Ranger as I was a Celt. When we clashed on the field we fought it out to the last. I faced him when he played at wing-half as well as at centre-half, and I got to know his many virtues. He was a skipper who did his job without fuss or round-table talks, a big-hearted man who made it clear to the rest of the side just what he wanted. And he got it.'

Rangers director and former team-mate Alan Morton said, 'Davie will go down in history as one of the greatest players ever to wear the light blue. No cause was ever lost when he was there behind you. I consider his finest position was right half, although there will be those who say he gained immortality as a centre half.'

Forty-eight hours before the funeral, Rangers played Queen's Park at Hampden and the players wore black armbands as a mark of respect. The admiration and respect commanded by Meiklejohn as a player with both Rangers and Scotland – and as a manager at Partick Thistle – was crystal clear as more than 2,000 people attended his funeral at Craigton Cemetery, less than a mile from Ibrox Stadium. Only a small portion of mourners were able to gain admittance to the crematorium, with the remainder standing outside till the close of the service.

It was a remarkable turnout considering it had been some 22 years since Meik's playing career had come to an end. All surviving members of the Rangers teams in which he played were present and mixing with them were some of his greatest opponents from Celtic. Representatives of every Scottish League club were in attendance. Equally, the SFA and Scottish League were represented by administrators past and present.

Cyril Horne, sports correspondent with the *Glasgow Herald*, paid tribute to Meik by saying, 'In the inevitable arguments about the past and present in football, the name of David Meiklejohn will continue to be introduced. Mr Meiklejohn was a great player for Rangers and Scotland in the 1920s and early 1930s – a period in which there were many fine players.

'Younger followers of football become irritated when comparisons with their heroes of today and those of previous generations are made. Football is so much faster today, they claim, that those of Meiklejohn's era would be run off their feet could the clock for them be turned back.

'I can recall as clearly as yesterday, a Celtic v Rangers match at Parkhead in which a Celtic forward line including a comparatively new player, Crum, led Rangers' defence, including Meiklejohn, a merry dance in the first half. Rangers were down 3-1 at one stage and though they further reduced the lead before half-time they did not seem capable of winning.

'But in the second half Meiklejohn inspired his side with his shrewd appraisal of the situation; he had paced the game to suit Rangers and himself and it was the right-half, never at any time of his career a man of much speed, who finished the match, which Rangers won 4-3, as fresh as a youth. The Celtic speed and enthusiasm had been curbed through the masterly use of the ball by Meiklejohn and his ability to spread the play to the best advantage of his side.

'Meiklejohn would have succeeded in any age of football so naturally gifted was he and so cunningly could he read a game. Rarely did he make a short pass with his foot; he believed in the far-flung pass and its effect on opponents who had to use their legs much more freely than he himself was pleased to do.

'The short passes he made were with his head, and he was uncannily accurate in directing with his brow forward, sideway or backward. Many a Rangers attack had begun with a flick from Meiklejohn's forehead from the centre-half position, which he occupied with as much distinction as he did at right-half.

'For a man who gained so many honours in football, he was remarkably reticent about his career. Indeed there has been no more reserved man in football. But David Meiklejohn, who became Partick Thistle manager in 1947, will forever be remembered first and foremost as one of Scotland's greatest ever players.'

It had been a wonderful career.

Epilogue

IMAGINE the great Franz Beckenbauer or Bobby Moore breaking from the centre of defence; ball never more than a couple of feet away, and carrying it over the halfway line before creating a real goalscoring opportunity for one of their team-mates. A sight to behold, and one that characterised both World Cup-winning captains.

It is fair to say that those reading this book will be too young to have seen Davie Meiklejohn play, but all the evidence points towards Meik being in the same mould as both Moore and Beckenbauer.

A master with or without the ball, Meiklejohn was seldom caught out of position and his strong tackling and pinpoint passes were features of his perfectly rounded game. He was normally one move ahead of opponents: the footballer with the chess-like mind who frowned upon kicking the ball aimlessly from defence.

He was also a tough man to pass and often talked about one particular tussle he had with legendary England striker Dixie Dean. It was in the 1931 Home International match between Scotland and England at Hampden, and both Goliaths enjoyed fearsome reputations for having perfected the art of the shoulder charge.

Meik said, 'There was nothing vicious about the clash, simply a private contest to settle who was boss. At the end of the game, we were both tired and sore, but shook hands with a genuine warmth and mutual admiration – and left it to others to decide who had come out on top.'

His career cut short by injury, he moved into journalism and gave his new profession the same commitment that had characterised his time in football. After a decade at one of Scotland's top newspapers he threw himself into football management and proved a more than capable boss at Partick Thistle. He handled the administrative side with relative ease while his great tactical brain and knowledge of the players' problems from the inside ensured success.

Davie Meiklejohn – a fine footballer and a successful manager, but more than anything else, a gentleman who always had time to speak to the man in the street about their mutual passion – the wonderful game of football.

The greatest ever Ranger? As Meiklejohn himself might have said, I'll leave that for others to decide.

Career stats

IN all competitive matches, Davie Meiklejohn played 635 times for Rangers and scored 53 goals. He also played 49 times in benefit, challenge or charity games and managed three goals, making a grand total of 684 games and 56 scored. It was an incredible tally for a player connected with the country's top club. A true one-club man.

A season-by-season breakdown of matches and goals for Rangers:

1919/20 14 matches 2 goals
1920/21 46 matches 5 goals
1921/22 45 matches 5 goals
1922/23 40 matches 1 goal
1923/24 45 matches 8 goals
1924/25 46 matches 5 goals
1925/26 12 matches 0 goals
1926/27 37 matches 2 goals
1927/28 43 matches 2 goals
1928/29 39 matches 5 goals
1929/30 46 matches 1 goal
1930/31 37 matches 2 goals
1931/32 47 matches 5 goals
1932/33 37 matches 2 goals
1933/34 38 matches 2 goals
1934/35 27 matches 3 goals
1935/36 36 matches 4 goals